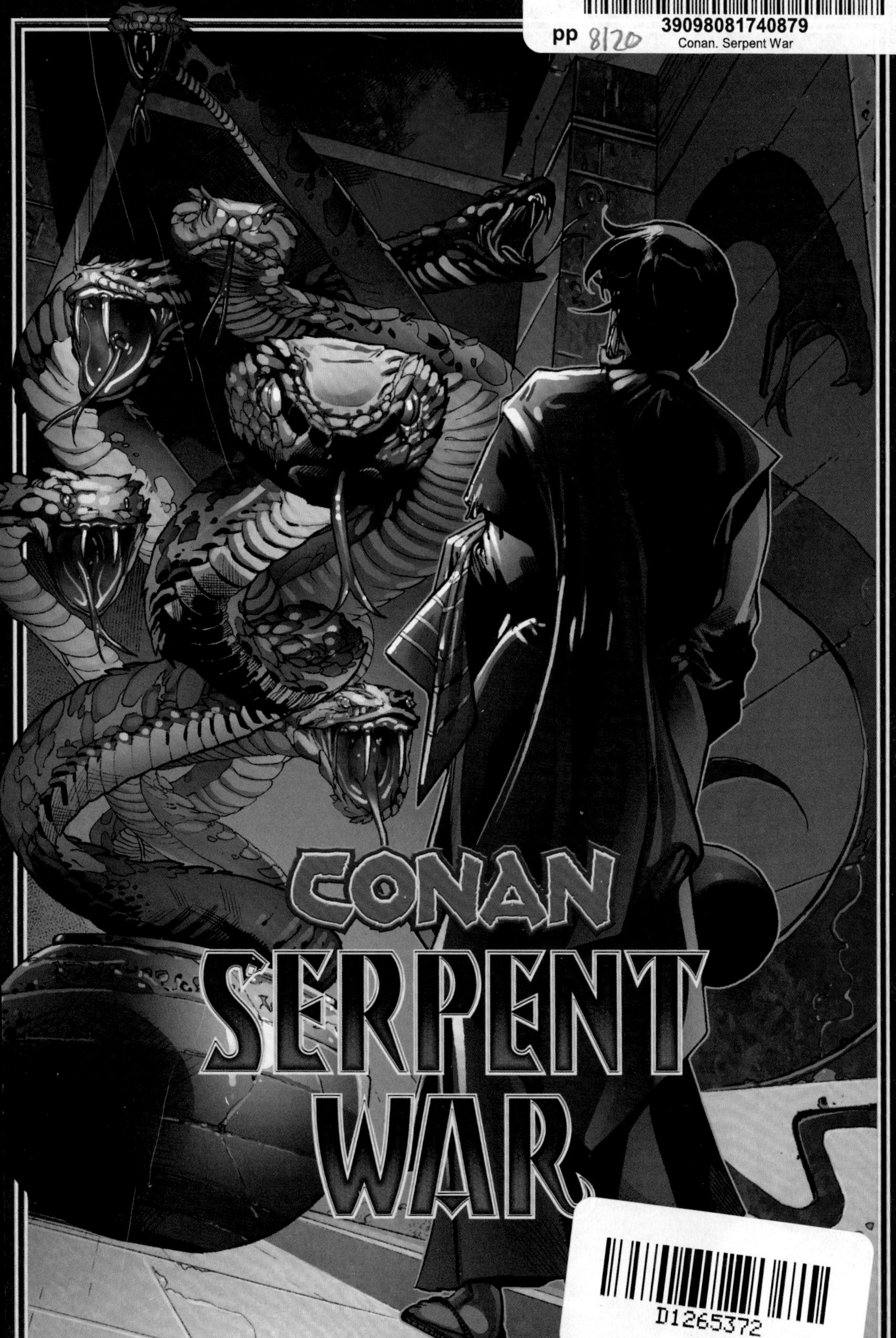
CONAN
SERPENT
WAR

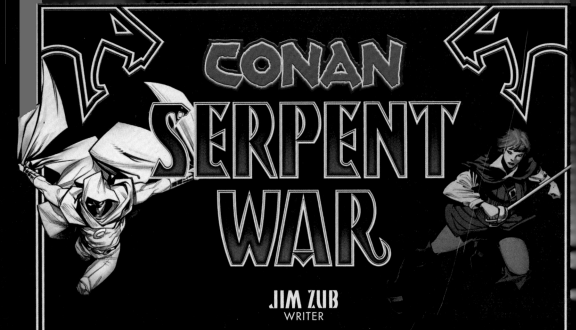

CONAN
SERPENT WAR

JIM ZUB
WRITER

#1	#2	#3	#4
SCOT EATON PENCILER	**STEPHEN SEGOVIA** ARTIST	**LUCA PIZZARI** ARTIST	**IG GUARA** ARTIST
SCOTT HANNA INKER	**FRANK D'ARMATA** COLORIST	**FRANK D'ARMATA** COLORIST	**FRANK D'ARMATA** COLORIST
FRANK D'ARMATA COLORIST			

VANESA R. DEL REY
ARTIST, JAMES ALLISON SEQUENCE

JEAN-FRANÇOIS BEAULIEU
COLORIST, JAMES ALLISON SEQUENCE

CARLOS PACHECO, ANEKE & FRANK D'ARMATA
COVER ART

VC's TRAVIS LANHAM
LETTERER

MARTIN BIRO
ASSISTANT EDITOR

MARK BASSO
EDITOR

RALPH MACCHIO
CONSULTING EDITOR

SPECIAL THANKS TO **BRIAN OVERTON**

CONAN CREATED BY **ROBERT E. HOWARD**

COLLECTION EDITOR **MARK D. BEAZLEY**
ASSISTANT MANAGING EDITOR **MAIA LOY**
ASSISTANT MANAGING EDITOR **LISA MONTALBANO**
SENIOR EDITOR, SPECIAL PROJECTS **JENNIFER GRÜNWALD**
VP PRODUCTION & SPECIAL PROJECTS **JEFF YOUNGQUIST**
BOOK DESIGNER **JAY BOWEN**
SVP PRINT, SALES & MARKETING **DAVID GABRIEL**
EDITOR IN CHIEF **C.B. CEBULSKI**

FOR CONAN PROPERTIES INTERNATIONAL

PRESIDENT **FRED MALMBERG**
EXECUTIVE VICE PRESIDENT **JAY ZETTERBERG**
CHIEF OPERATING OFFICER **STEVE BOOTH**
COORDINATOR **MIKE JACOBSEN**

CONAN: SERPENT WAR. Contains material originally published in magazine form as CONAN: SERPENT WAR (2019) #1-4 and SUPERNATURAL THRILLERS (1972) #3. First printing 2020. ISBN 978-1-302-92307-5. Published by MARVEL WORLDWIDE, INC., a subsidiary of MARVEL ENTERTAINMENT, LLC. OFFICE OF PUBLICATION: 1290 Avenue of the Americas, New York, NY 10104. **Printed in Canada.** KEVIN FEIGE, Chief Creative Officer; DAN BUCKLEY, President, Marvel Entertainment; JOHN NEE, Publisher; JOE QUESADA, EVP & Creative Director; TOM BREVOORT, SVP of Publishing; DAVID BOGART, Associate Publisher & SVP of Talent Affairs; Publishing & Partnership; DAVID GABRIEL, VP of Print & Digital Publishing; JEFF YOUNGQUIST, VP of Production & Special Projects; DAN CARR, Executive Director of Publishing Technology; ALEX MORALES, Director of Publishing Operations; DAN EDINGTON, Managing Editor; SUSAN CRESPI, Production Manager; STAN LEE, Chairman Emeritus. For information regarding advertising in Marvel Comics or on Marvel.com, please contact Vit DeBellis, Custom Solutions & Integrated Advertising Manager, at vdebellis@marvel.com. For Marvel subscription inquiries, please call 888-511-5480. **Manufactured between 2/28/2020 and 3/31/2020 by SOLISCO PRINTERS, SCOTT, QC, CANADA.**

10 9 8 7 6 5 4 3 2 1

"Let them build me a cairn where I lie and lay me therein with my bow and sword at hand, to guard this valley forever; so if the ghost of the god I slew comes up from below, my ghost will ever be ready to give it battle."

Sometimes you read a story, and it hits you like a thunderclap.

This was one of those times.

Conan Editor Mark Basso contacted me to see if I might be interested in spinning a tale that brought together several of Robert E. Howard's finest fantasy creations under the umbrella of an epic event. The players and the plot were mine to pitch, but the sooner I had something for them to look over, the better.

It was such an amazing and intimidating opportunity, rife with the potential to go oh so wrong, but also the kind of project I'd be insane to turn down because it played to so many of my strengths — pulp fantasy, crazy quests, deep-dive continuity and a flare for the dramatically violent.

So I did what I always do — I dug into the source material and looked for lightning; some kind of energetic *something* that could spark a story idea and power the mad machine we were trying to build.

And then I read "Valley of the Worm."

It's not a long story by any stretch, somewhere just over 8,700 words, but packed into that terrific text is a stirring stretch of fantastic fury laid bare with unexpected intensity. James Allison is a broken man living in (at that point) contemporary Texas, an author whose dreams are haunted by nightmarish past lives stretched across days of yore. It might be one of the first meta narratives, a thinly veiled self-insert author frothing with frustration, unable to contain the stories bursting forth from his brain.

That thunderclap went off, and I knew I had a framing device for our event. James as the beginning and the end. Niord as the connective tissue that could bring these disparate heroes together on a quest to save reality itself from unimaginable horror.

The Marvel Universe was built from a webwork of story ideas crisscrossing one another at unexpected angles, old stories informing new ones and old characters coming back with new twists and turns.

Doing the same kind of thing with Robert E. Howard's creations would be audacious, but also in line with the way pulp authors riffed on one another's tales or created parallel heroes to fill classic roles made famous by someone else.

Conan the Barbarian, Solomon Kane, Dark Agnes, James Allison...and let's add in Moon Knight for good measure. The Fist of Khonshu would have an important role to play here and his past conflicts with Set made for a natural fit alongside the rest of our cast.

When I formalized the concept into a pitch called "Kingdom of the Wyrm," Mark and the Conan Properties crew jumped on board, and I realized we were really doing this thing. The pitch became the plan, and our storm clouds were ready to rumble.

The last piece of the puzzle came from Brian Overton and Consulting Editor Ralph Macchio. They remembered that way back in 1972 Roy Thomas and Gerry Conway adapted "Valley of the Worm" in an issue of *Supernatural Thrillers* with artwork by the legendary Gil Kane. Brian tracked down the issue and we immediately knew we could use it to fill out our backstory, bridging past and present by re-presenting that original tale. What an absolute honor and a fun forgotten bit of Marvel comics history.

Writing comics is a gift. When you get to collaborate with top-notch talent like Scot Eaton, Stephen Segovia, Luca Pizzari, Ig Guara, Vanesa R. Del Rey, Frank D'Armata, Jean-François Beaulieu and everyone else who contributed to this very special project, that gift is delivered back to you in a stunning package you could hardly have imagined when you started.

Robert E. Howard's potent prose has inspired countless stories over the years, and all I can hope is that this yarn of gods and men versus ancient evil does right by the man and his myth. If not, then I'm sure I'll have the Wyrm to contend with when next I close my eyes...

Jim Zub
January 27, 2020

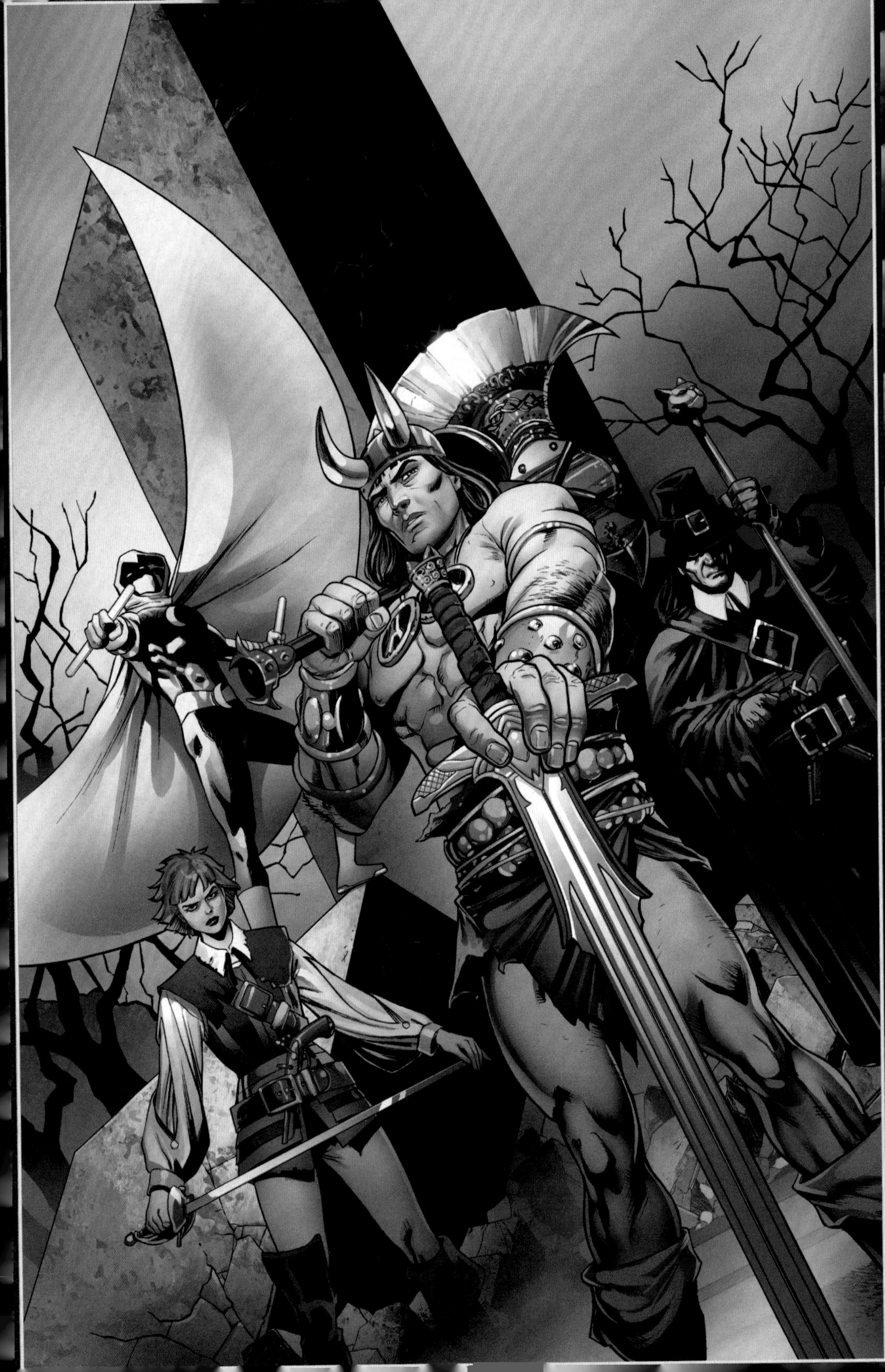

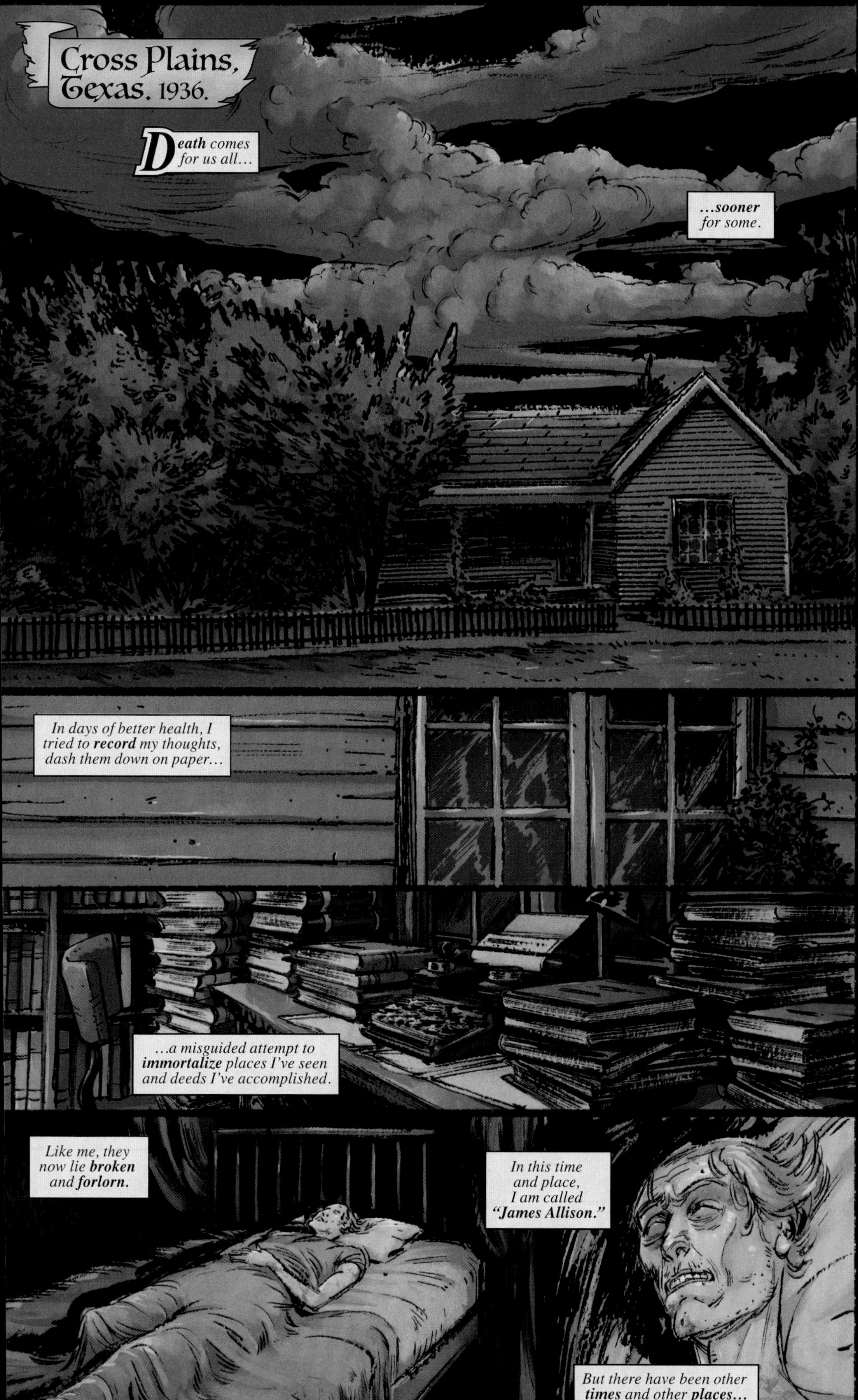
Cross Plains, Texas. 1936.
Death comes for us all...
...sooner for some.
In days of better health, I tried to record my thoughts, dash them down on paper...
...a misguided attempt to immortalize places I've seen and deeds I've accomplished.
Like me, they now lie broken and forlorn.
In this time and place, I am called "James Allison."
But there have been other times and other places...

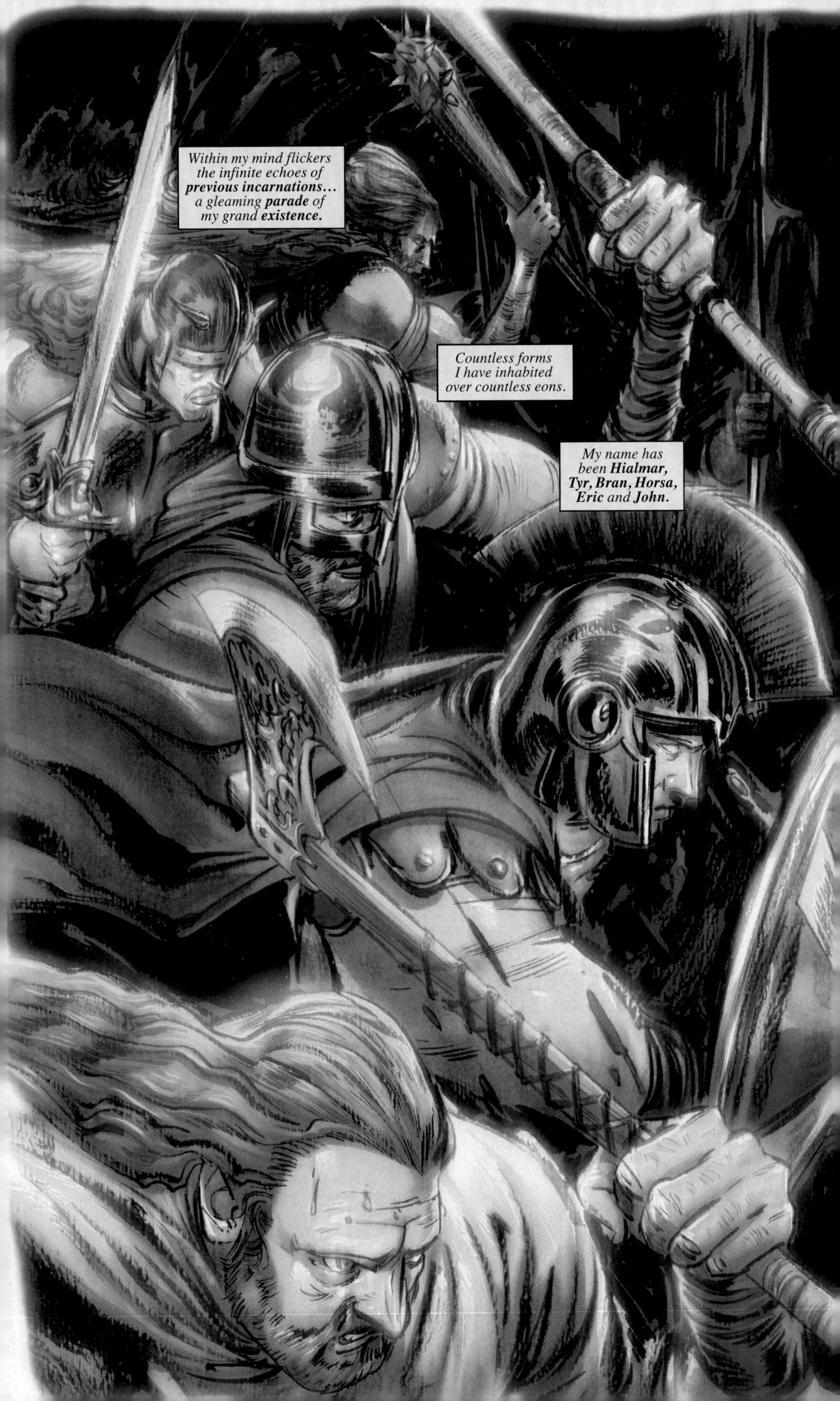
Within my mind flickers the infinite echoes of **previous incarnations...** a gleaming **parade** of my grand **existence.**
Countless forms I have inhabited over countless eons.
My name has been **Hialmar, Tyr, Bran, Horsa, Eric** and **John.**

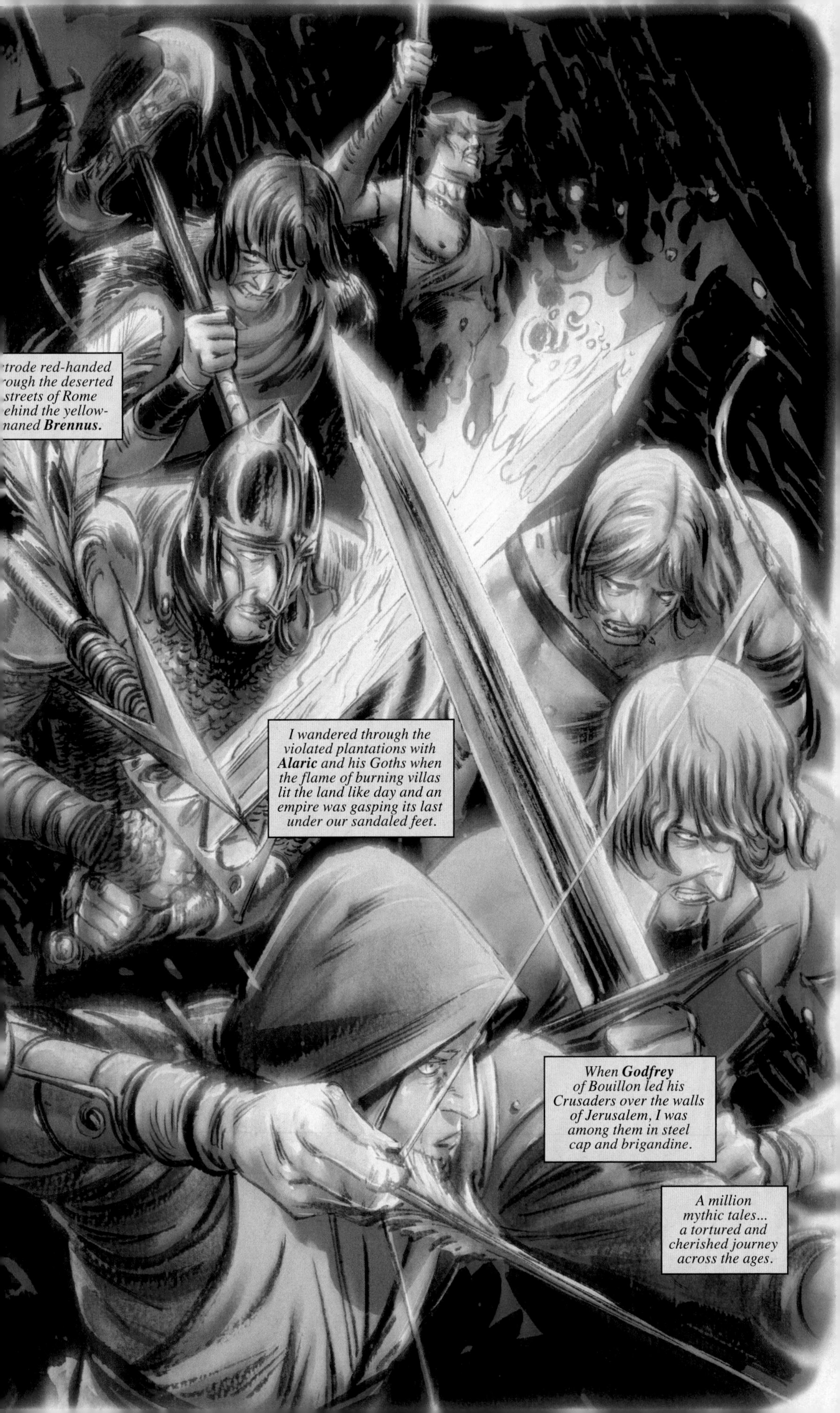

trode red-handed rough the deserted streets of Rome ehind the yellow-naned **Brennus.**
I wandered through the violated plantations with **Alaric** and his Goths when the flame of burning villas lit the land like day and an empire was gasping its last under our sandaled feet.
When **Godfrey** of Bouillon led his Crusaders over the walls of Jerusalem, I was among them in steel cap and brigandine.
A million mythic tales... a tortured and cherished journey across the ages.

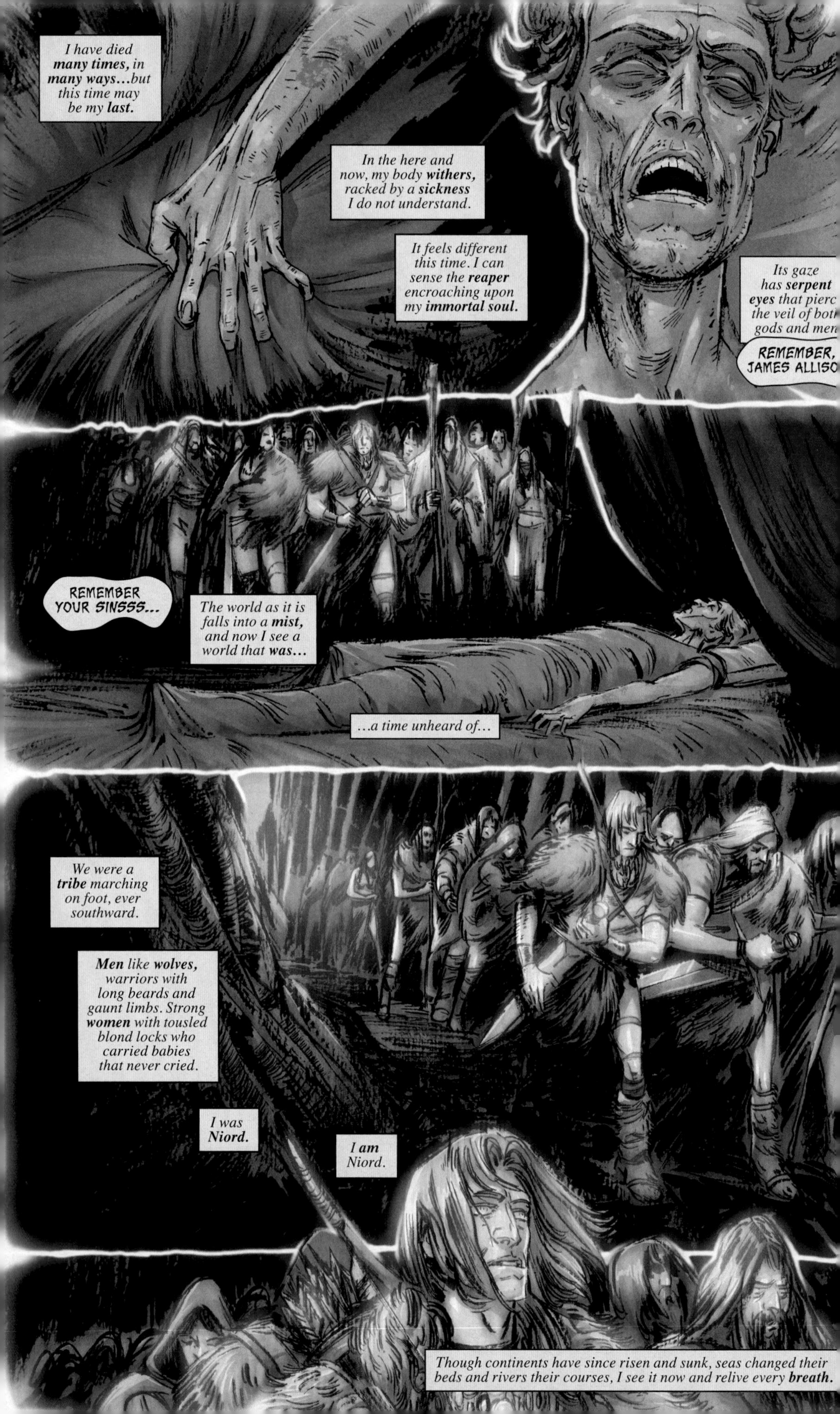
I have died ***many times,*** in ***many ways…***but this time may be my ***last.***
In the here and now, my body ***withers,*** racked by a ***sickness*** I do not understand.
It feels different this time. I can sense the ***reaper*** encroaching upon my ***immortal soul.***
Its gaze has ***serpent eyes*** that pierc
the veil of bot
gods and men
REMEMBER, JAMES ALLISO
REMEMBER YOUR SINSSS…
The world as it is falls into a ***mist,*** and now I see a world that ***was…***
…a time unheard of…
We were a ***tribe*** marching on foot, ever southward.
Men like ***wolves,*** warriors with long beards and gaunt limbs. Strong ***women*** with tousled blond locks who carried babies that never cried.
I was ***Niord.***
I am Niord.
Though continents have since risen and sunk, seas changed their beds and rivers their courses, I see it now and relive every ***breath.***

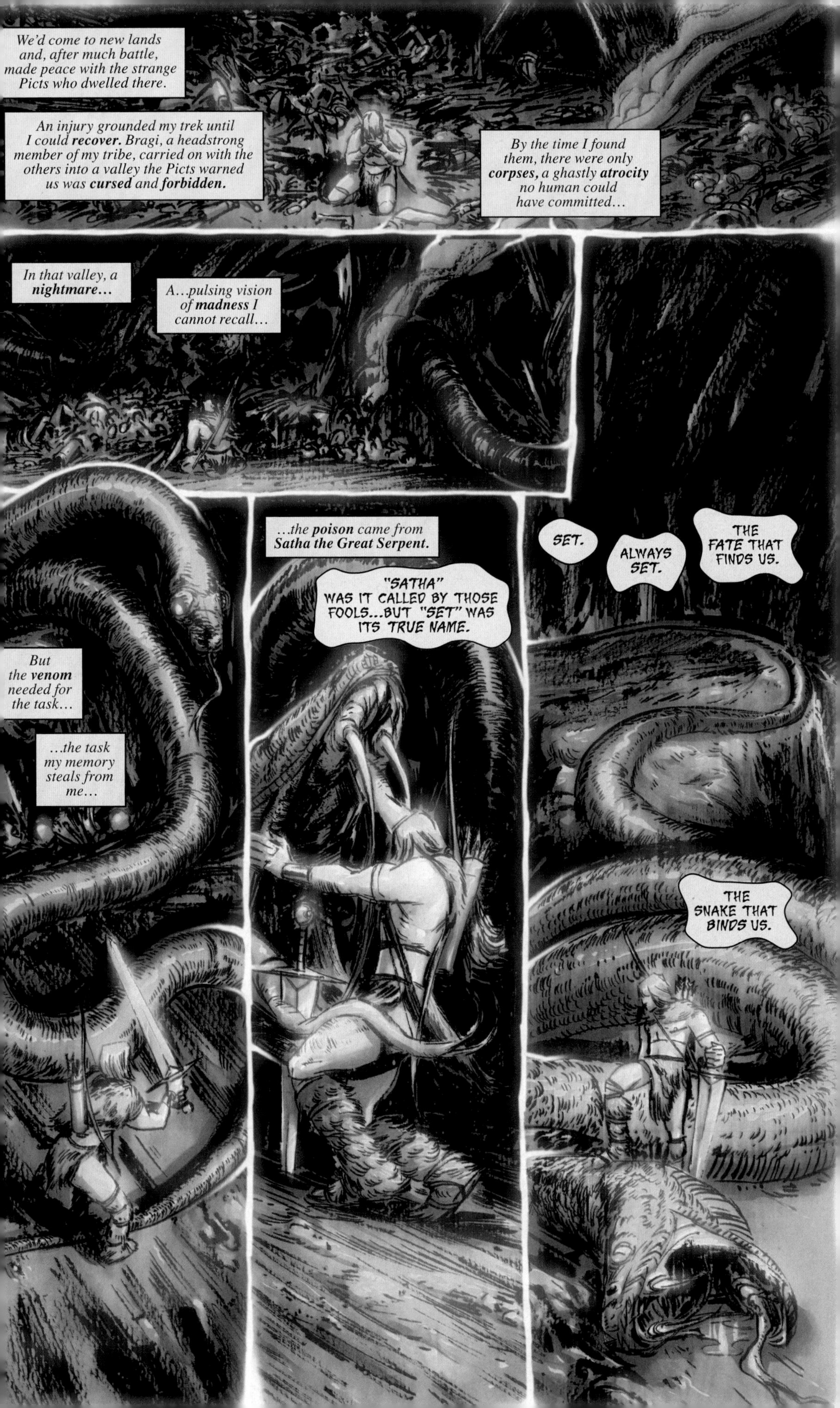
We'd come to new lands and, after much battle, made peace with the strange Picts who dwelled there.
An injury grounded my trek until I could **recover.** Bragi, a headstrong member of my tribe, carried on with the others into a valley the Picts warned us was **cursed** and **forbidden.**
By the time I found them, there were only **corpses,** a ghastly **atrocity** no human could have committed…
In that valley, a **nightmare…**
A…pulsing vision of **madness** I cannot recall…
But the **venom** needed for the task…
…the task my memory steals from me…
…the **poison** came from **Satha the Great Serpent**.
"SATHA" WAS IT CALLED BY THOSE FOOLS...BUT "SET" WAS ITS TRUE NAME.
SET.
ALWAYS SET.
THE FATE THAT FINDS US.
THE SNAKE THAT BINDS US.

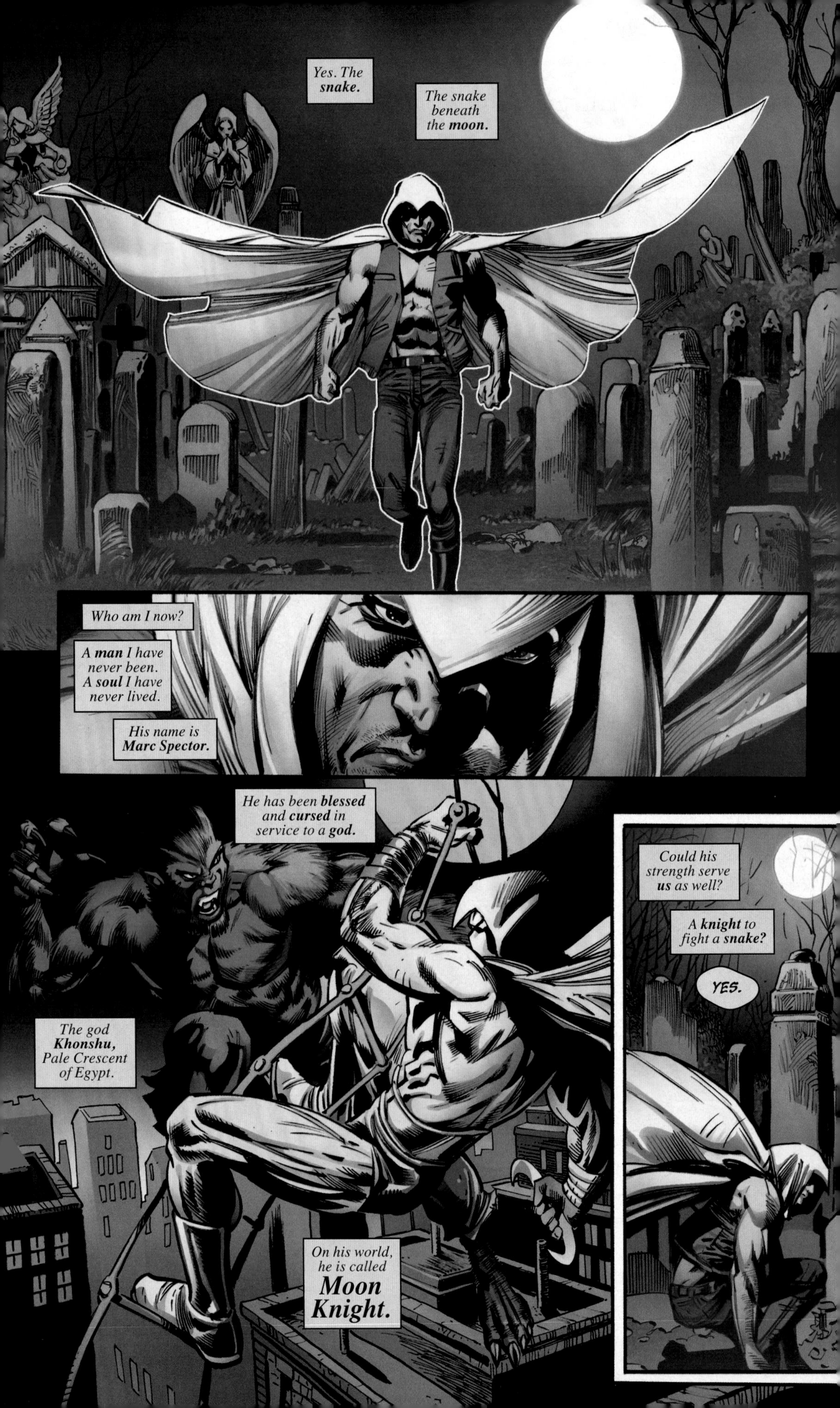
Yes. The **snake.**
The snake beneath the **moon.**
Who am I now?
A **man** I have never been. A **soul** I have never lived.
His name is **Marc Spector.**
He has been **blessed** and **cursed** in service to a **god.**
The god **Khonshu,** Pale Crescent of Egypt.
On his world, he is called **Moon Knight.**
Could his strength serve **us** as well?
A **knight** to fight a **snake?**
YES.

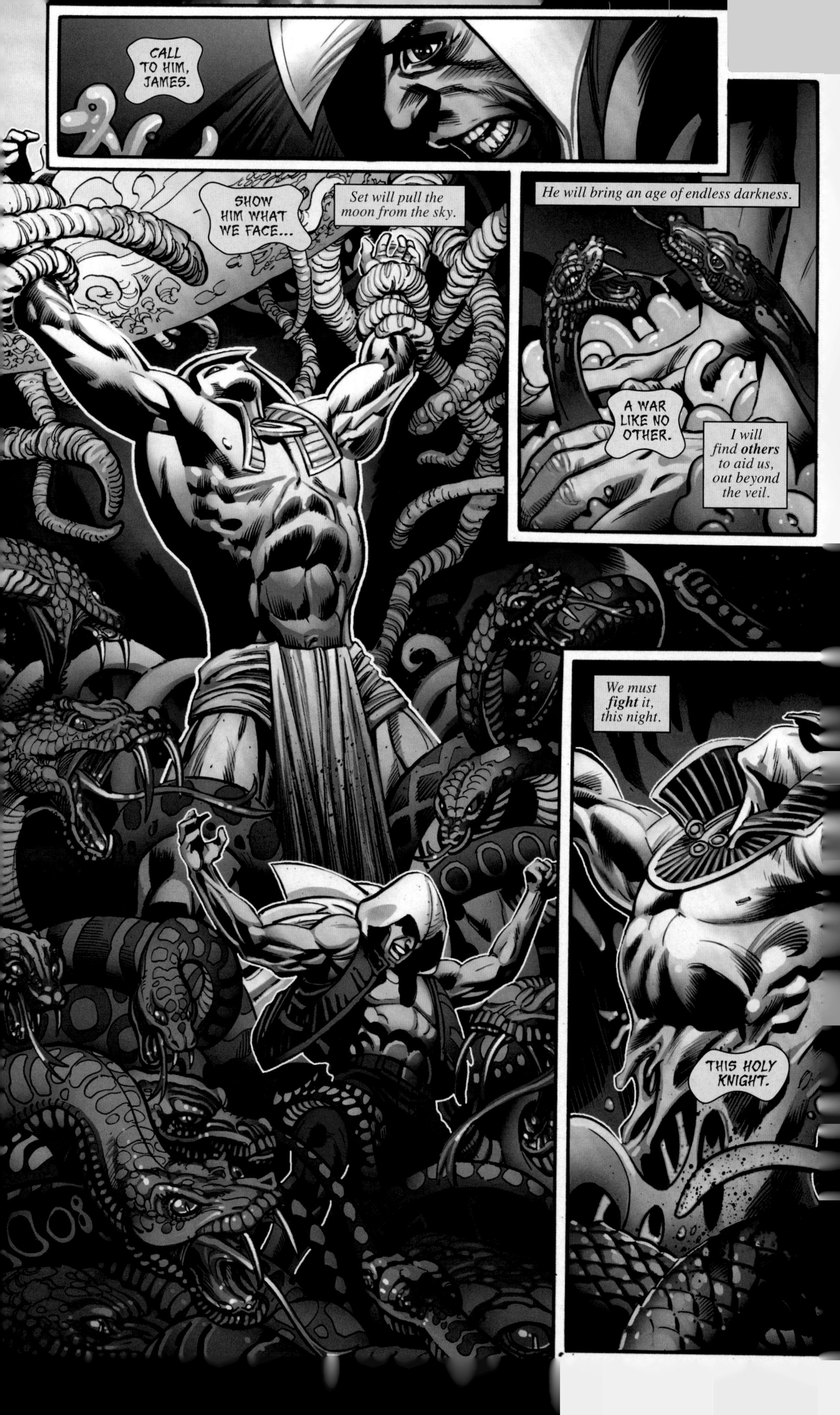
CALL TO HIM, JAMES.
SHOW HIM WHAT WE FACE...
Set will pull the moon from the sky.
He will bring an age of endless darkness.
A WAR LIKE NO OTHER.
I will find **others** to aid us, out beyond the veil.
We must **fight** it, this night.
THIS HOLY KNIGHT.

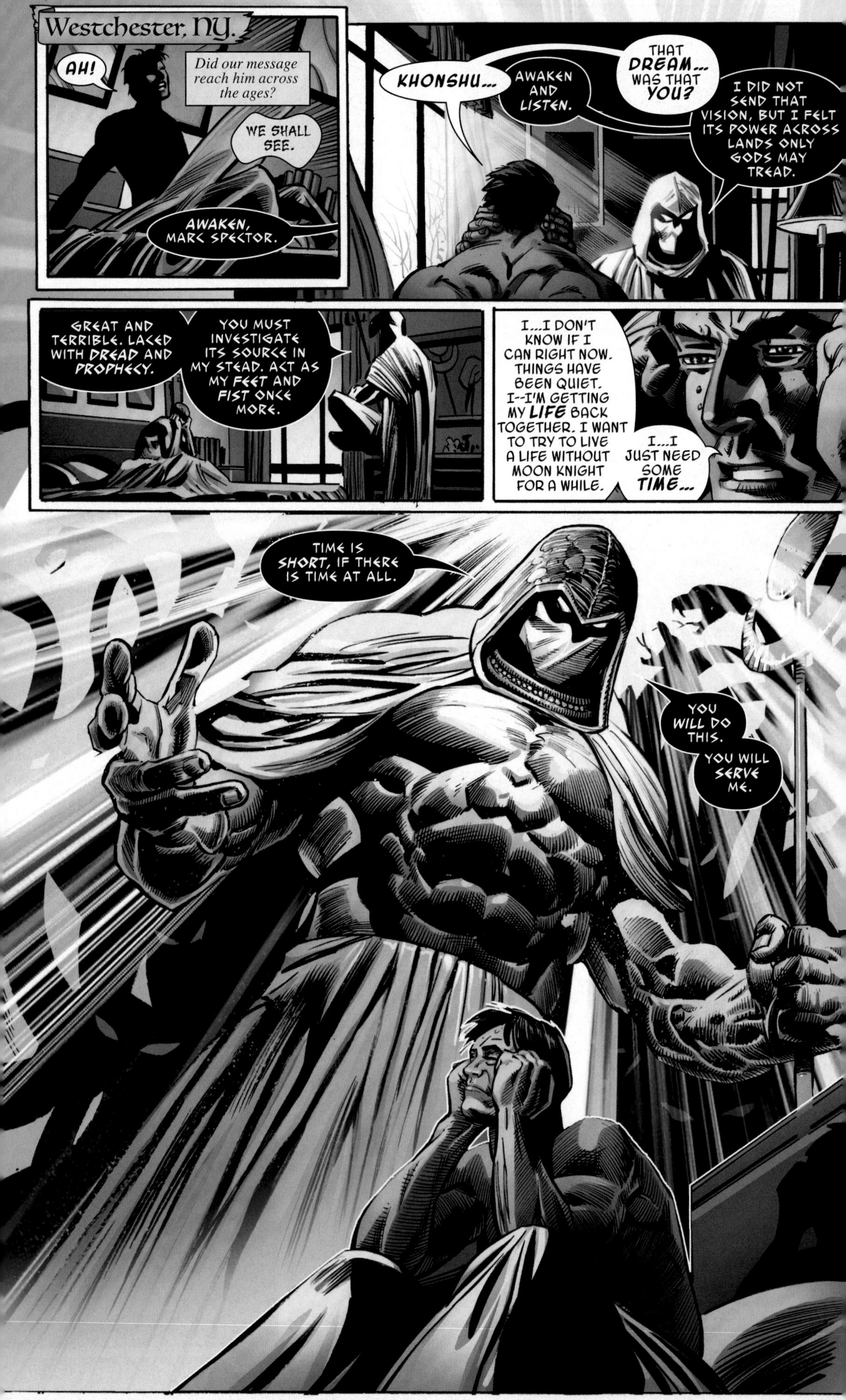
Westchester, NY.
AH!
Did our message reach him across the ages?
WE SHALL SEE.
AWAKEN, MARC SPECTOR.
KHONSHU...
AWAKEN AND LISTEN.
THAT DREAM... WAS THAT YOU?
I DID NOT SEND THAT VISION, BUT I FELT ITS POWER ACROSS LANDS ONLY GODS MAY TREAD.
GREAT AND TERRIBLE. LACED WITH DREAD AND PROPHECY.
YOU MUST INVESTIGATE ITS SOURCE IN MY STEAD. ACT AS MY FEET AND FIST ONCE MORE.
I...I DON'T KNOW IF I CAN RIGHT NOW. THINGS HAVE BEEN QUIET. I--I'M GETTING MY LIFE BACK TOGETHER. I WANT TO TRY TO LIVE A LIFE WITHOUT MOON KNIGHT FOR A WHILE.
I...I JUST NEED SOME TIME...
TIME IS SHORT, IF THERE IS TIME AT ALL.
YOU WILL DO THIS.
YOU WILL SERVE ME.

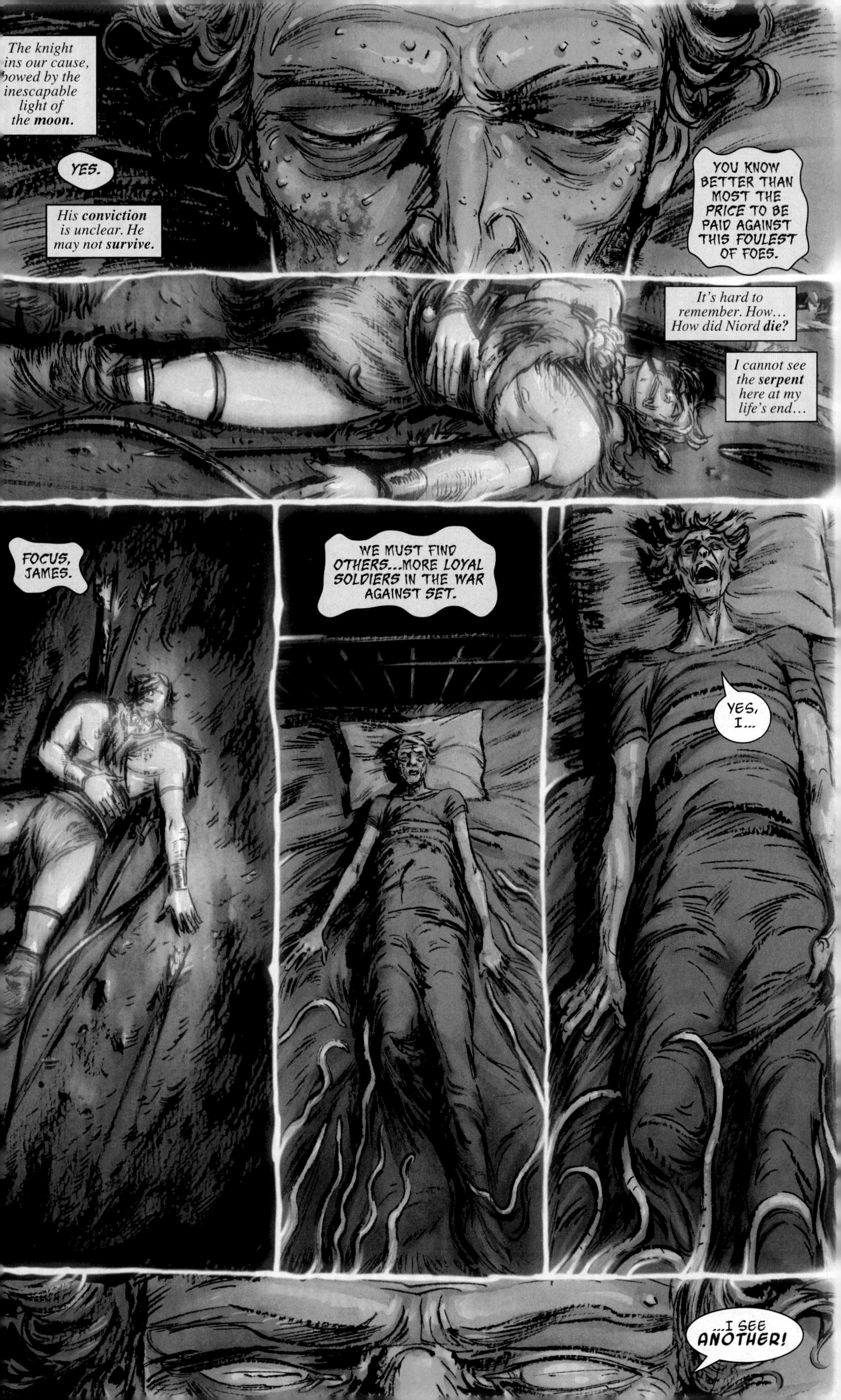

The knight
ins our cause,
bowed by the
inescapable
light of
the **moon**.
YES.
His **conviction**
is unclear. He
may not **survive**.
YOU KNOW
BETTER THAN
MOST THE
PRICE TO BE
PAID AGAINST
THIS *FOULEST*
OF FOES.
It's hard to
remember. How…
How did Niord **die**?
I cannot see
the **serpent**
here at my
life's end…
FOCUS,
JAMES.
WE MUST FIND
OTHERS...MORE LOYAL
SOLDIERS IN THE WAR
AGAINST SET.
YES,
I...
...I SEE
ANOTHER!

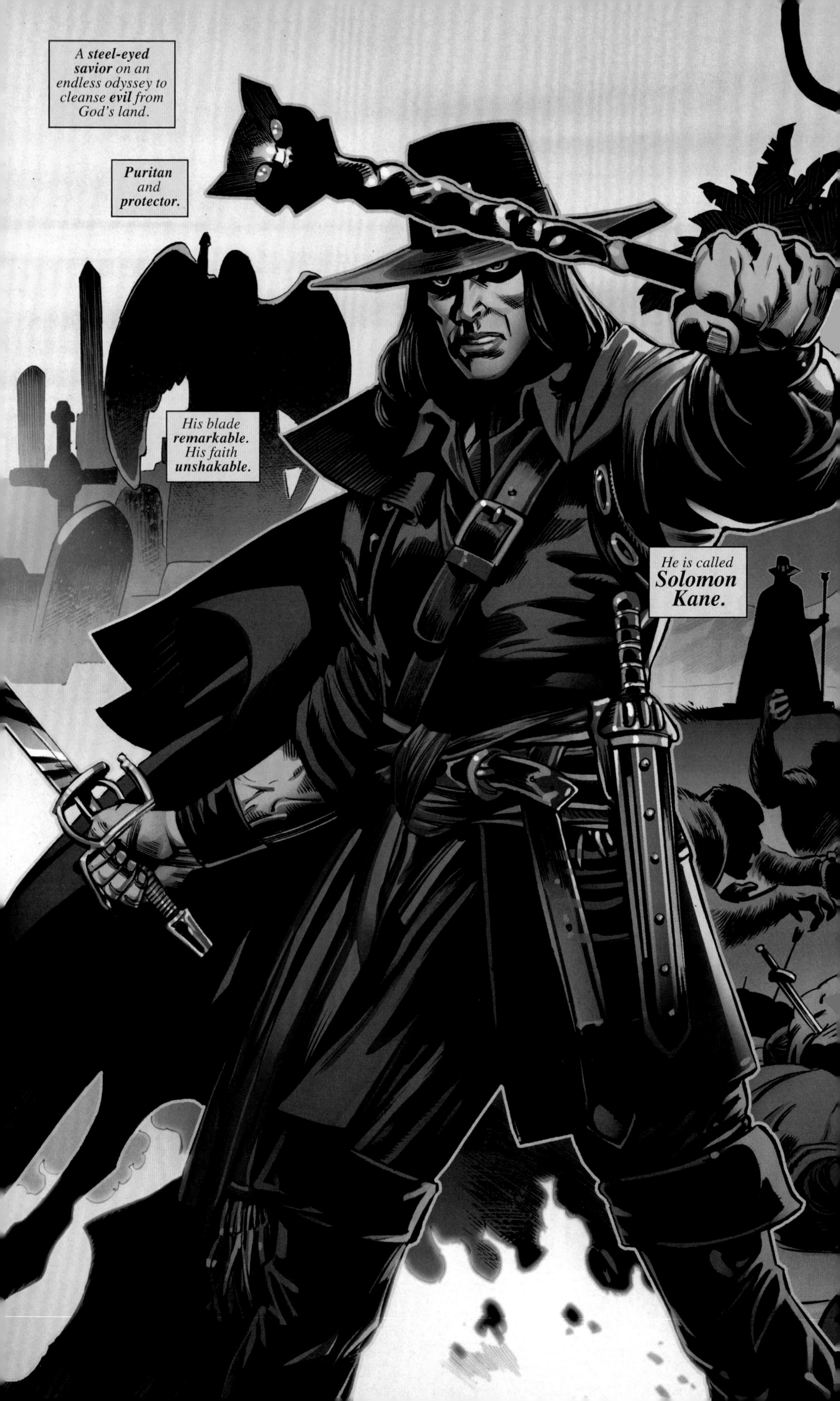
A **steel-eyed savior** on an endless odyssey to cleanse **evil** from God's land.
Puritan and **protector.**
His blade **remarkable.** His faith **unshakable.**
He is called **Solomon Kane.**

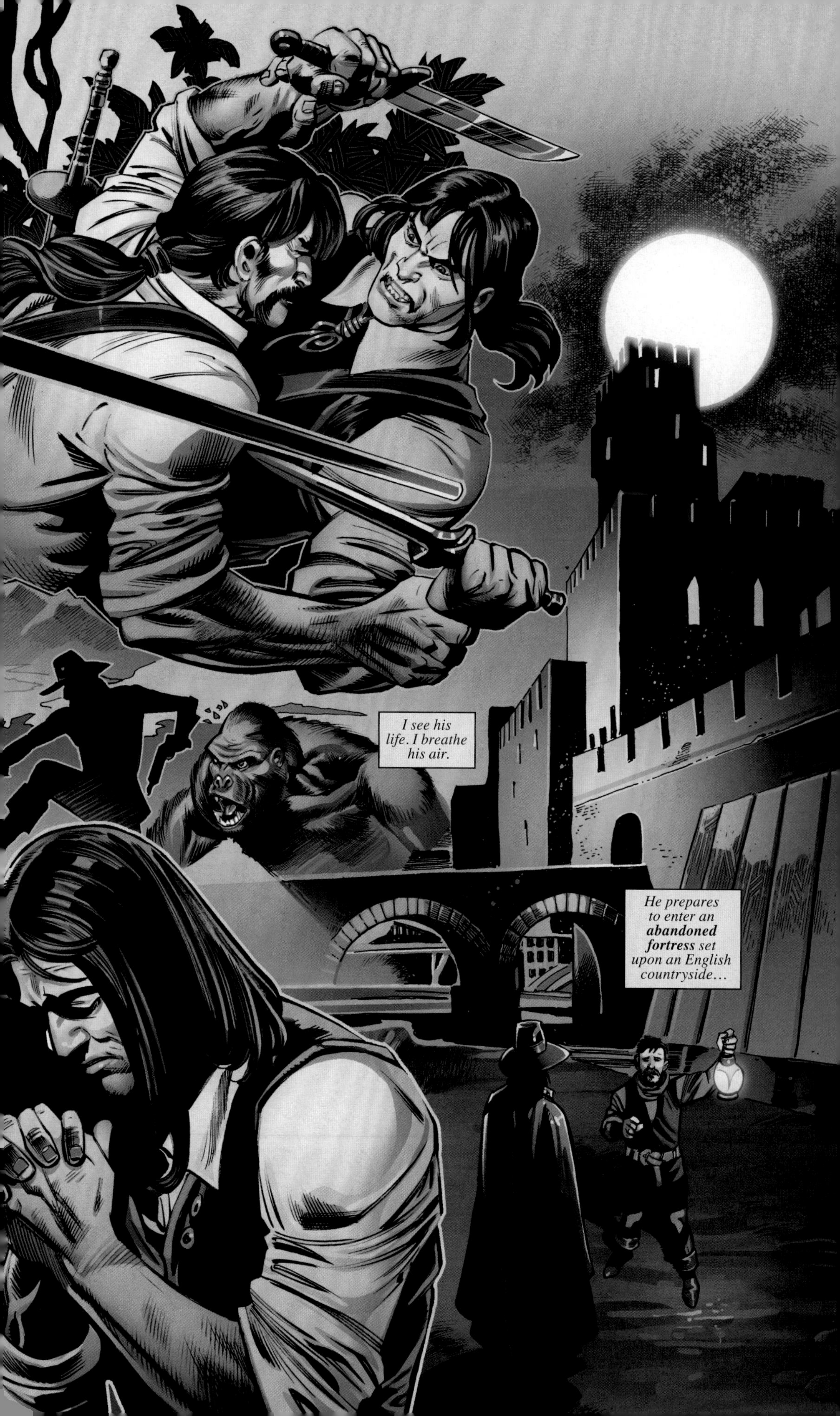

I see his life. I breathe his air.
He prepares to enter an **abandoned fortress** set upon an English countryside…

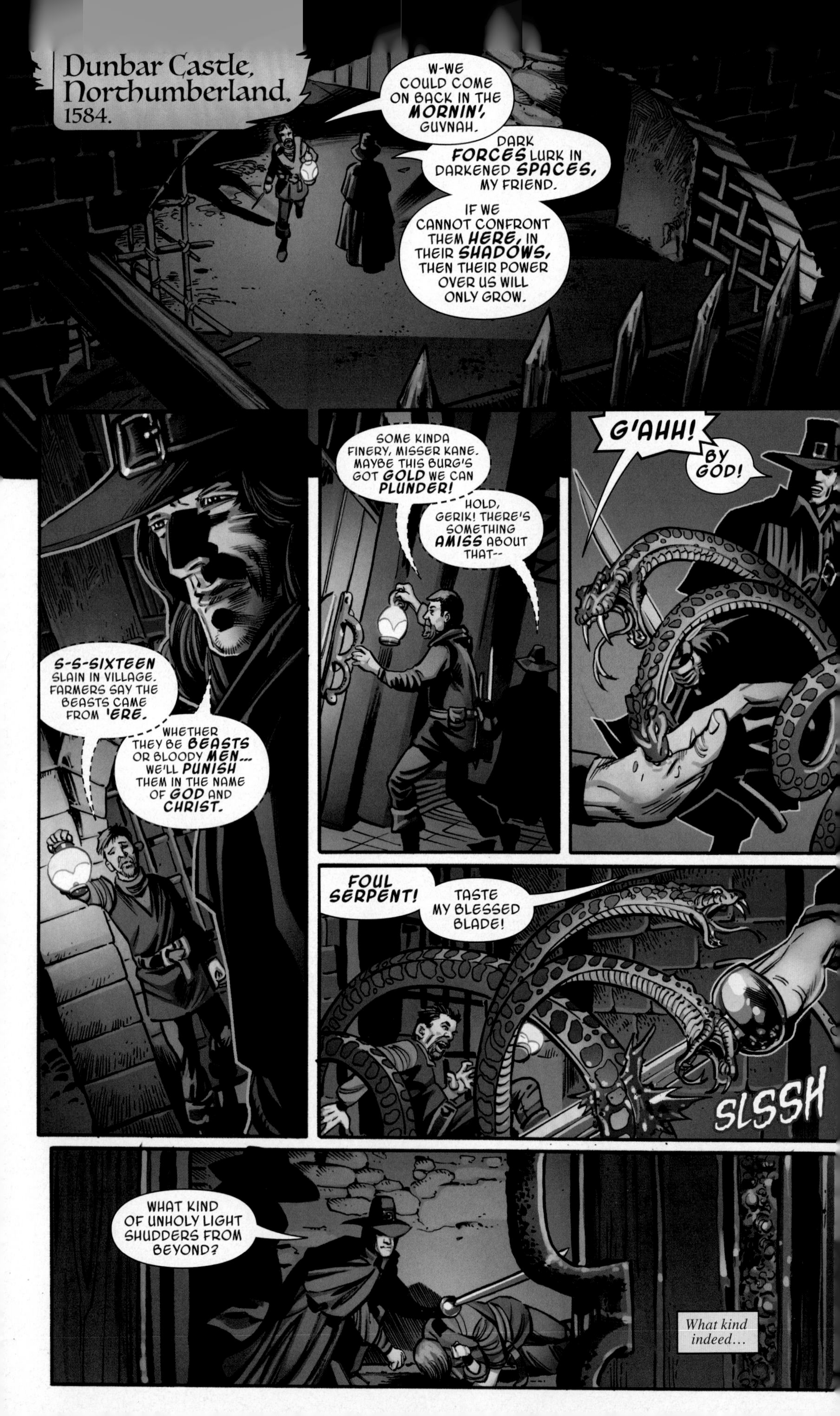
Dunbar Castle, Northumberland. 1584.
W-WE COULD COME ON BACK IN THE MORNIN', GUVNAH.
DARK FORCES LURK IN DARKENED SPACES, MY FRIEND.
IF WE CANNOT CONFRONT THEM HERE, IN THEIR SHADOWS, THEN THEIR POWER OVER US WILL ONLY GROW.
S-S-SIXTEEN SLAIN IN VILLAGE. FARMERS SAY THE BEASTS CAME FROM 'ERE.
WHETHER THEY BE BEASTS OR BLOODY MEN... WE'LL PUNISH THEM IN THE NAME OF GOD AND CHRIST.
SOME KINDA FINERY, MISSER KANE. MAYBE THIS BURG'S GOT GOLD WE CAN PLUNDER!
HOLD, GERIK! THERE'S SOMETHING AMISS ABOUT THAT--
G'AHH!
BY GOD!
FOUL SERPENT!
TASTE MY BLESSED BLADE!
SLSSH
WHAT KIND OF UNHOLY LIGHT SHUDDERS FROM BEYOND?
What kind indeed...

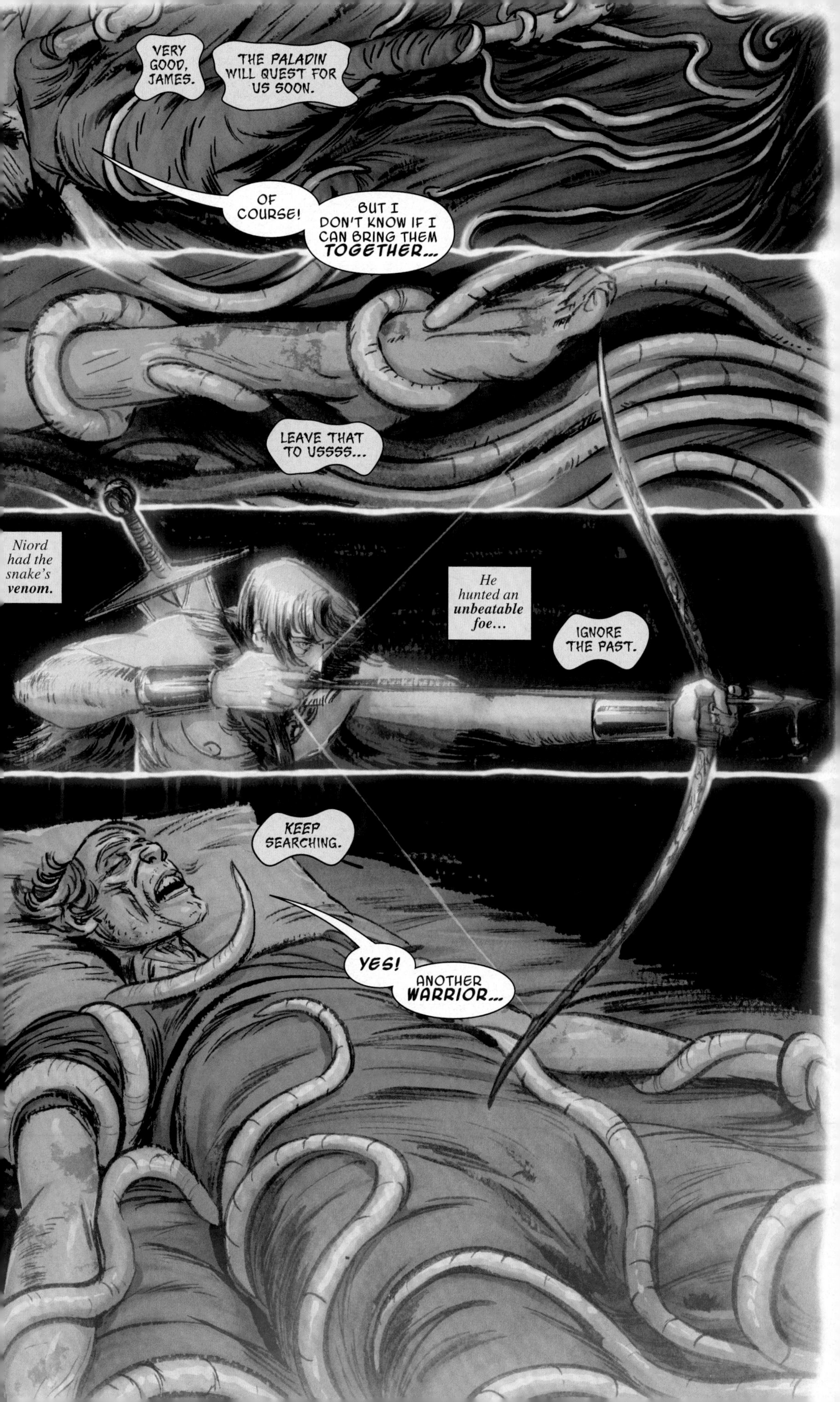
VERY GOOD, JAMES.
THE *PALADIN* WILL QUEST FOR US SOON.
OF COURSE!
BUT I DON'T KNOW IF I CAN BRING THEM ***TOGETHER...***
LEAVE THAT TO USSSS...
*Niord had the snake's **venom.***
*He hunted an **unbeatable foe...***
IGNORE THE PAST.
KEEP SEARCHING.
YES!
ANOTHER **WARRIOR...**

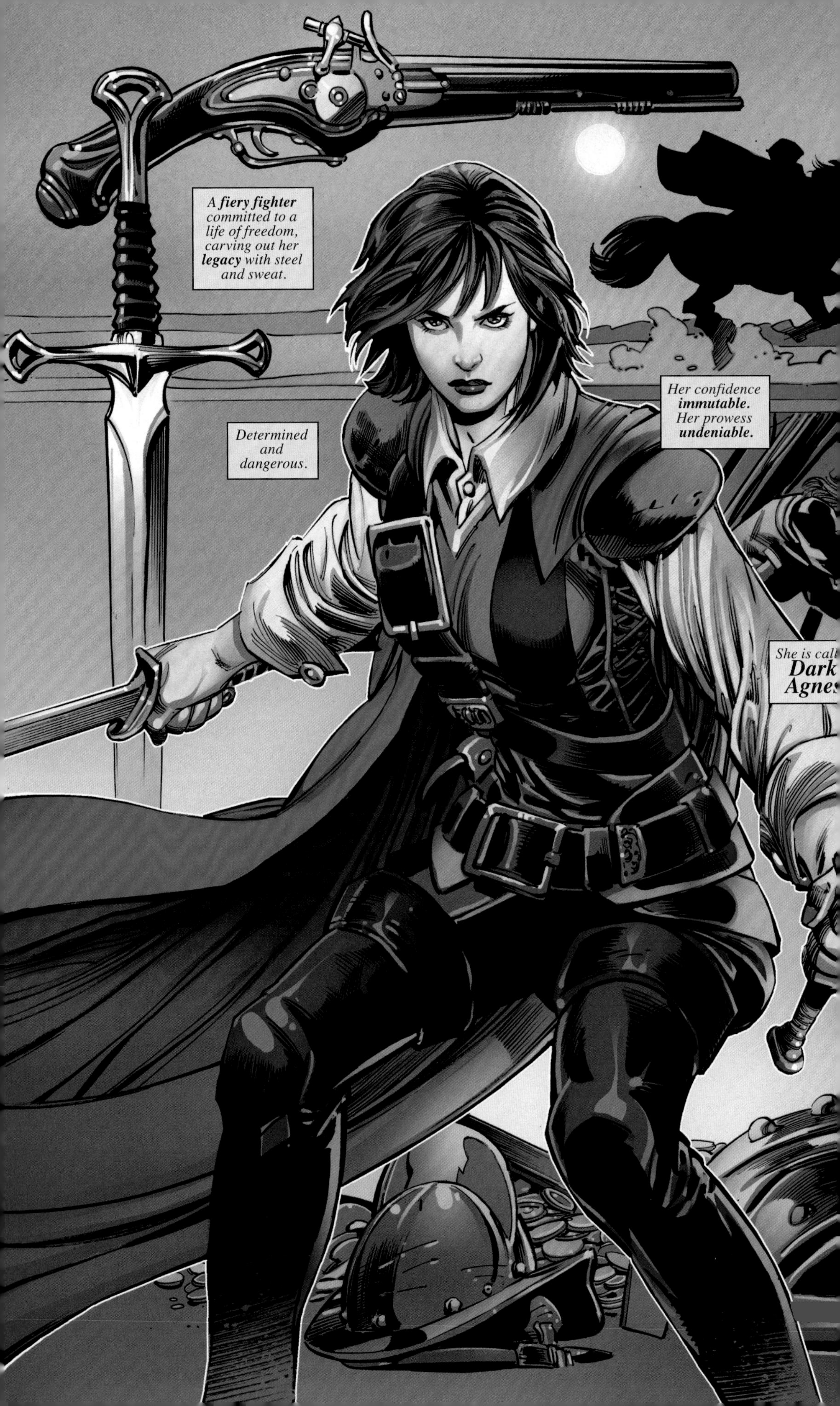
A **fiery fighter** committed to a life of freedom, carving out her **legacy** with steel and sweat.
Determined and dangerous.
Her confidence **immutable.** Her prowess **undeniable.**
She is cal
Dark
Agne

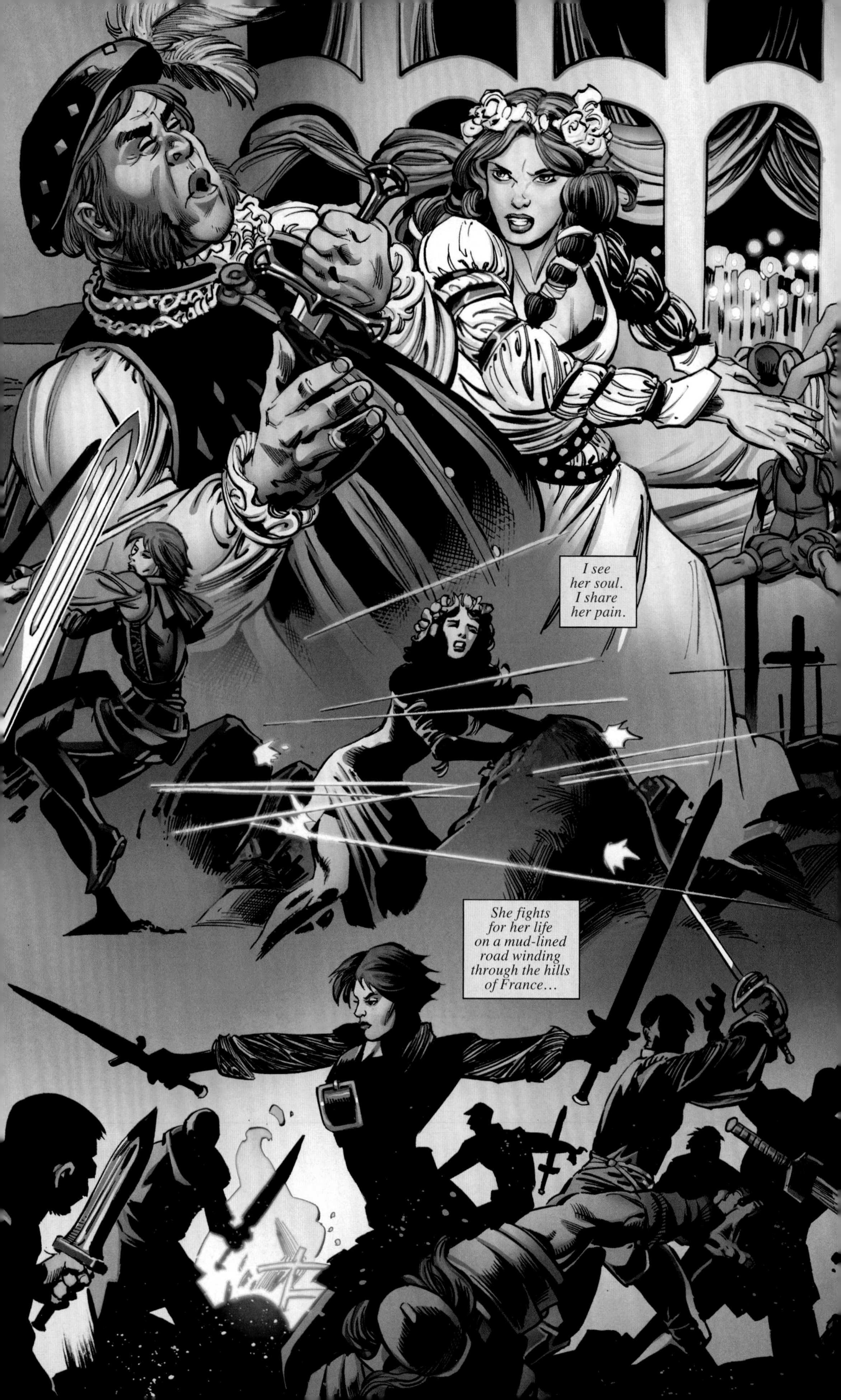
I see her soul. I share her pain.
She fights for her life on a mud-lined road winding through the hills of France…

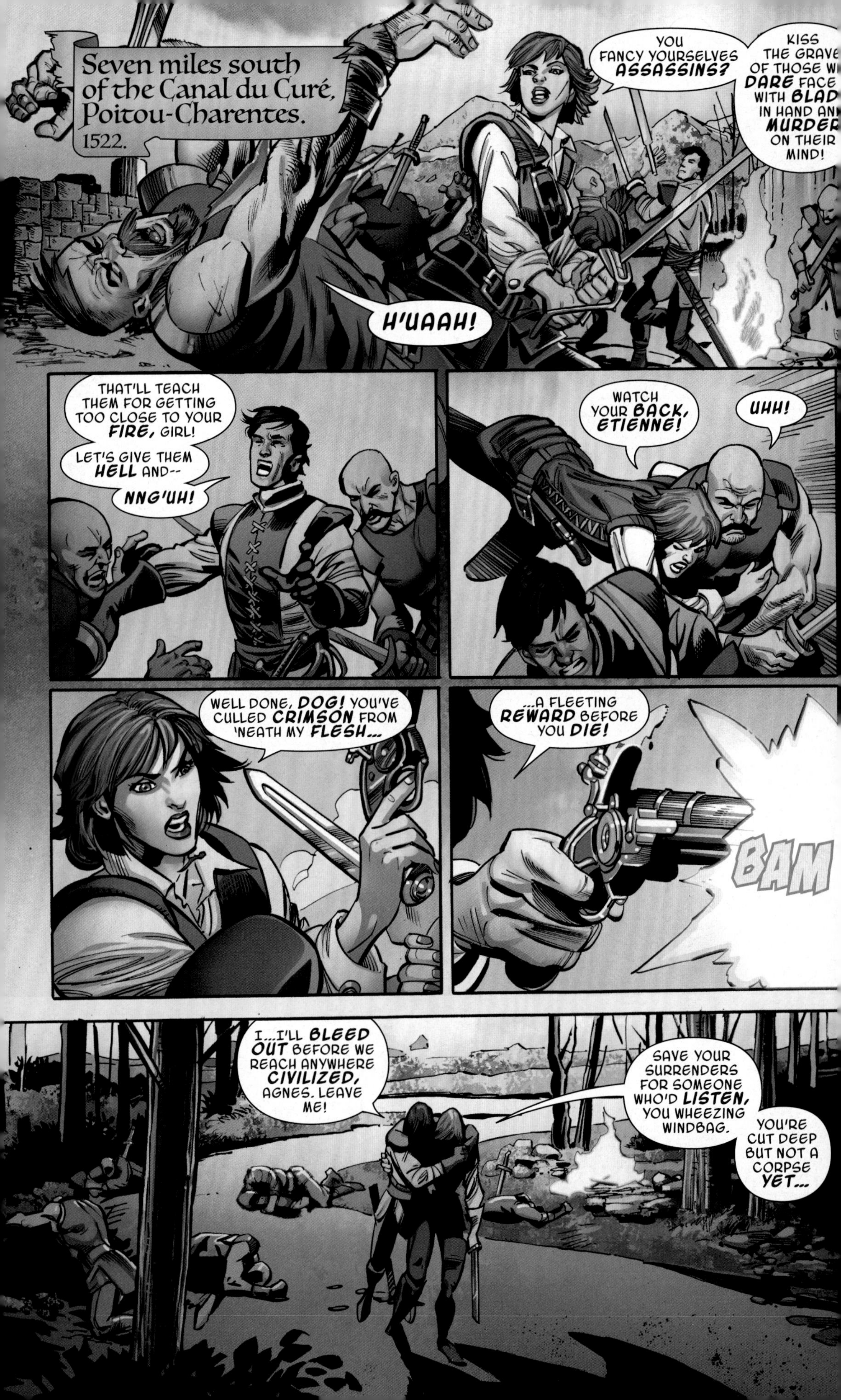

Seven miles south of the Canal du Curé, Poitou-Charentes. 1522.
YOU FANCY YOURSELVES ASSASSINS?
KISS THE GRAVE OF THOSE WH DARE FACE WITH BLAD IN HAND AN MURDER ON THEIR MIND!
H'UAAH!
THAT'LL TEACH THEM FOR GETTING TOO CLOSE TO YOUR FIRE, GIRL!
LET'S GIVE THEM HELL AND--
NNG'UH!
WATCH YOUR BACK, ETIENNE!
UHH!
WELL DONE, DOG! YOU'VE CULLED CRIMSON FROM 'NEATH MY FLESH...
...A FLEETING REWARD BEFORE YOU DIE!
BAM
I...I'LL BLEED OUT BEFORE WE REACH ANYWHERE CIVILIZED, AGNES. LEAVE ME!
SAVE YOUR SURRENDERS FOR SOMEONE WHO'D LISTEN, YOU WHEEZING WINDBAG.
YOU'RE CUT DEEP BUT NOT A CORPSE YET...

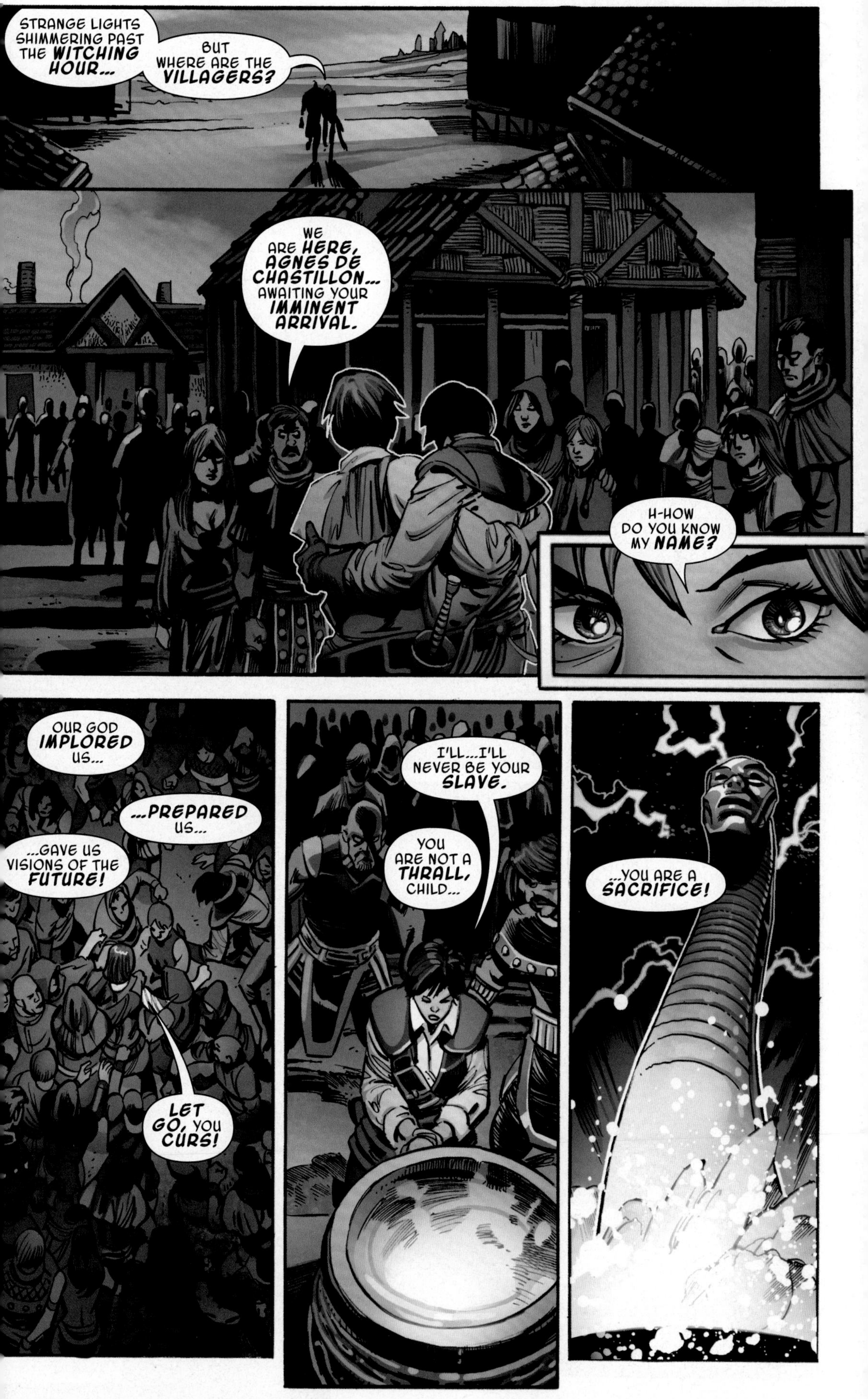
STRANGE LIGHTS SHIMMERING PAST THE WITCHING HOUR...
BUT WHERE ARE THE VILLAGERS?
WE ARE HERE, AGNES DE CHASTILLON... AWAITING YOUR IMMINENT ARRIVAL.
H-HOW DO YOU KNOW MY NAME?
OUR GOD IMPLORED US...
...PREPARED US...
...GAVE US VISIONS OF THE FUTURE!
LET GO, YOU CURS!
I'LL...I'LL NEVER BE YOUR SLAVE.
YOU ARE NOT A THRALL, CHILD...
...YOU ARE A SACRIFICE!

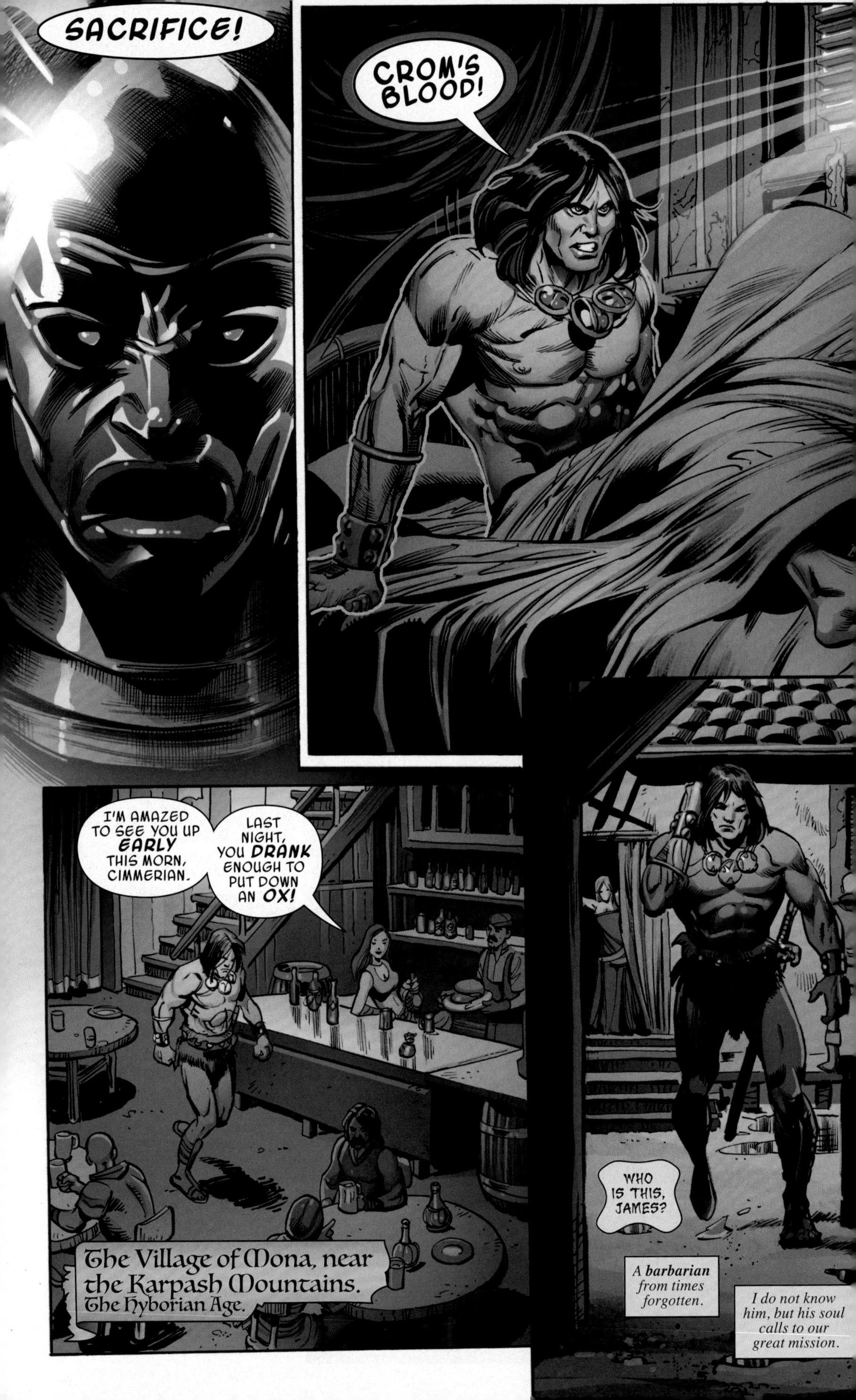

SACRIFICE!
CROM'S BLOOD!
The Village of Mona, near the Karpash Mountains.
The Hyborian Age.
I'M AMAZED TO SEE YOU UP EARLY THIS MORN, CIMMERIAN.
LAST NIGHT, YOU DRANK ENOUGH TO PUT DOWN AN OX!
WHO IS THIS, JAMES?
A barbarian from times forgotten.
I do not know him, but his soul calls to our great mission.

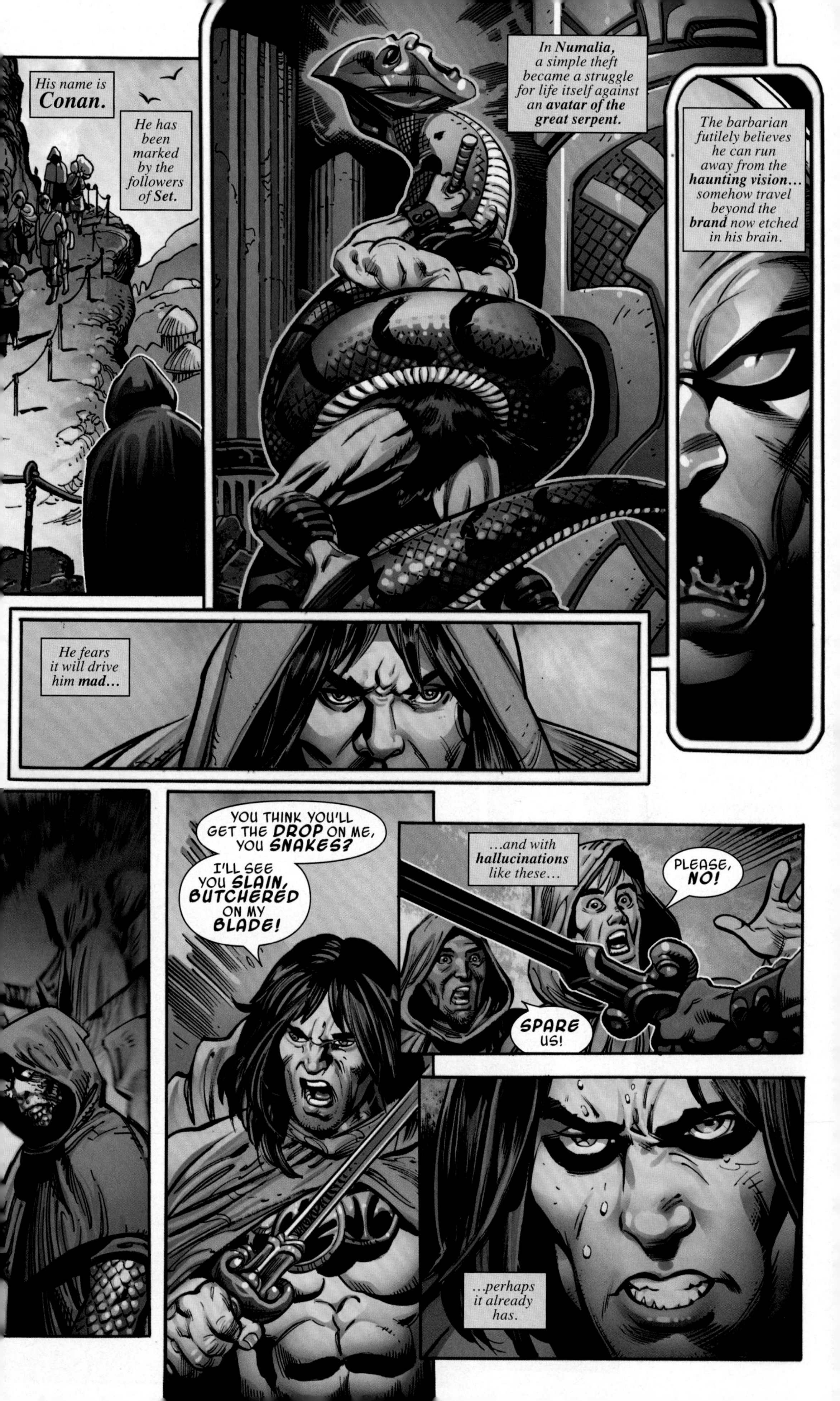

His name is Conan.
He has been marked by the followers of Set.
In Numalia, a simple theft became a struggle for life itself against an avatar of the great serpent.
The barbarian futilely believes he can run away from the haunting vision... somehow travel beyond the brand now etched in his brain.
He fears it will drive him mad...
YOU THINK YOU'LL GET THE DROP ON ME, YOU SNAKES?
I'LL SEE YOU SLAIN, BUTCHERED ON MY BLADE!
...and with hallucinations like these...
PLEASE, NO!
SPARE US!
...perhaps it already has.

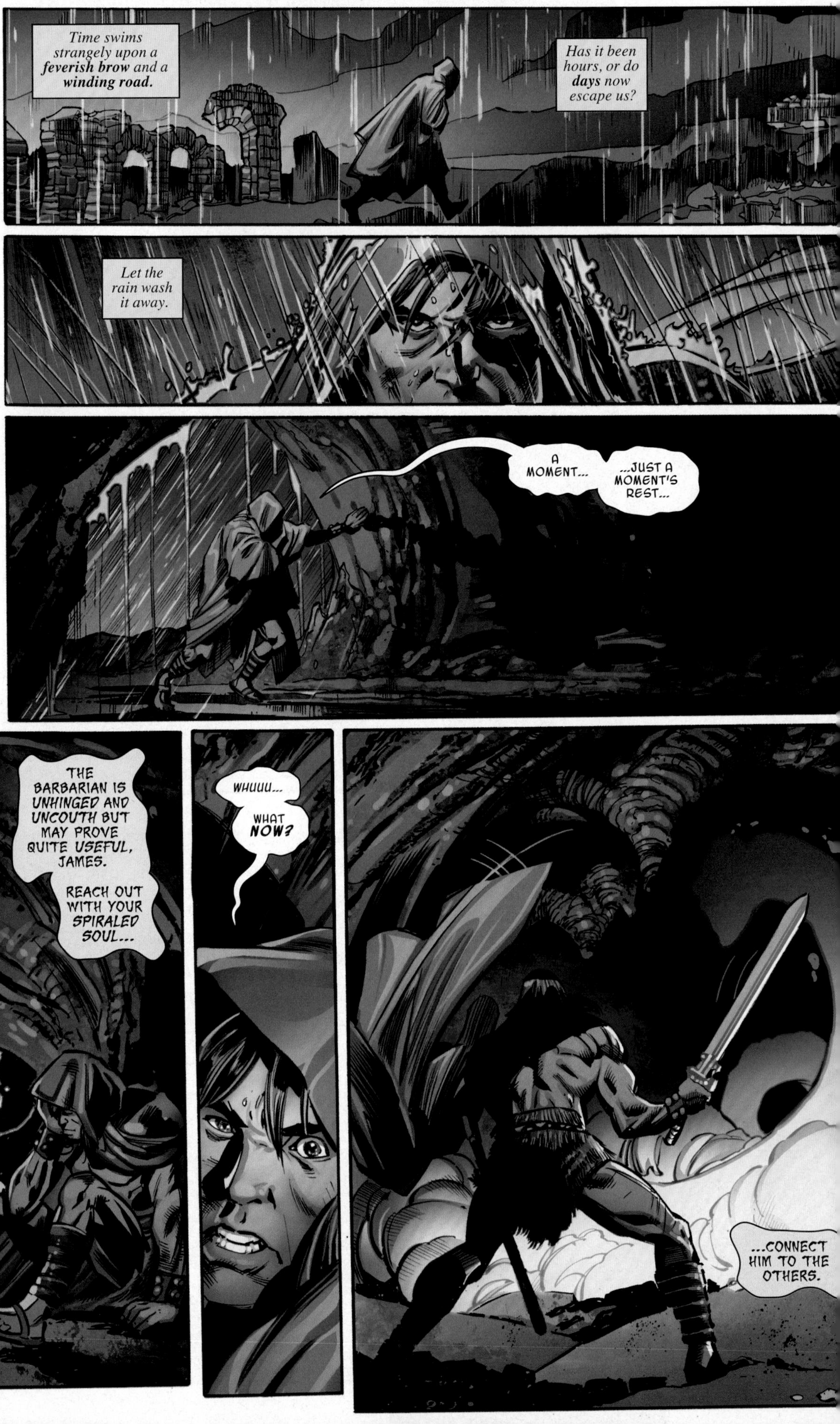

Time swims strangely upon a **feverish brow** and a **winding road.**
Has it been hours, or do **days** now escape us?
Let the rain wash it away.
A MOMENT...
...JUST A MOMENT'S REST...
THE BARBARIAN IS UNHINGED AND UNCOUTH BUT MAY PROVE QUITE USEFUL, JAMES.
REACH OUT WITH YOUR SPIRALED SOUL...
WHUUU...
WHAT **NOW?**
...CONNECT HIM TO THE OTHERS.

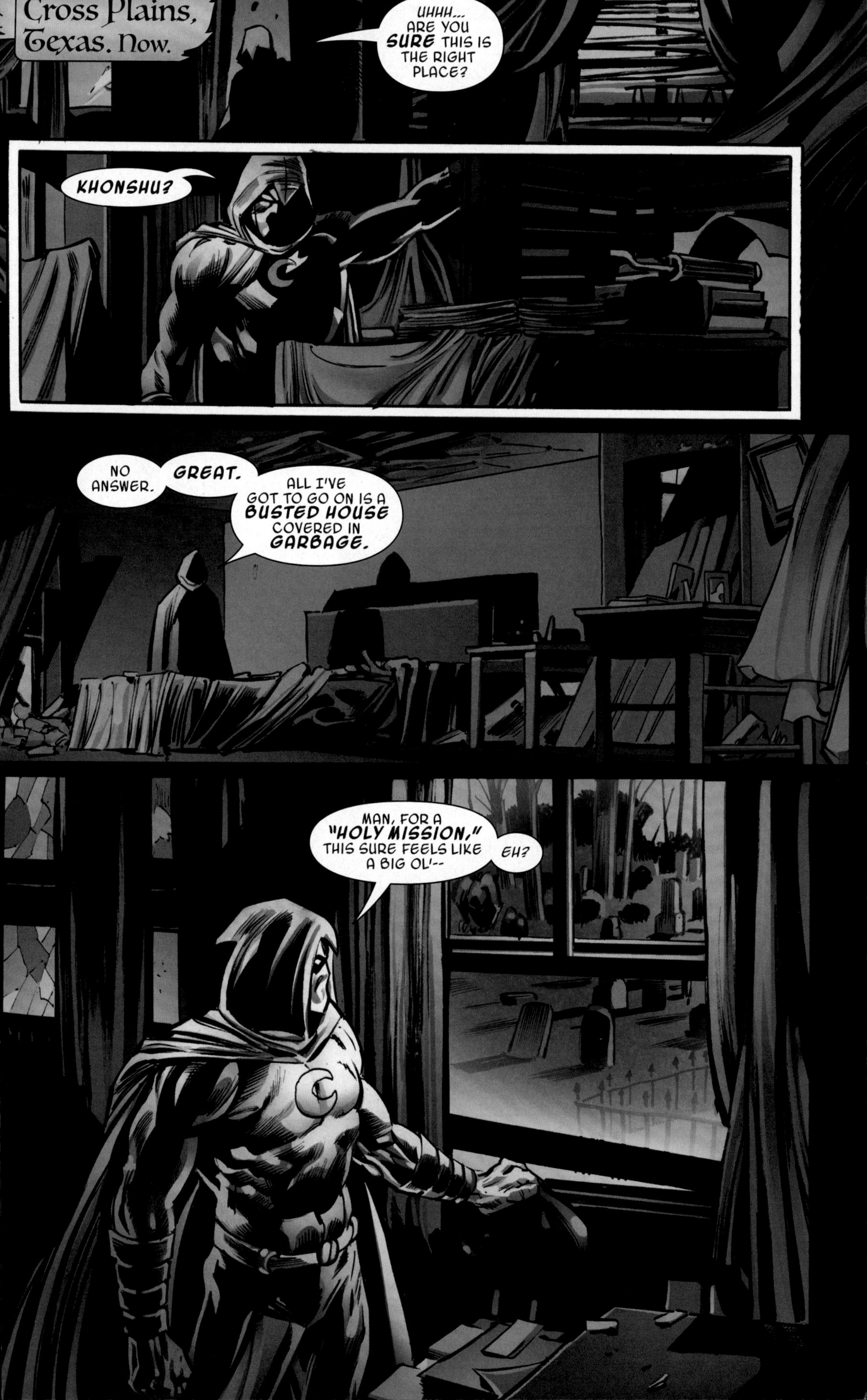
Cross Plains, Texas. Now.
UHHH... ARE YOU SURE THIS IS THE RIGHT PLACE?
KHONSHU?
NO ANSWER.
GREAT.
ALL I'VE GOT TO GO ON IS A BUSTED HOUSE COVERED IN GARBAGE.
MAN, FOR A "HOLY MISSION," THIS SURE FEELS LIKE A BIG OL'--
EH?

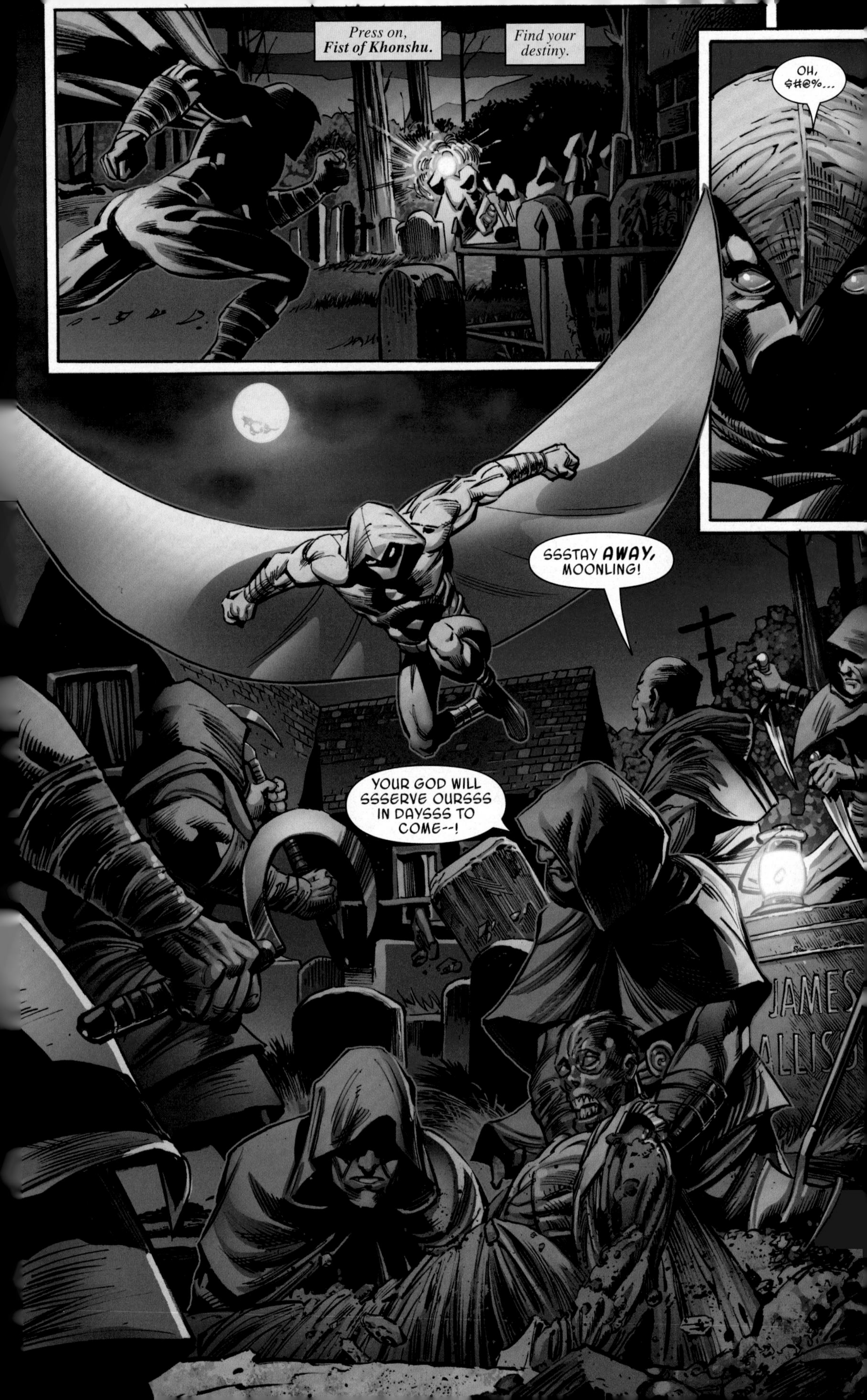
Press on, **Fist of Khonshu.**
Find your destiny.
OH, $#@%...
SSSTAY **AWAY,** MOONLING!
YOUR GOD WILL SSSERVE OURSSS IN DAYSSS TO COME--!
JAMES

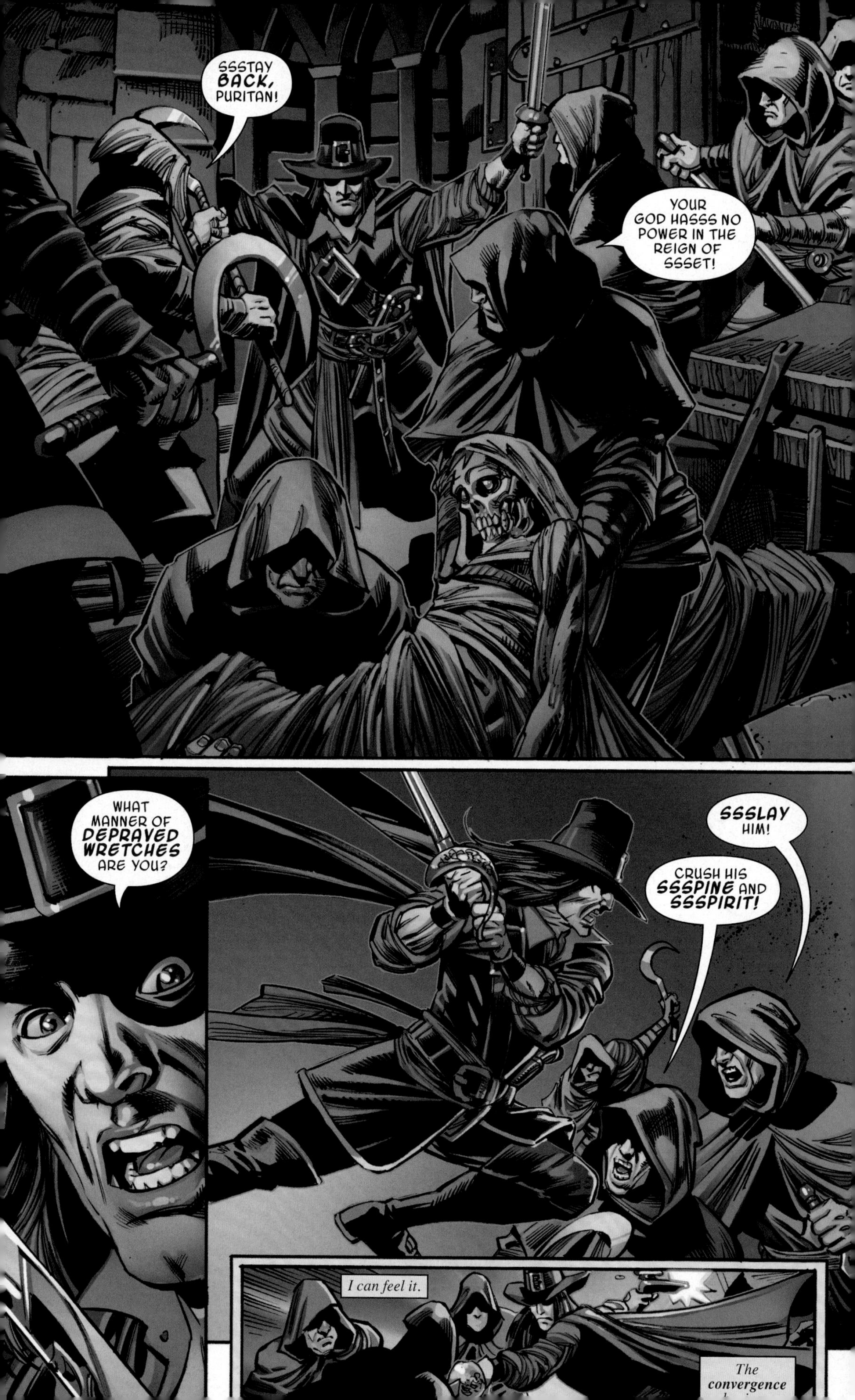
SSSTAY BACK, PURITAN!
YOUR GOD HASSS NO POWER IN THE REIGN OF SSSET!
WHAT MANNER OF DEPRAVED WRETCHES ARE YOU?
SSSLAY HIM!
CRUSH HIS SSSPINE AND SSSPIRIT!
I can feel it.
The convergence

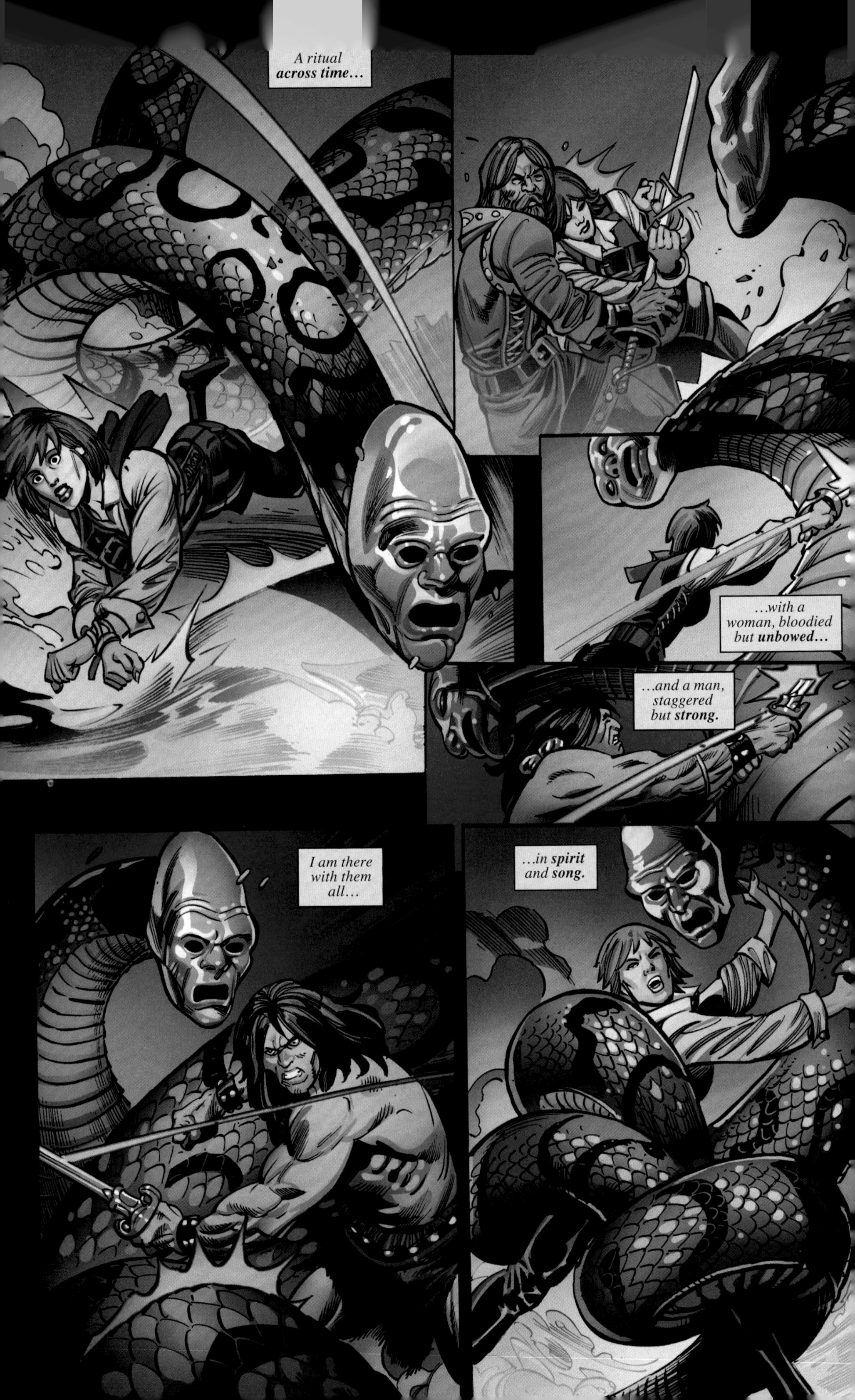
A ritual
across time…
…with a
woman, bloodied
but unbowed…
…and a man,
staggered
but strong.
I am there
with them
all…
…in spirit
and song.

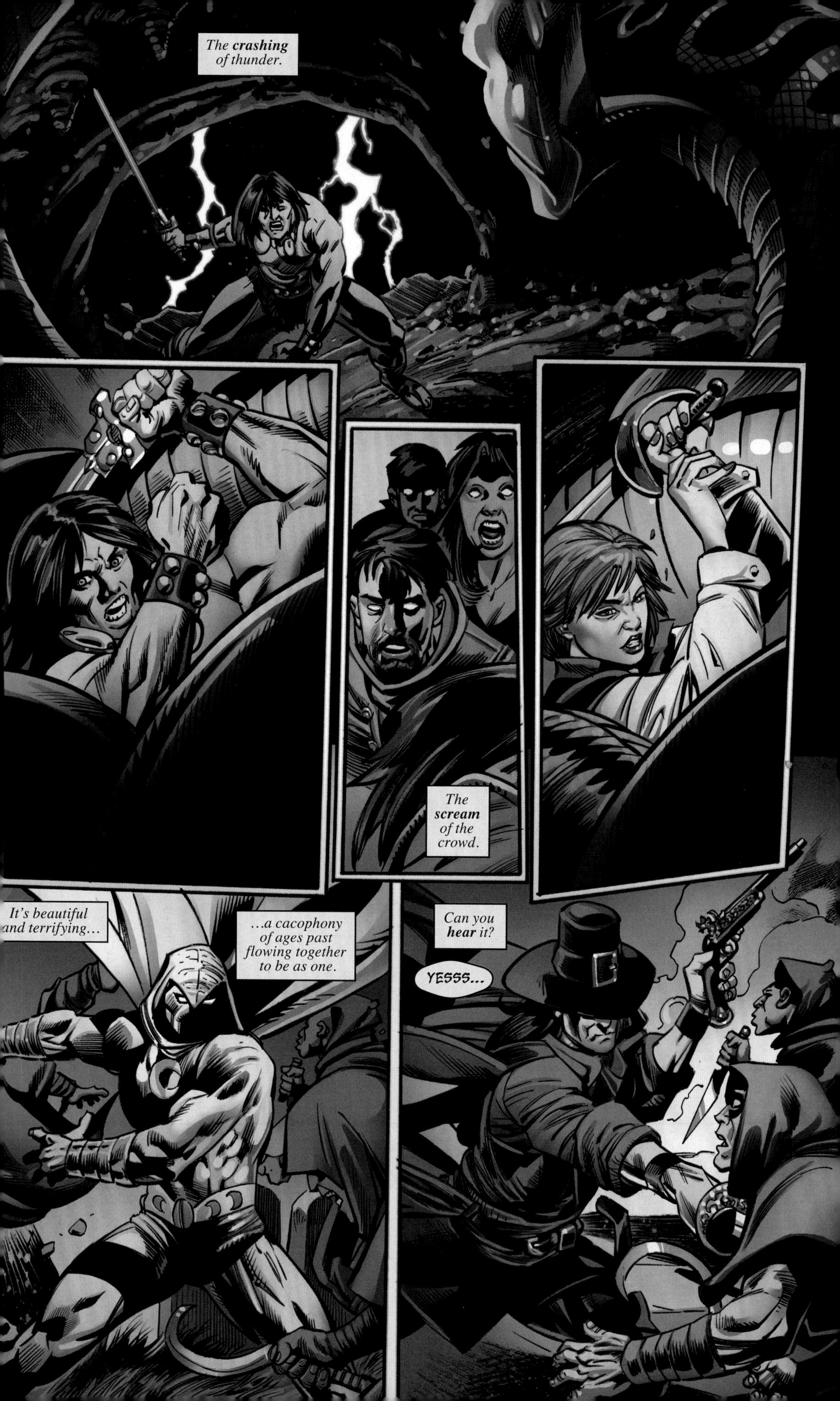
The crashing of thunder.
The scream of the crowd.
It's beautiful and terrifying...
...a cacophony of ages past flowing together to be as one.
Can you hear it?
YESSS...

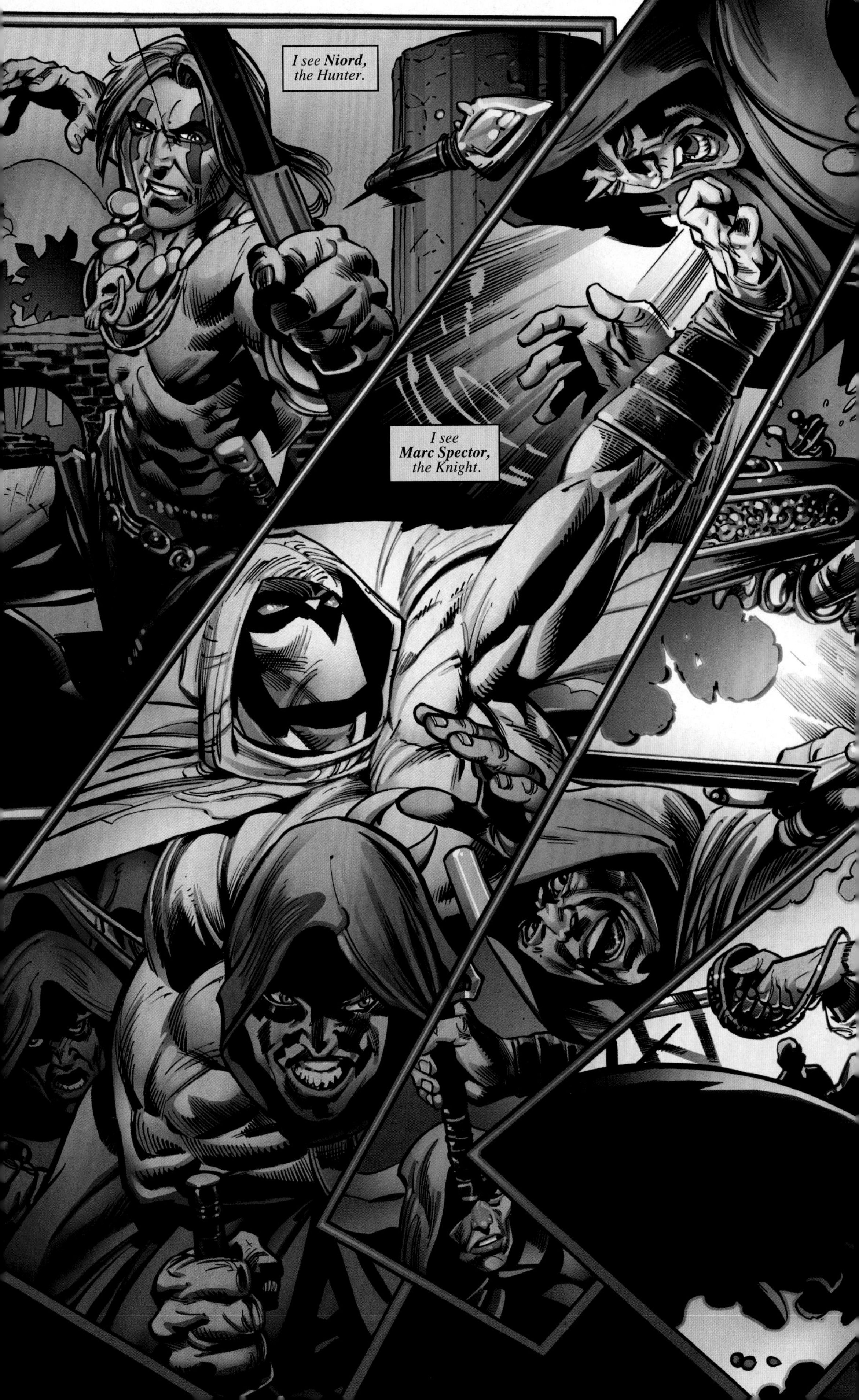
I see **Niord,** the Hunter.
I see **Marc Spector,** the Knight.

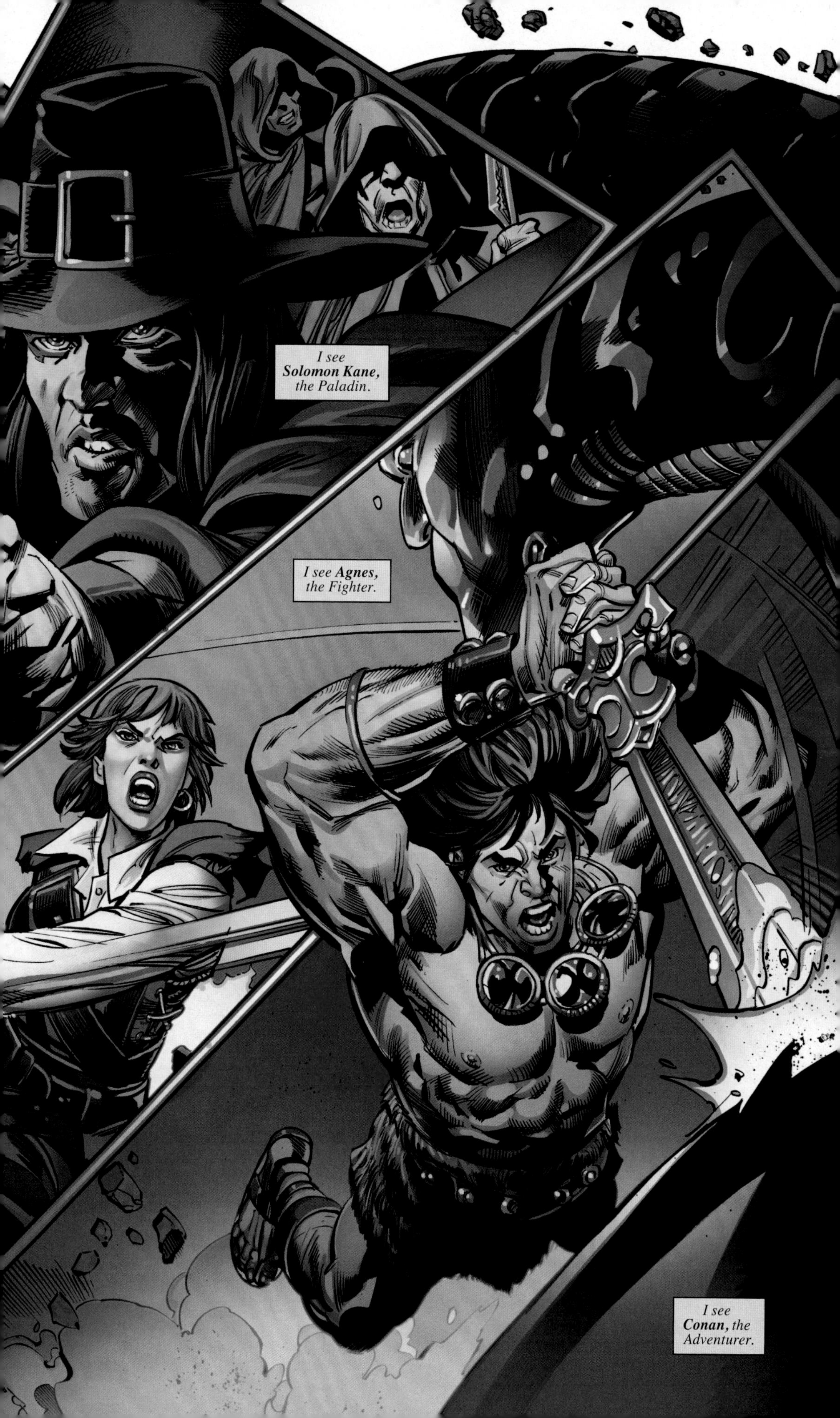
I see **Solomon Kane,** the Paladin.
I see **Agnes,** the Fighter.
I see **Conan,** the Adventurer.

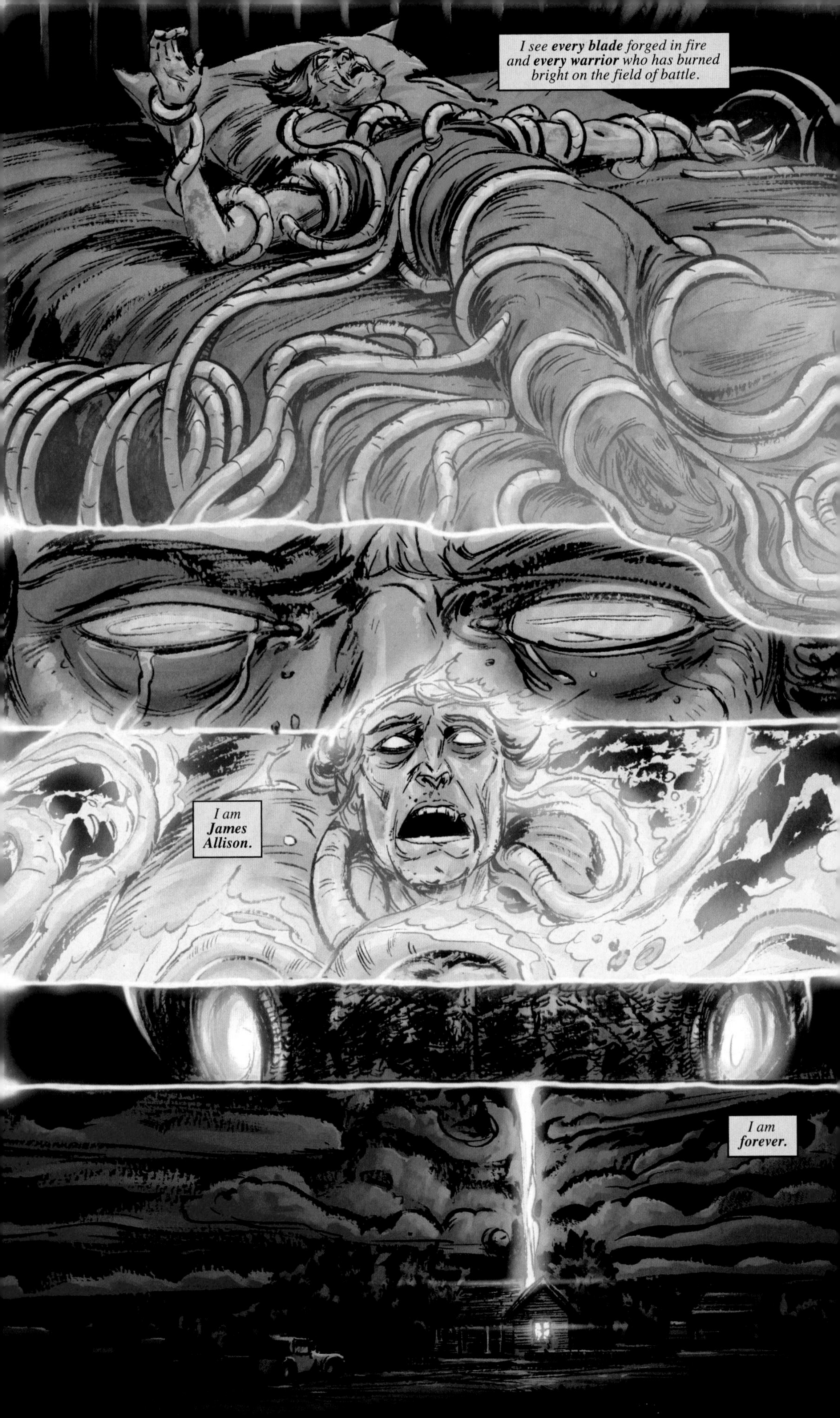
I see **every blade** forged in fire and **every warrior** who has burned bright on the field of battle.
I am **James Allison.**
I am **forever.**

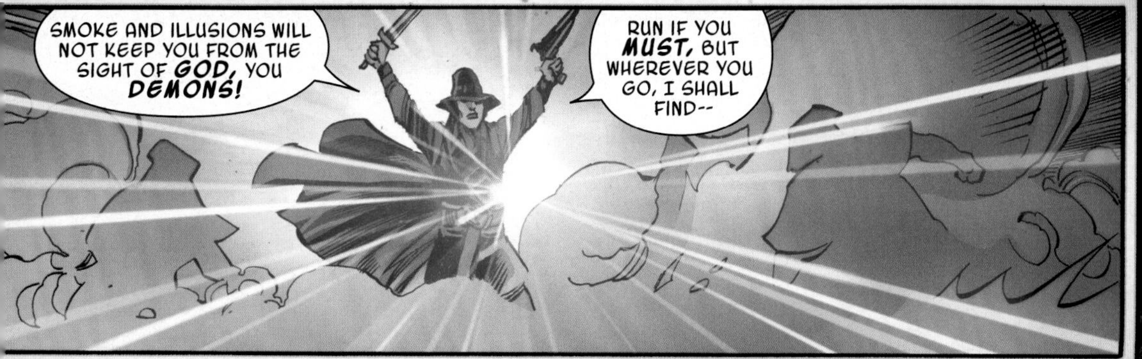
SMOKE AND ILLUSIONS WILL NOT KEEP YOU FROM THE SIGHT OF **GOD,** YOU **DEMONS!**
RUN IF YOU **MUST,** BUT WHEREVER YOU GO, I SHALL FIND--

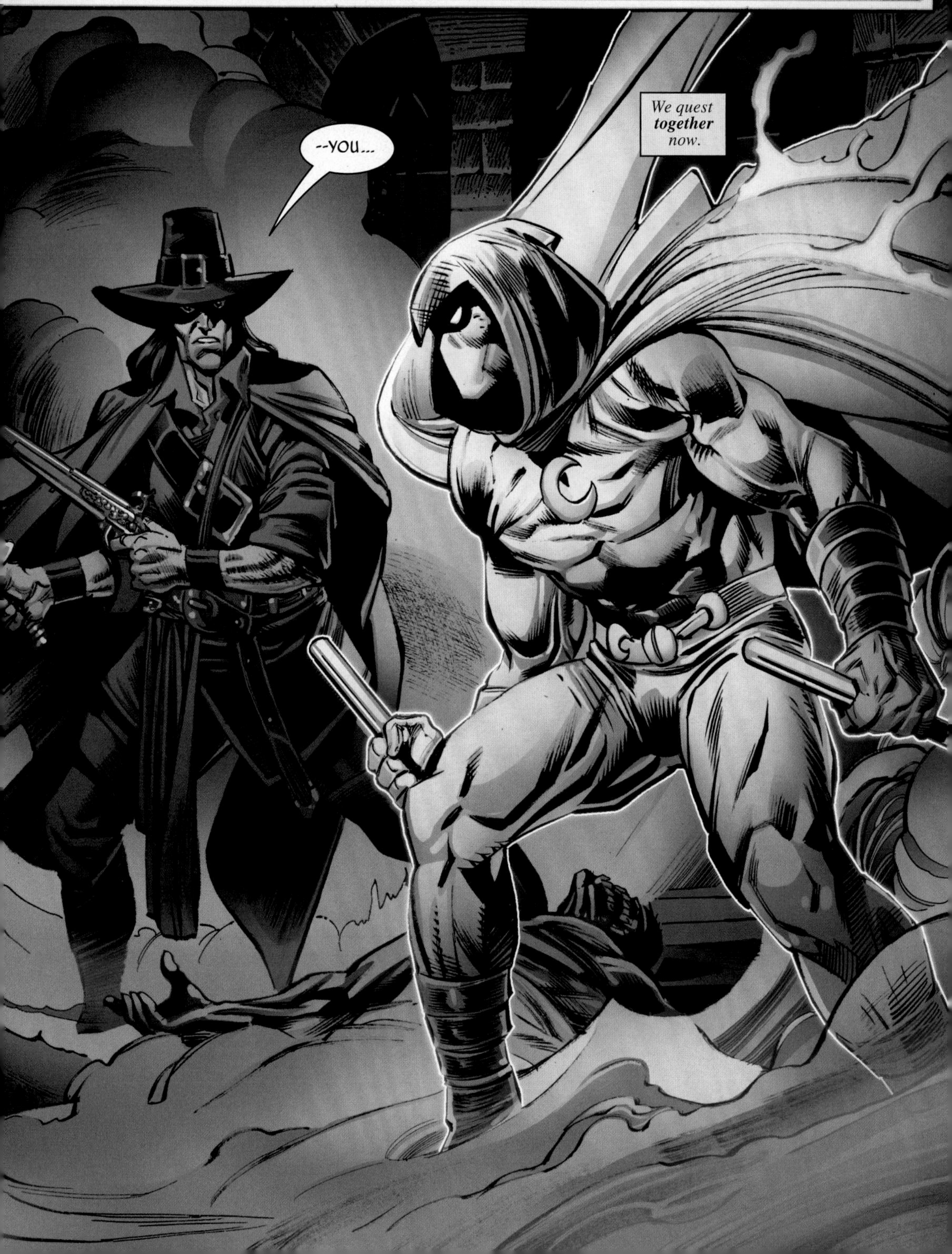
--YOU...
We quest **together** now.

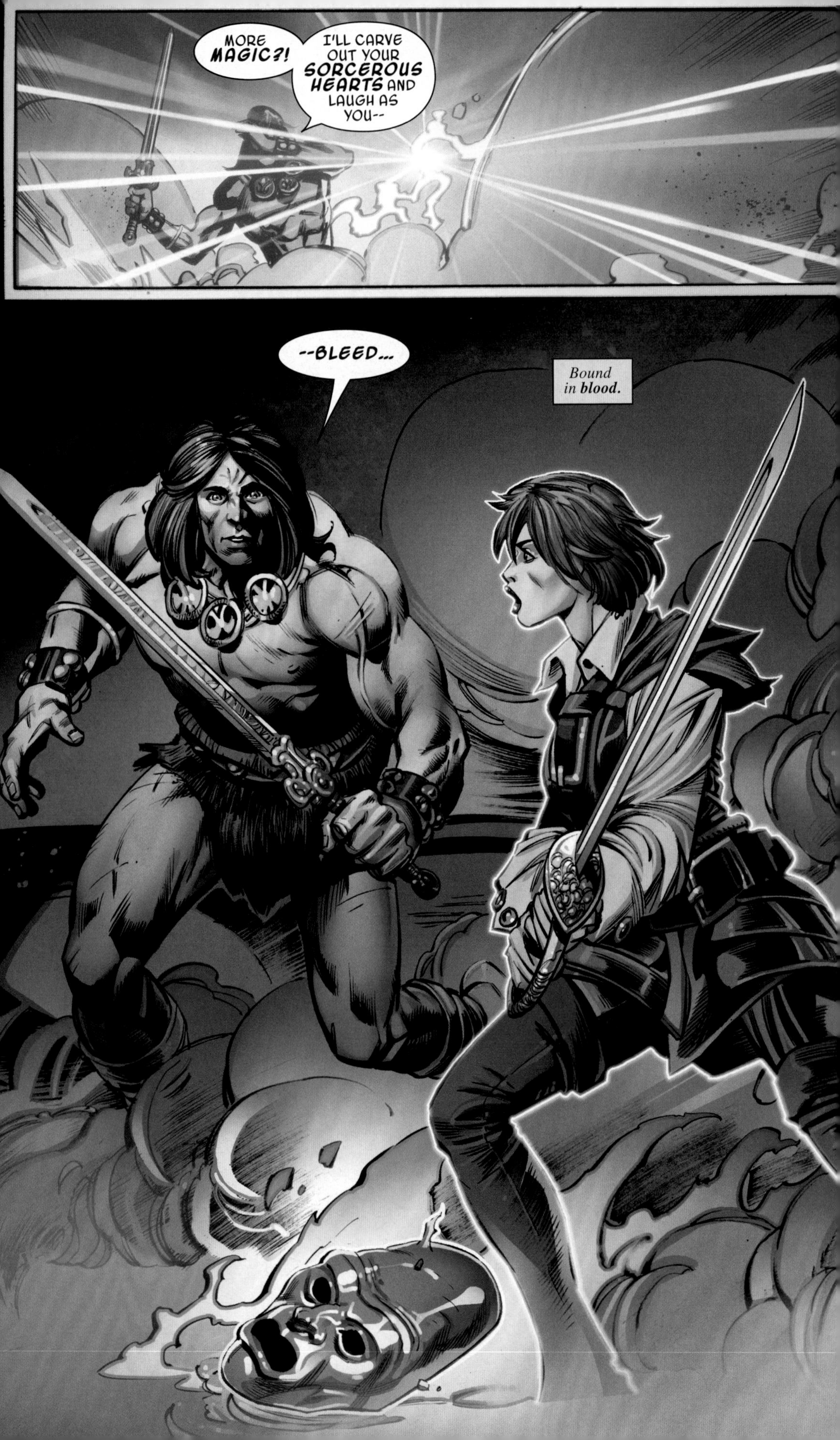
MORE MAGIC?!
I'LL CARVE OUT YOUR SORCEROUS HEARTS AND LAUGH AS YOU--
--BLEED...
Bound in blood.

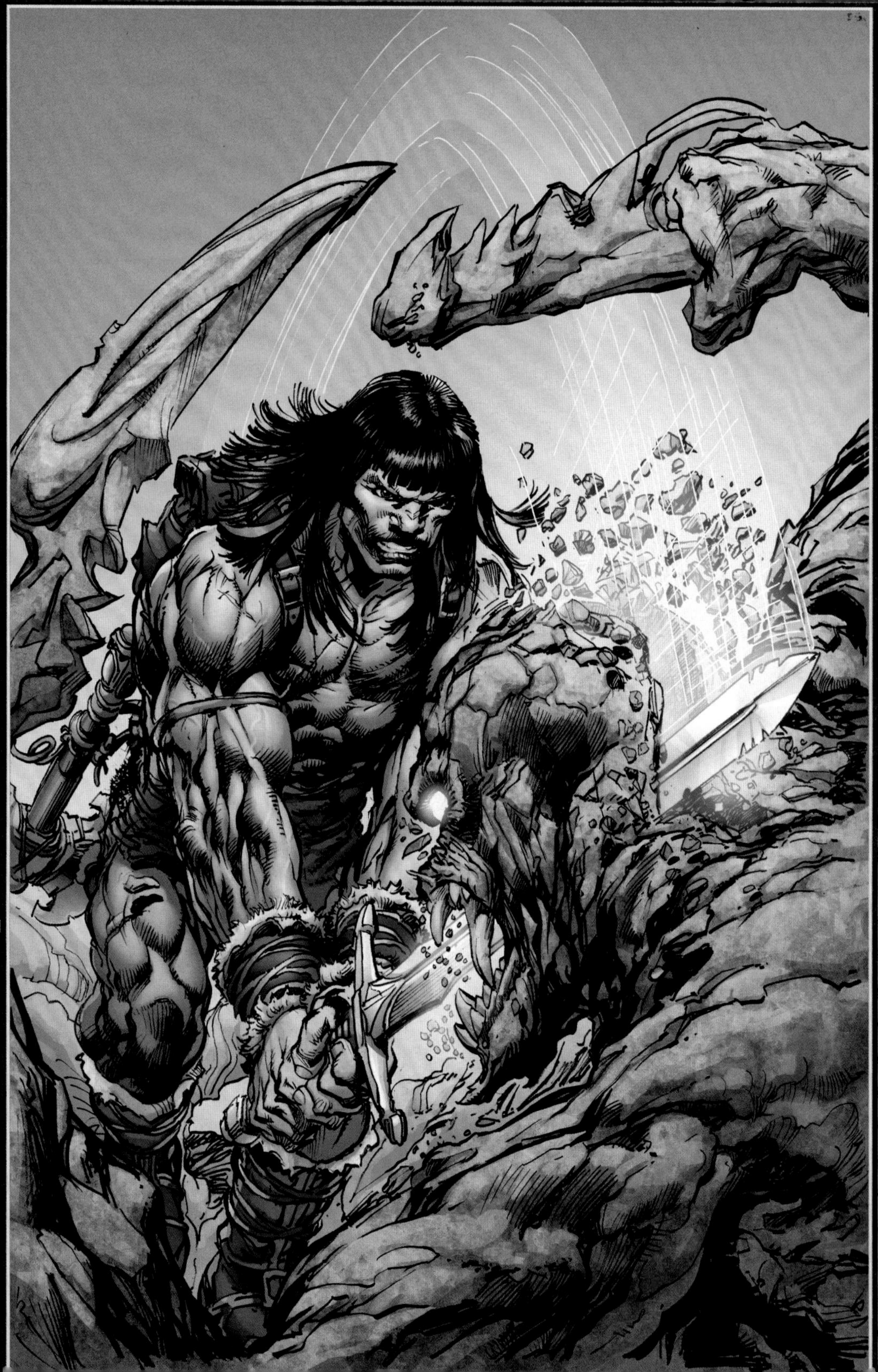

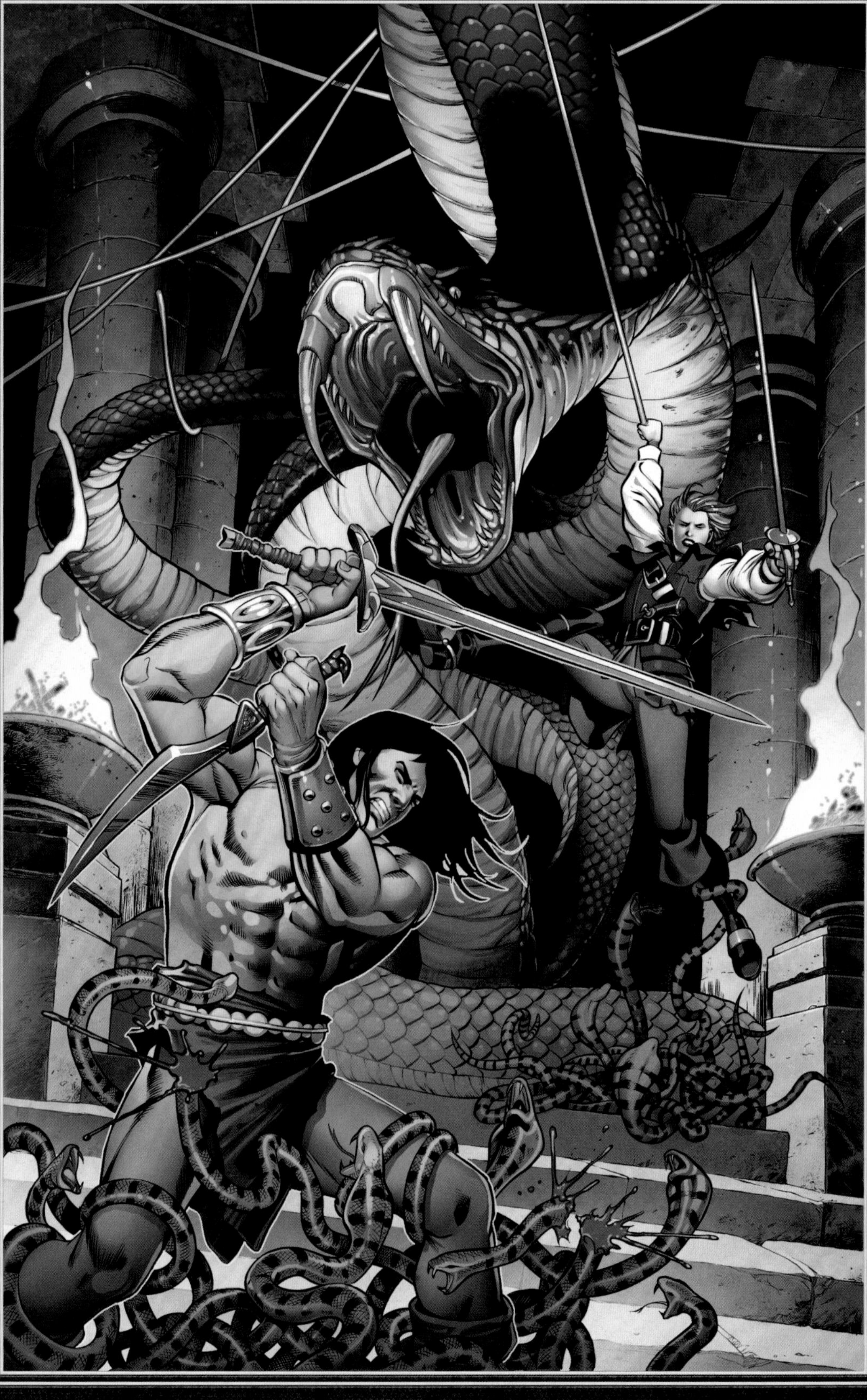

CHAPTER II: RELICS OF THE GODS

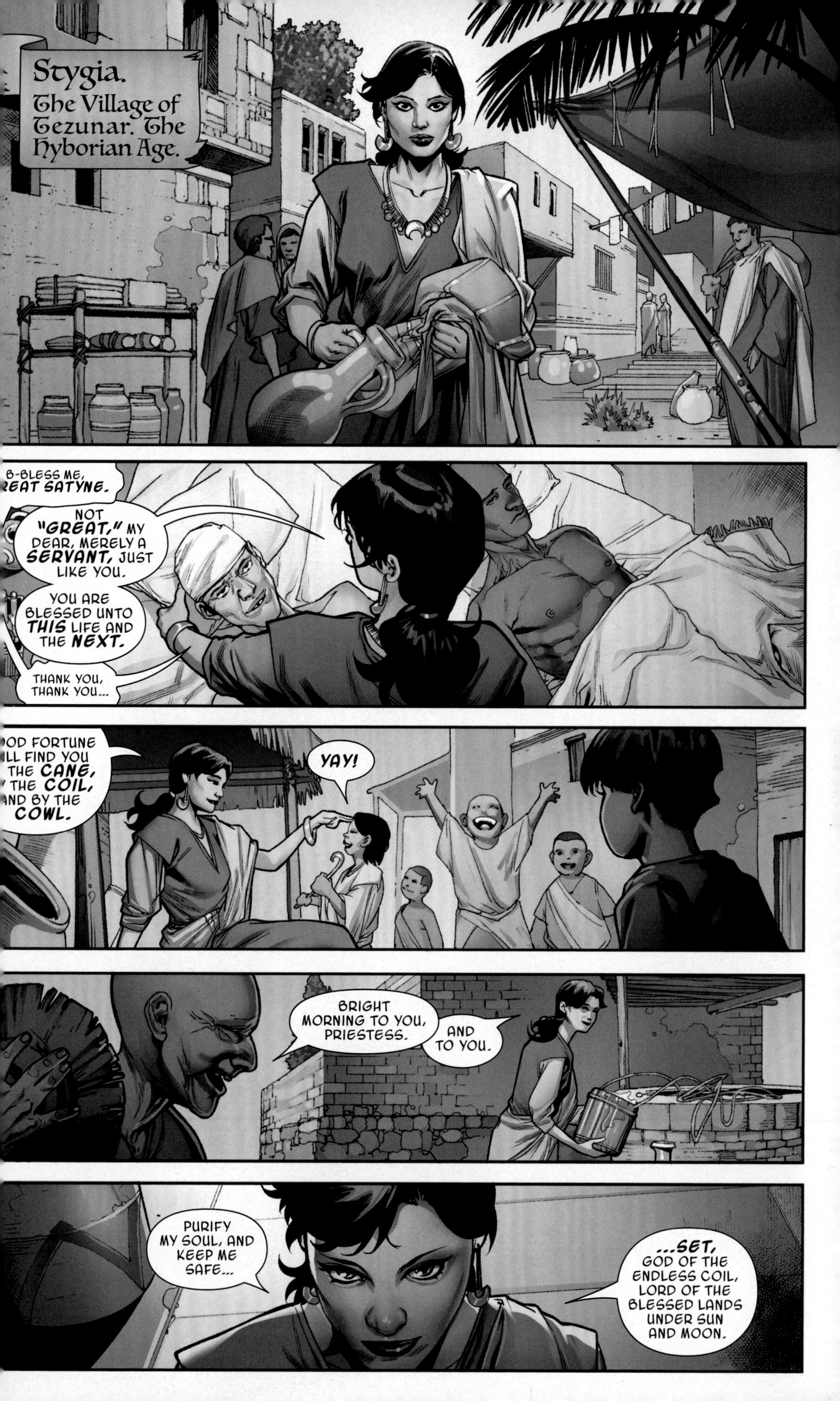
Stygia.
The Village of Tezunar. The Hyborian Age.
B-BLESS ME, REAT SATYNE.
NOT "GREAT," MY DEAR, MERELY A SERVANT, JUST LIKE YOU.
YOU ARE BLESSED UNTO THIS LIFE AND THE NEXT.
THANK YOU, THANK YOU...
OD FORTUNE LL FIND YOU THE CANE, THE COIL, AND BY THE COWL.
YAY!
BRIGHT MORNING TO YOU, PRIESTESS.
AND TO YOU.
PURIFY MY SOUL, AND KEEP ME SAFE...
...SET, GOD OF THE ENDLESS COIL, LORD OF THE BLESSED LANDS UNDER SUN AND MOON.

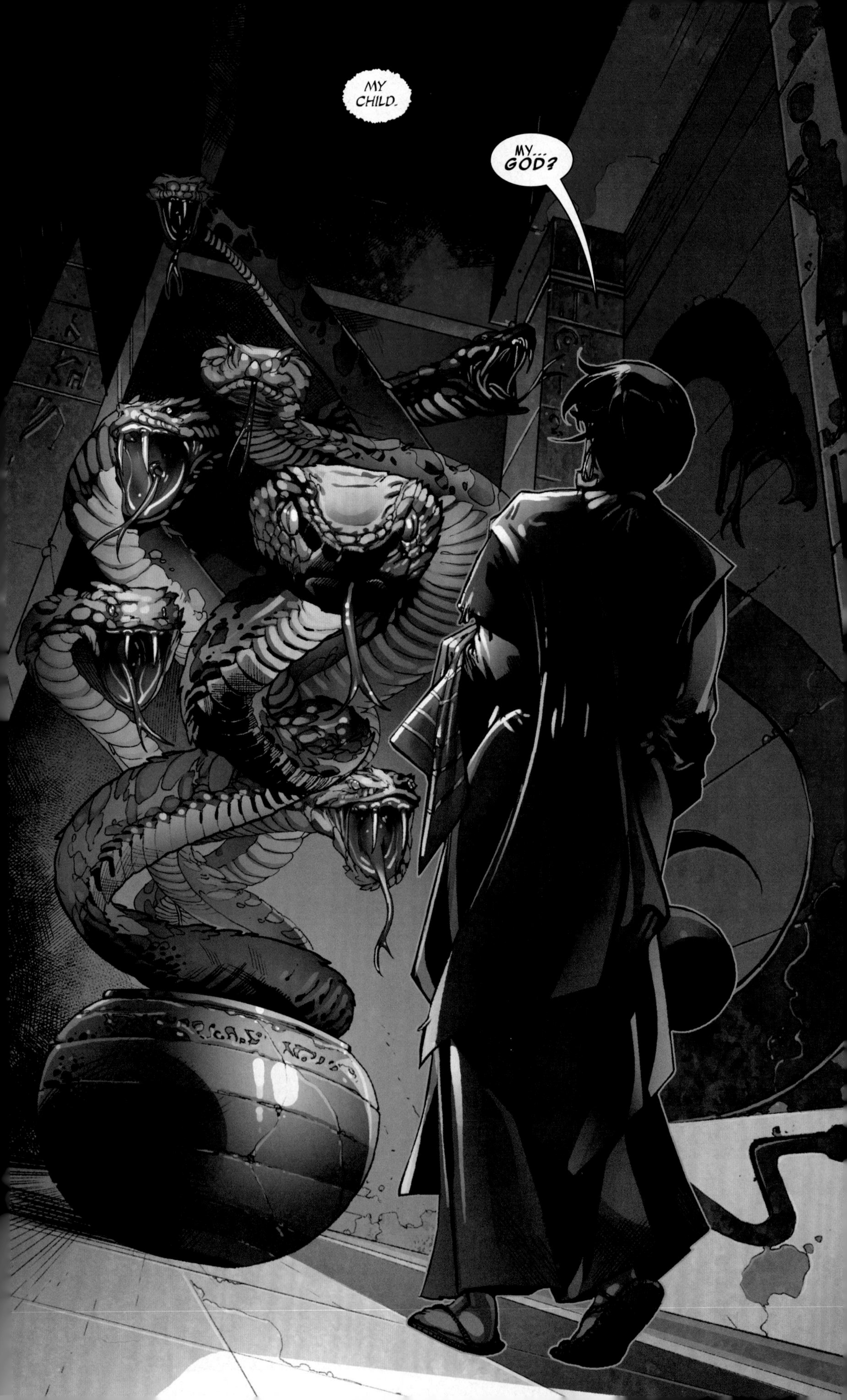
MY CHILD.
MY... GOD?

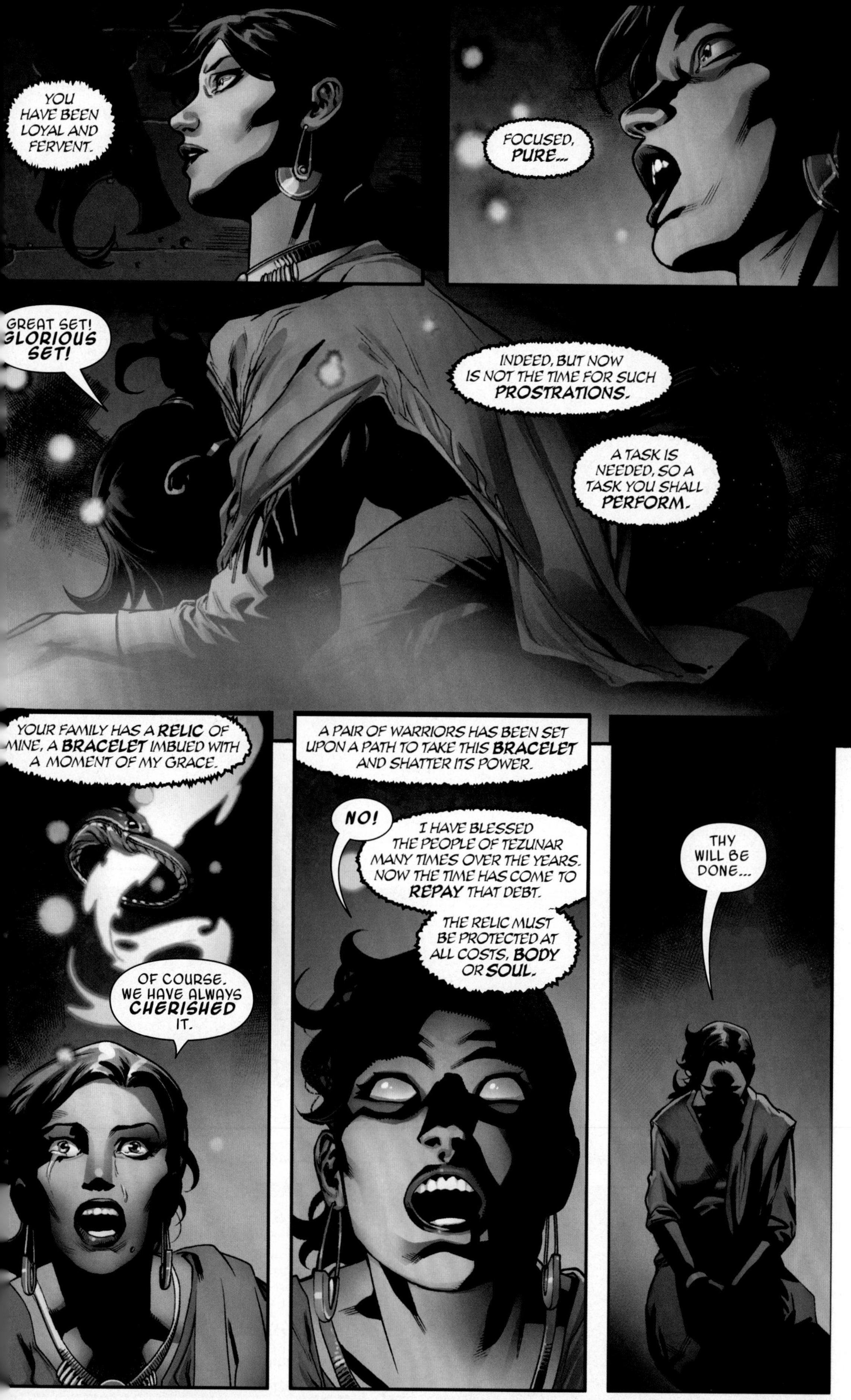

YOU HAVE BEEN LOYAL AND FERVENT.
FOCUSED, PURE...
GREAT SET! GLORIOUS SET!
INDEED, BUT NOW IS NOT THE TIME FOR SUCH PROSTRATIONS.
A TASK IS NEEDED, SO A TASK YOU SHALL PERFORM.
YOUR FAMILY HAS A RELIC OF MINE, A BRACELET IMBUED WITH A MOMENT OF MY GRACE.
OF COURSE. WE HAVE ALWAYS CHERISHED IT.
A PAIR OF WARRIORS HAS BEEN SET UPON A PATH TO TAKE THIS BRACELET AND SHATTER ITS POWER.
NO!
I HAVE BLESSED THE PEOPLE OF TEZUNAR MANY TIMES OVER THE YEARS. NOW THE TIME HAS COME TO REPAY THAT DEBT.
THE RELIC MUST BE PROTECTED AT ALL COSTS, BODY OR SOUL.
THY WILL BE DONE...

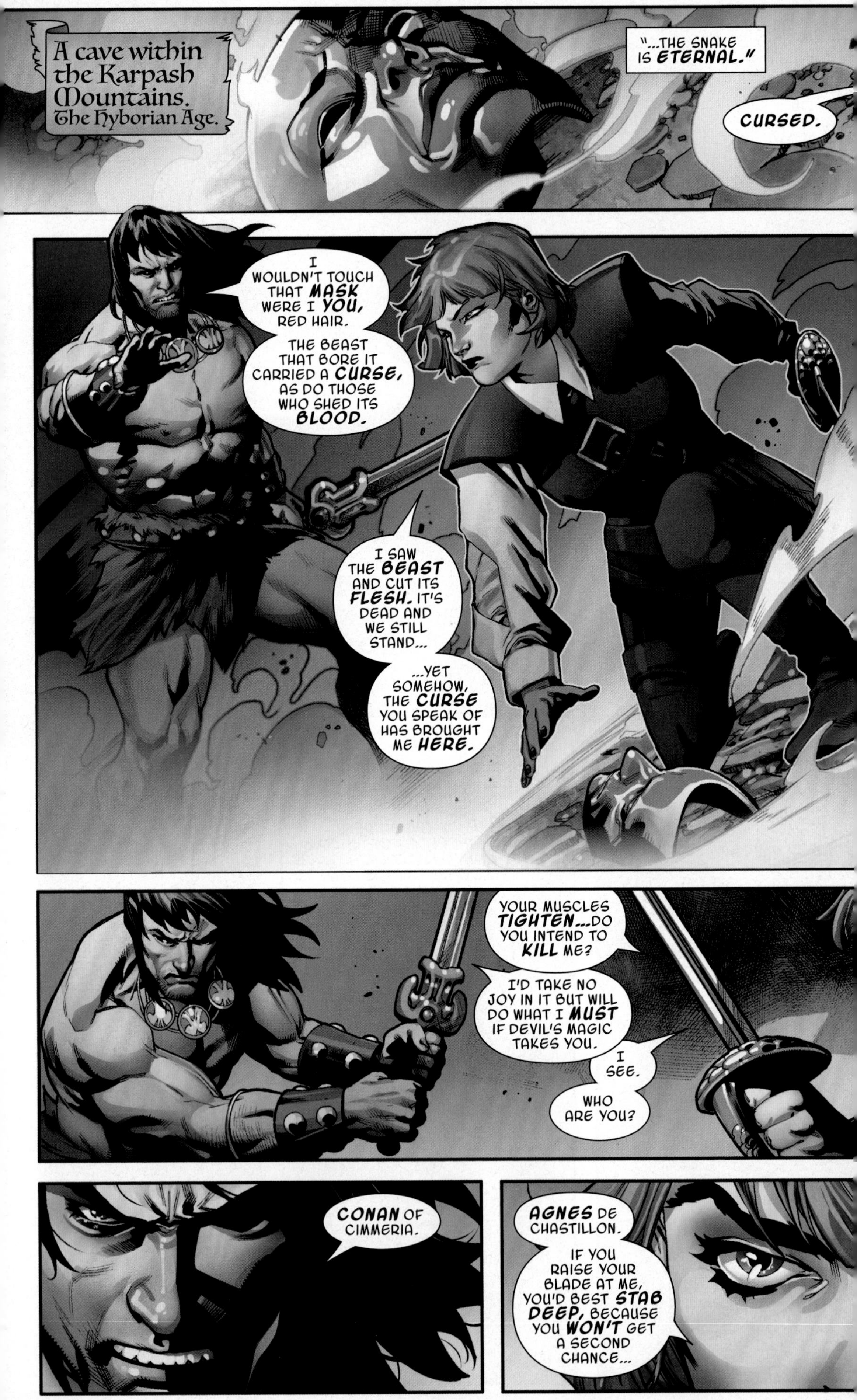
A cave within the Karpash Mountains. The Hyborian Age.
"...THE SNAKE IS ETERNAL."
CURSED.
I WOULDN'T TOUCH THAT MASK WERE I YOU, RED HAIR.
THE BEAST THAT BORE IT CARRIED A CURSE, AS DO THOSE WHO SHED ITS BLOOD.
I SAW THE BEAST AND CUT ITS FLESH. IT'S DEAD AND WE STILL STAND...
...YET SOMEHOW, THE CURSE YOU SPEAK OF HAS BROUGHT ME HERE.
YOUR MUSCLES TIGHTEN...DO YOU INTEND TO KILL ME?
I'D TAKE NO JOY IN IT BUT WILL DO WHAT I MUST IF DEVIL'S MAGIC TAKES YOU.
I SEE.
WHO ARE YOU?
CONAN OF CIMMERIA.
AGNES DE CHASTILLON.
IF YOU RAISE YOUR BLADE AT ME, YOU'D BEST STAB DEEP, BECAUSE YOU WON'T GET A SECOND CHANCE...

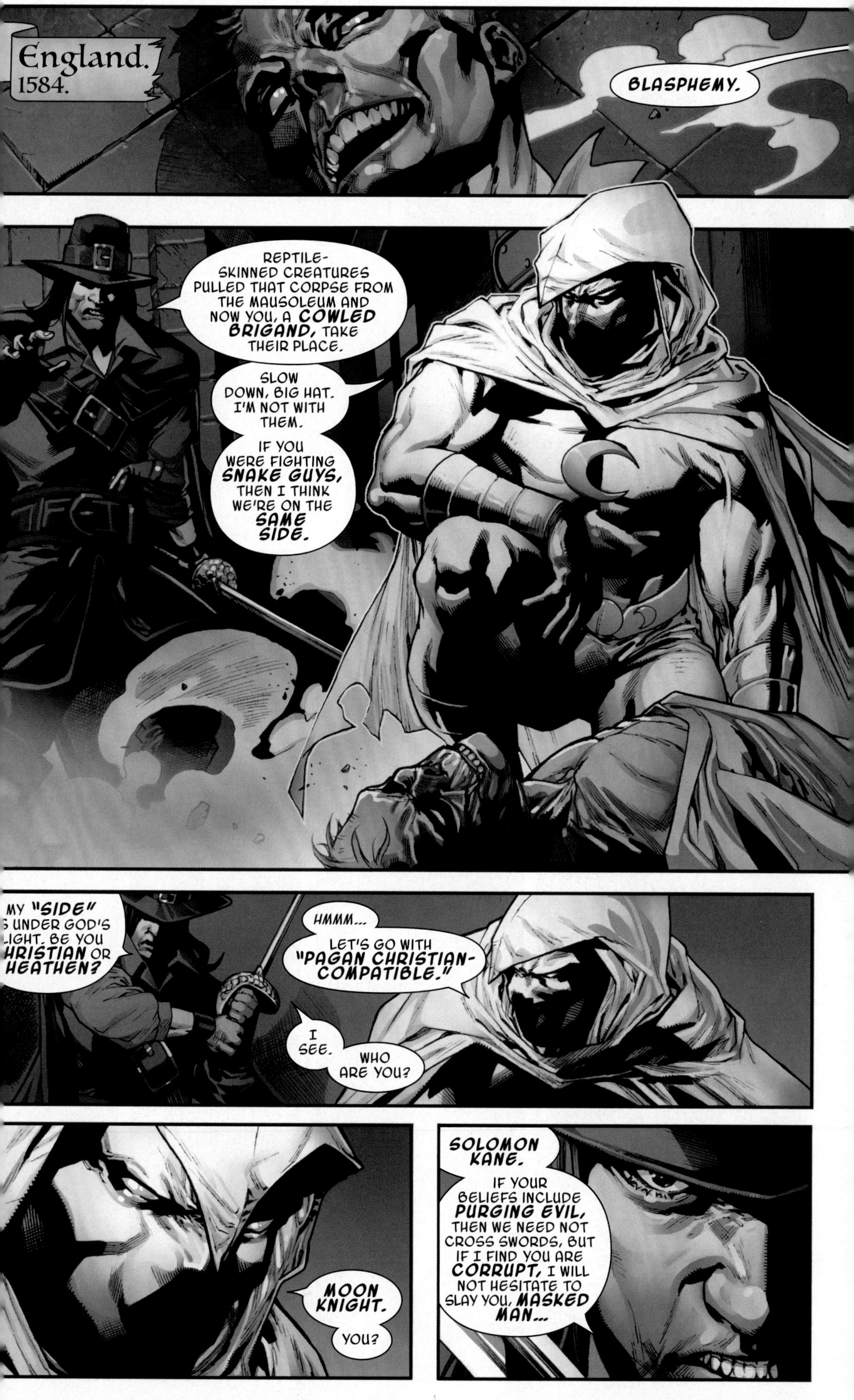
England.
1584.
BLASPHEMY.
REPTILE-SKINNED CREATURES PULLED THAT CORPSE FROM THE MAUSOLEUM AND NOW YOU, A COWLED BRIGAND, TAKE THEIR PLACE.
SLOW DOWN, BIG HAT. I'M NOT WITH THEM.
IF YOU WERE FIGHTING SNAKE GUYS, THEN I THINK WE'RE ON THE SAME SIDE.
MY "SIDE" IS UNDER GOD'S LIGHT. BE YOU CHRISTIAN OR HEATHEN?
HMMM...
LET'S GO WITH "PAGAN CHRISTIAN-COMPATIBLE."
I SEE.
WHO ARE YOU?
MOON KNIGHT.
YOU?
SOLOMON KANE.
IF YOUR BELIEFS INCLUDE PURGING EVIL, THEN WE NEED NOT CROSS SWORDS, BUT IF I FIND YOU ARE CORRUPT, I WILL NOT HESITATE TO SLAY YOU, MASKED MAN...

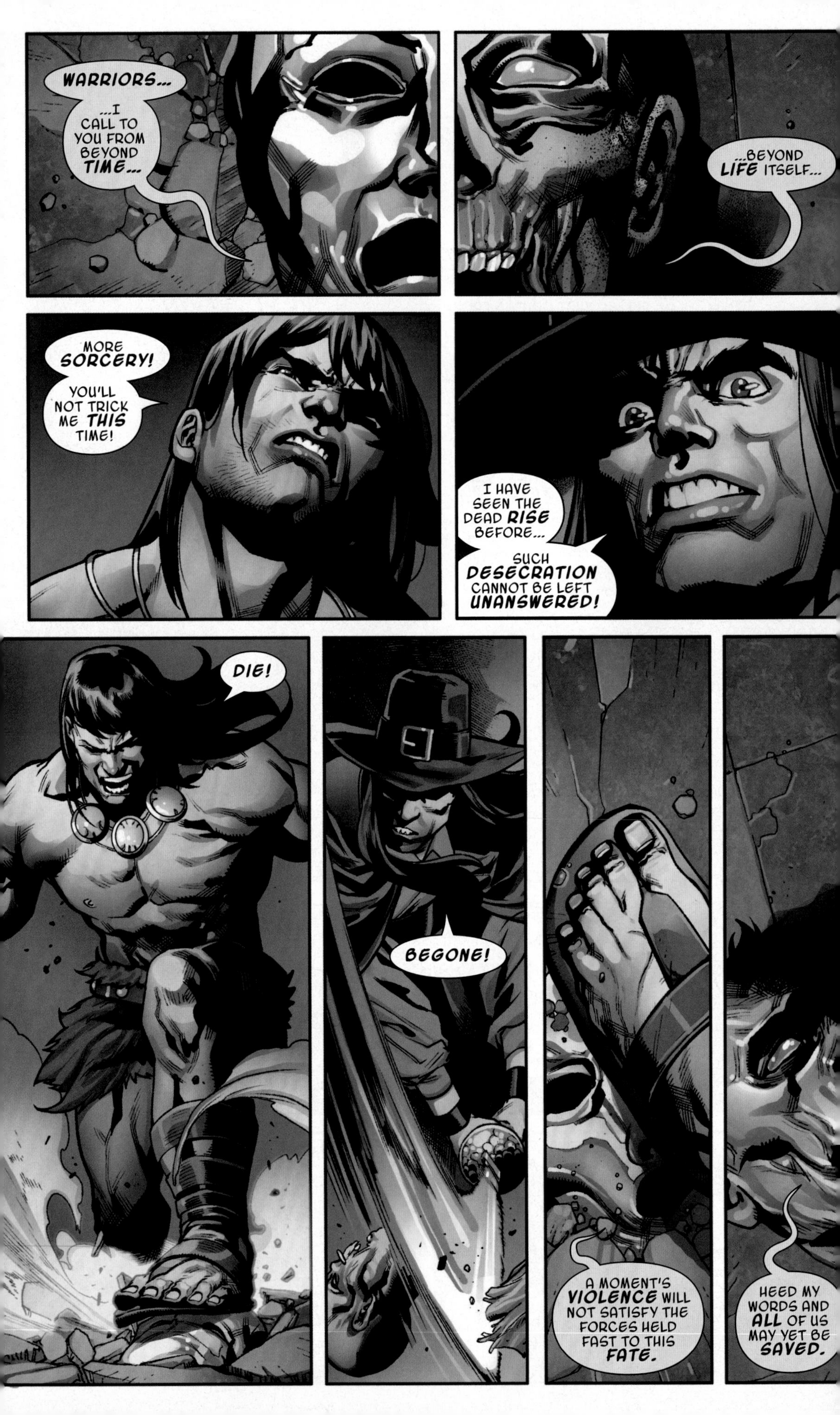
WARRIORS...
...I CALL TO YOU FROM BEYOND TIME...
...BEYOND LIFE ITSELF...
MORE SORCERY!
YOU'LL NOT TRICK ME THIS TIME!
I HAVE SEEN THE DEAD RISE BEFORE...
SUCH DESECRATION CANNOT BE LEFT UNANSWERED!
DIE!
BEGONE!
A MOMENT'S VIOLENCE WILL NOT SATISFY THE FORCES HELD FAST TO THIS FATE.
HEED MY WORDS AND ALL OF US MAY YET BE SAVED.

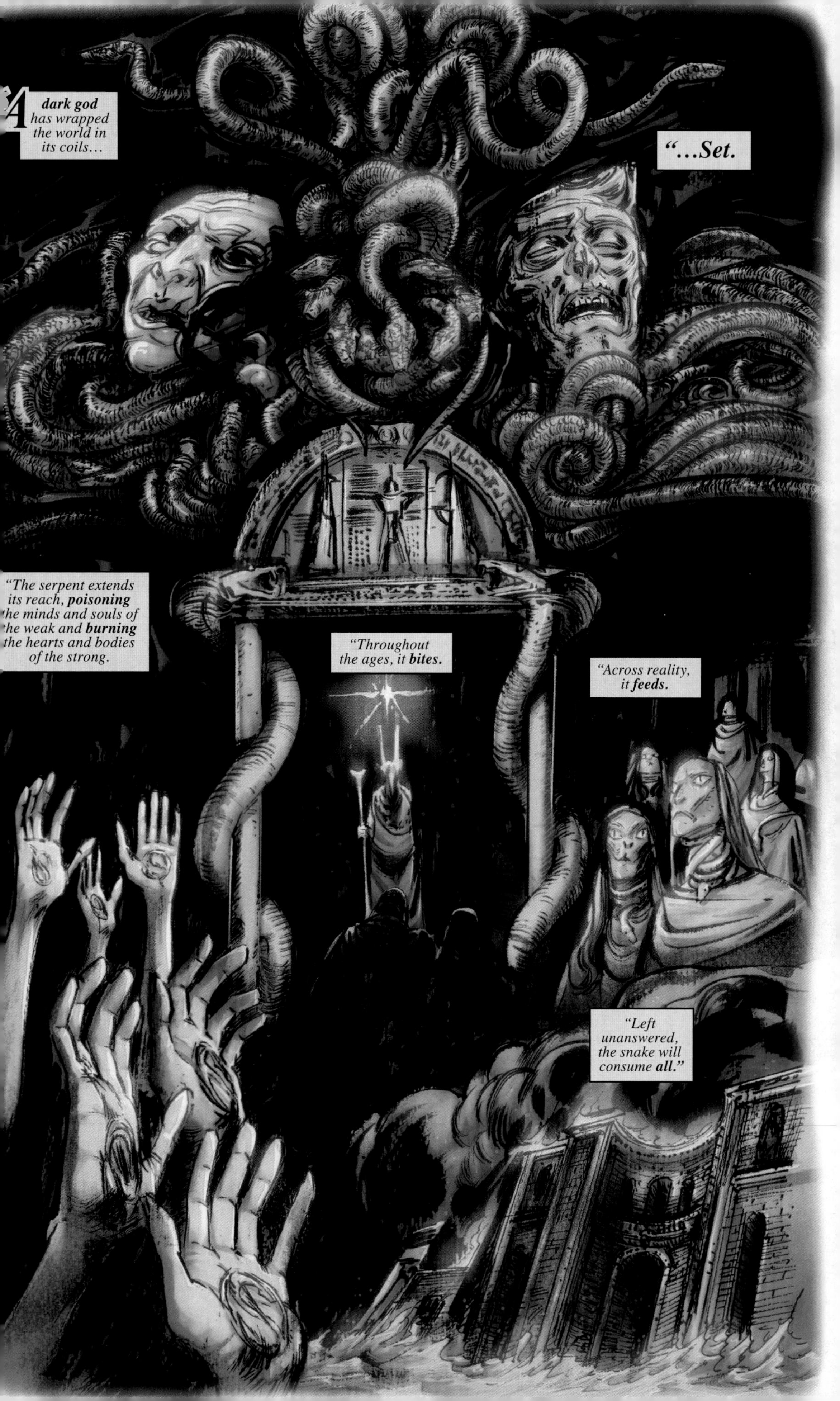
A dark god has wrapped the world in its coils…
"…Set.
"The serpent extends its reach, poisoning the minds and souls of the weak and burning the hearts and bodies of the strong.
"Throughout the ages, it bites.
"Across reality, it feeds.
"Left unanswered, the snake will consume all."

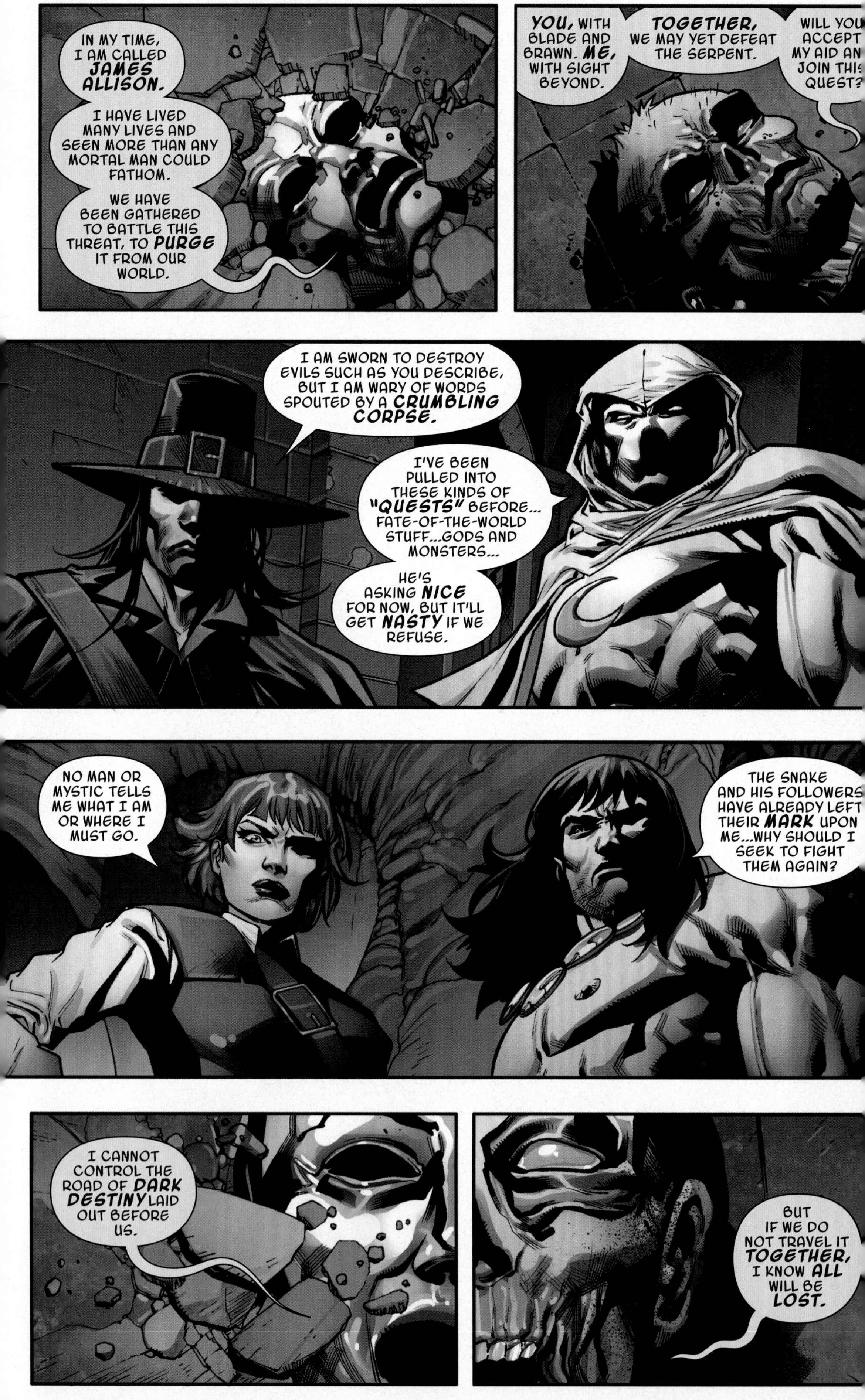

IN MY TIME, I AM CALLED JAMES ALLISON.
I HAVE LIVED MANY LIVES AND SEEN MORE THAN ANY MORTAL MAN COULD FATHOM.
WE HAVE BEEN GATHERED TO BATTLE THIS THREAT, TO PURGE IT FROM OUR WORLD.
YOU, WITH BLADE AND BRAWN. ME, WITH SIGHT BEYOND.
TOGETHER, WE MAY YET DEFEAT THE SERPENT.
WILL YOU ACCEPT MY AID AN JOIN THIS QUEST?
I AM SWORN TO DESTROY EVILS SUCH AS YOU DESCRIBE, BUT I AM WARY OF WORDS SPOUTED BY A CRUMBLING CORPSE.
I'VE BEEN PULLED INTO THESE KINDS OF "QUESTS" BEFORE... FATE-OF-THE-WORLD STUFF...GODS AND MONSTERS...
HE'S ASKING NICE FOR NOW, BUT IT'LL GET NASTY IF WE REFUSE.
NO MAN OR MYSTIC TELLS ME WHAT I AM OR WHERE I MUST GO.
THE SNAKE AND HIS FOLLOWERS HAVE ALREADY LEFT THEIR MARK UPON ME...WHY SHOULD I SEEK TO FIGHT THEM AGAIN?
I CANNOT CONTROL THE ROAD OF DARK DESTINY LAID OUT BEFORE US.
BUT IF WE DO NOT TRAVEL IT TOGETHER, I KNOW ALL WILL BE LOST.

YOU SEE IT TOO, DON'T YOU?

THE **FAITH** YOU CHERISH, SET **AFLAME.**

THE **MIND** YOU SHEPHERD, FRAGMENTED **BEYOND REPAIR.**

THE **FREEDOM** YOU FOUGHT FOR, CRUSHED **UNDERFOOT.**

THE **NIGHTMARES** YOU'VE GLIMPSED, CONQUERING YOUR SOUL AND THE LAND YOU WALK UPON.

WE CAN STOP IT.

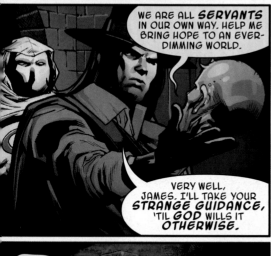

WE ARE ALL **SERVANTS** IN OUR OWN WAY. HELP ME BRING HOPE TO AN EVER-DIMMING WORLD.

VERY WELL, JAMES. I'LL TAKE YOUR **STRANGE GUIDANCE,** 'TIL **GOD** WILLS IT **OTHERWISE.**

LET US **SAVE** THOSE WHO NEED US AND **SLAY** THOSE WHO BRING DARKNESS.

IF WE ARE **BOUND** TO THIS PATH AS YOU SPEAK, THEN KEEP MY SWORD FED WITH **BLOOD** AND **BATTLE,** BUT **CROSS** ME AT YOUR OWN **PERIL.**

COMPELLING WORDS, JAMES.

A WORTHY CALL TO ACTION.

THEY HAVE DOUBTS BUT FOLLOW NONETHELESS...

O f course.

They are **soldiers,** *and this is a* **war.**

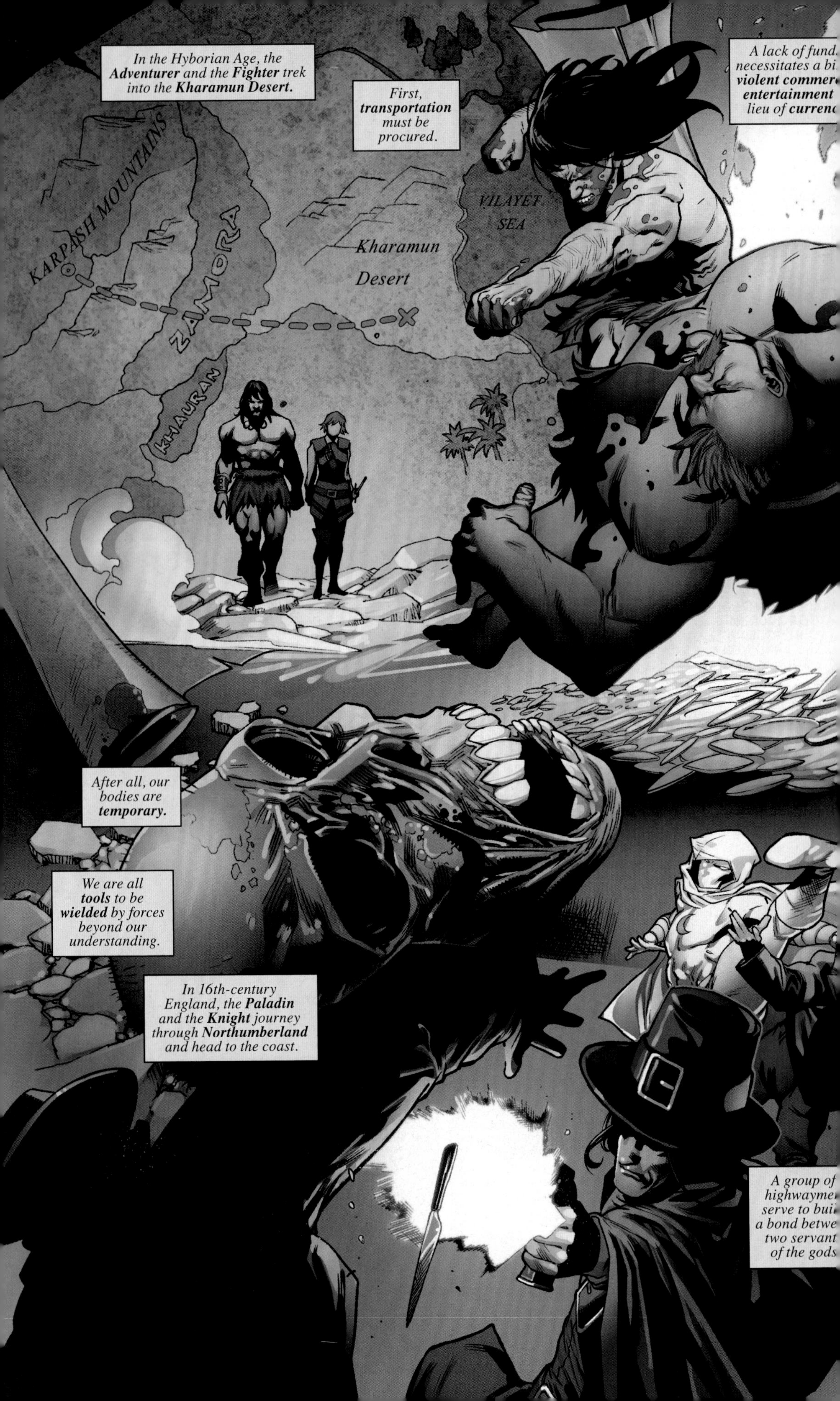
In the Hyborian Age, the Adventurer and the Fighter trek into the Kharamun Desert.
First, transportation must be procured.
A lack of fund necessitates a bi violent commer entertainment lieu of curren
KARPASH MOUNTAINS
ZAMORA
KHAURAN
Kharamun Desert
VILAYET SEA
After all, our bodies are temporary.
We are all tools to be wielded by forces beyond our understanding.
In 16th-century England, the Paladin and the Knight journey through Northumberland and head to the coast.
A group of highwayme serve to bui a bond betwe two servant of the gods

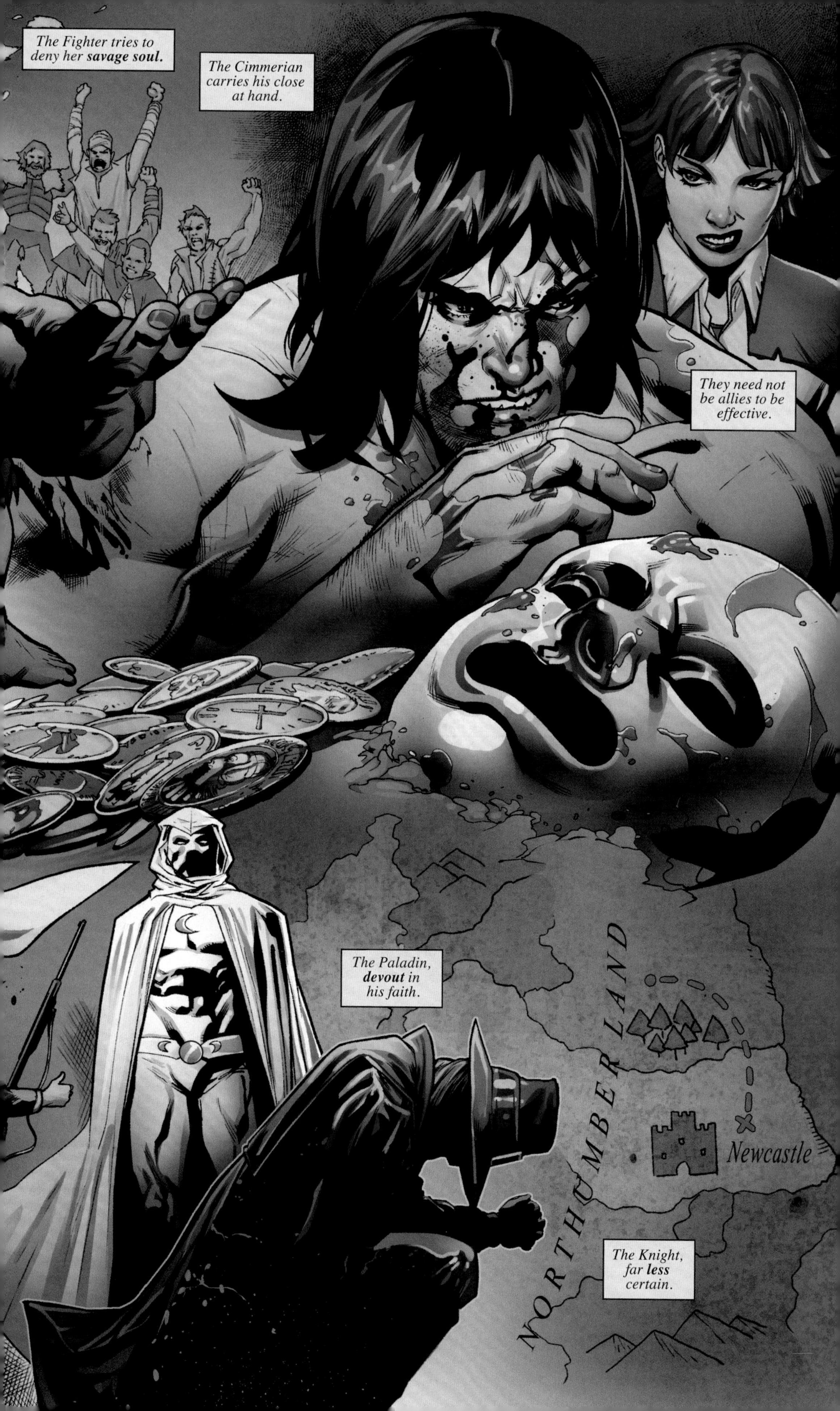
The Fighter tries to deny her **savage soul.**
The Cimmerian carries his close at hand.
They need not be allies to be effective.
The Paladin, **devout** in his faith.
NORTHUMBERLAND
Newcastle
The Knight, far **less** certain.

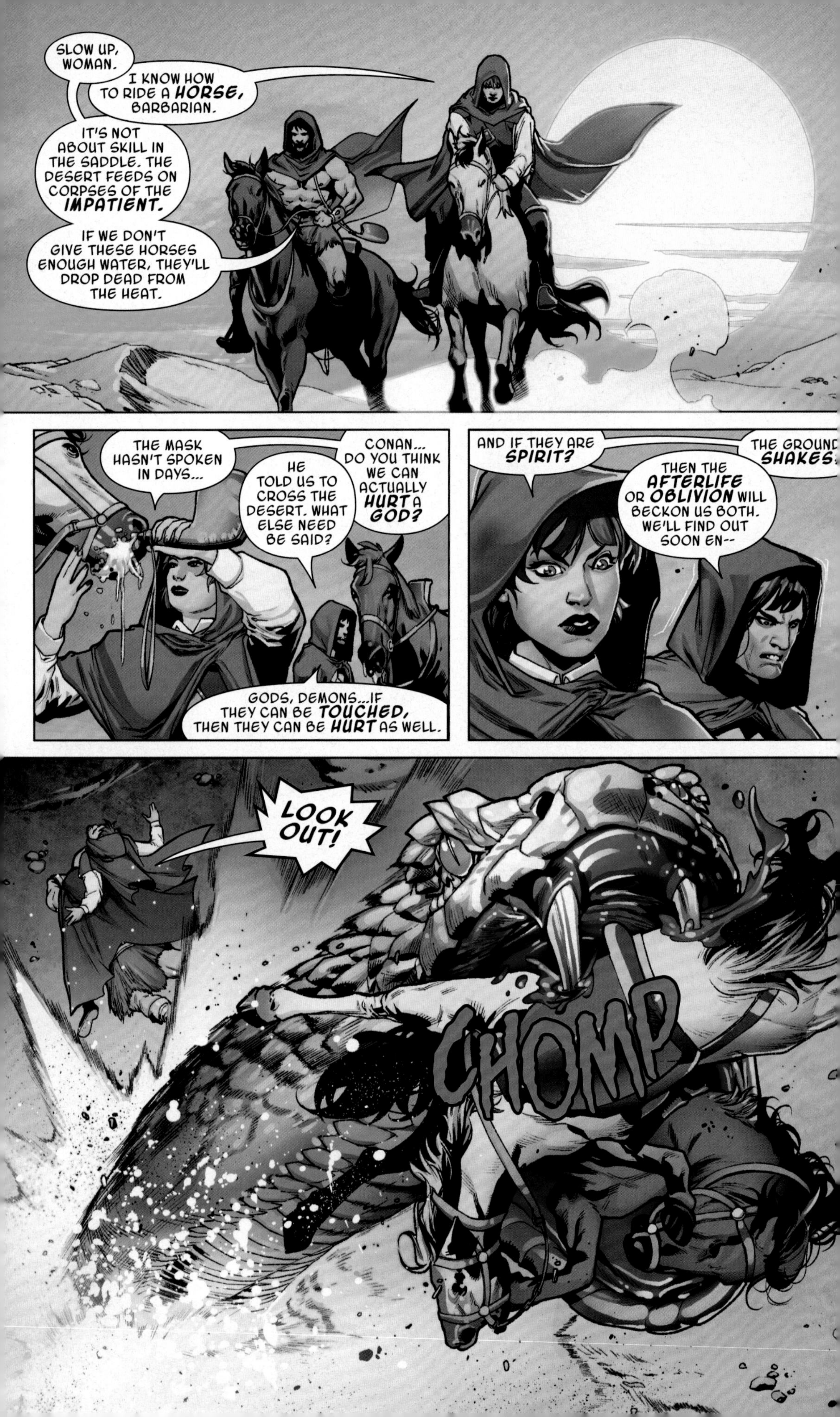
SLOW UP, WOMAN.
I KNOW HOW TO RIDE A HORSE, BARBARIAN.
IT'S NOT ABOUT SKILL IN THE SADDLE. THE DESERT FEEDS ON CORPSES OF THE IMPATIENT.
IF WE DON'T GIVE THESE HORSES ENOUGH WATER, THEY'LL DROP DEAD FROM THE HEAT.
THE MASK HASN'T SPOKEN IN DAYS...
CONAN... DO YOU THINK WE CAN ACTUALLY HURT A GOD?
HE TOLD US TO CROSS THE DESERT. WHAT ELSE NEED BE SAID?
GODS, DEMONS...IF THEY CAN BE TOUCHED, THEN THEY CAN BE HURT AS WELL.
AND IF THEY ARE SPIRIT?
THEN THE AFTERLIFE OR OBLIVION WILL BECKON US BOTH. WE'LL FIND OUT SOON EN--
THE GROUND SHAKES!
LOOK OUT!
CHOMP

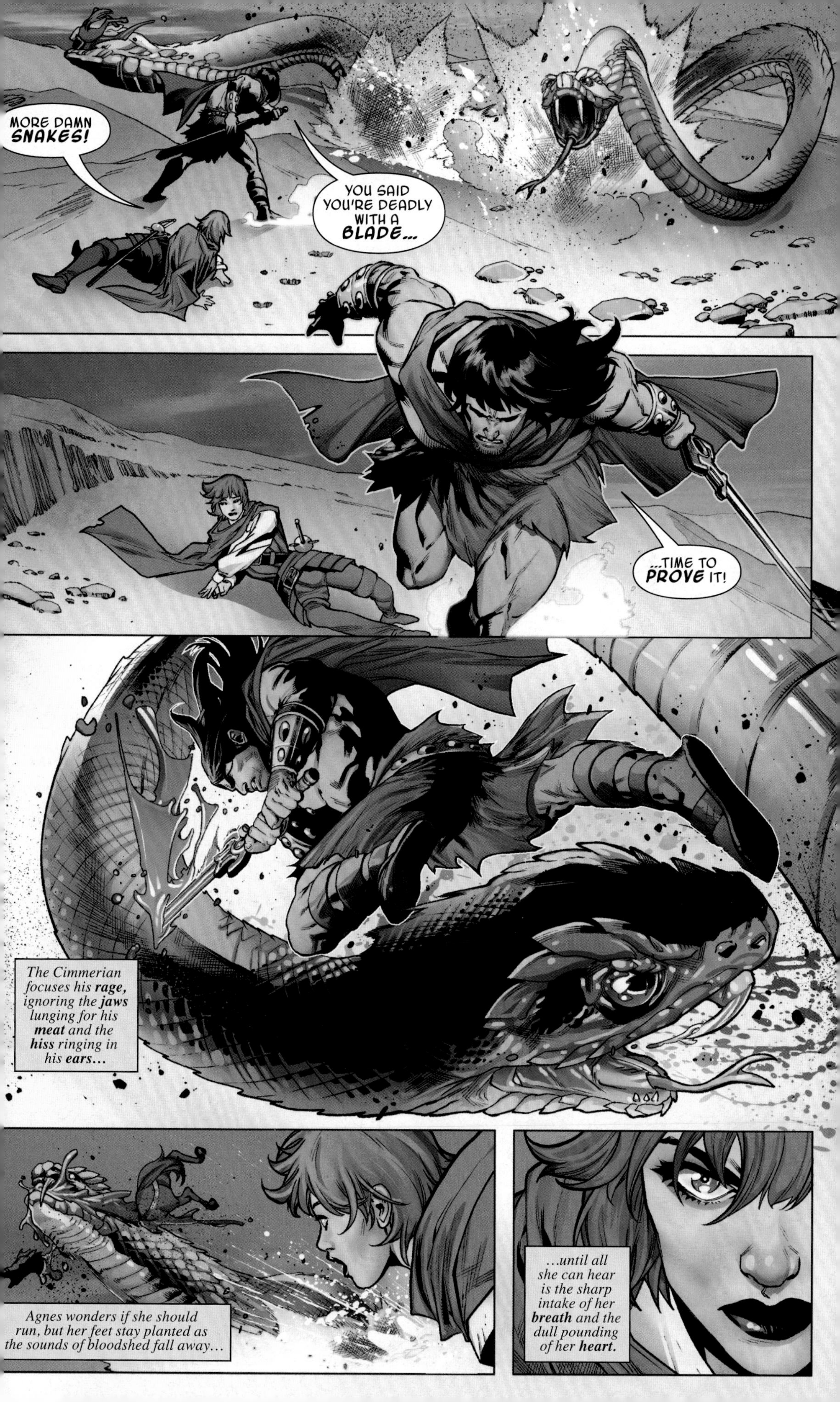
MORE DAMN SNAKES!
YOU SAID YOU'RE DEADLY WITH A BLADE...
...TIME TO PROVE IT!
The Cimmerian focuses his rage, ignoring the jaws lunging for his meat and the hiss ringing in his ears...
Agnes wonders if she should run, but her feet stay planted as the sounds of bloodshed fall away...
...until all she can hear is the sharp intake of her breath and the dull pounding of her heart.

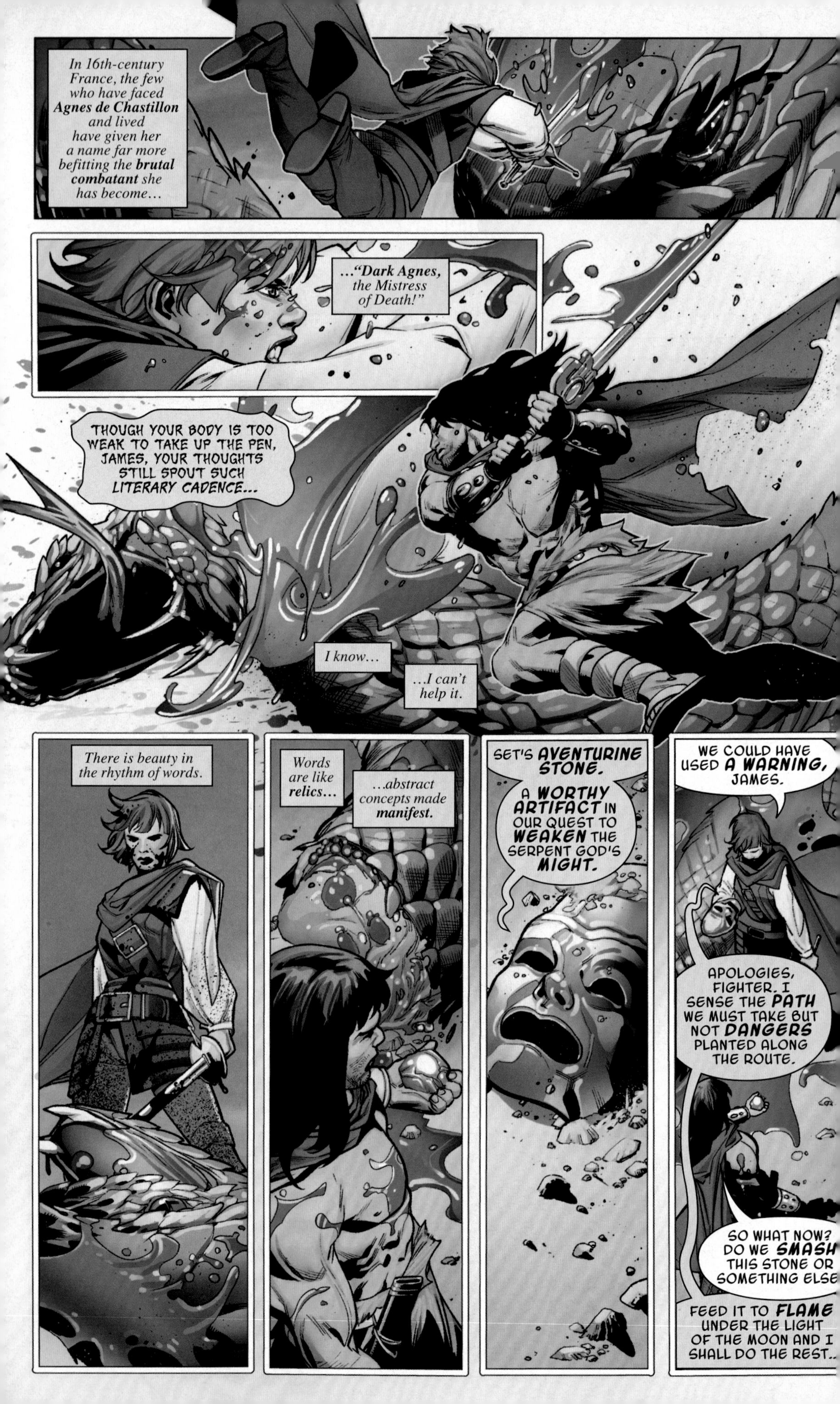
In 16th-century France, the few who have faced Agnes de Chastillon and lived have given her a name far more befitting the brutal combatant she has become…
…"Dark Agnes, the Mistress of Death!"
THOUGH YOUR BODY IS TOO WEAK TO TAKE UP THE PEN, JAMES, YOUR THOUGHTS STILL SPOUT SUCH LITERARY CADENCE…
I know…
…I can't help it.
There is beauty in the rhythm of words.
Words are like relics…
…abstract concepts made manifest.
SET'S AVENTURINE STONE.
A WORTHY ARTIFACT IN OUR QUEST TO WEAKEN THE SERPENT GOD'S MIGHT.
WE COULD HAVE USED A WARNING, JAMES.
APOLOGIES, FIGHTER. I SENSE THE PATH WE MUST TAKE BUT NOT DANGERS PLANTED ALONG THE ROUTE.
SO WHAT NOW? DO WE SMASH THIS STONE OR SOMETHING ELSE
FEED IT TO FLAME UNDER THE LIGHT OF THE MOON AND I SHALL DO THE REST…

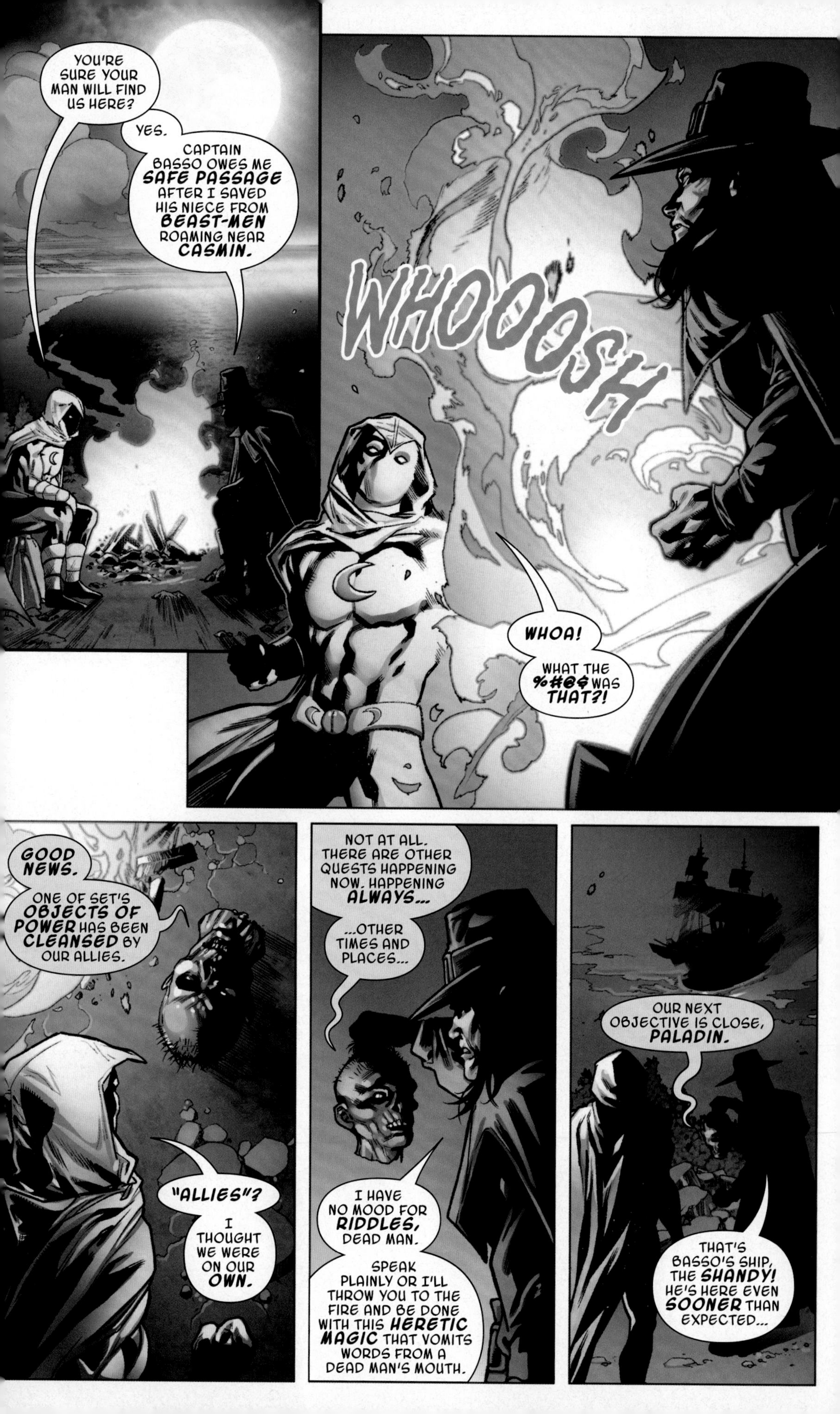
YOU'RE SURE YOUR MAN WILL FIND US HERE?
YES.
CAPTAIN BASSO OWES ME SAFE PASSAGE AFTER I SAVED HIS NIECE FROM BEAST-MEN ROAMING NEAR CASMIN.
WHOOOSH
WHOA!
WHAT THE %#@$ WAS THAT?!
GOOD NEWS.
ONE OF SET'S OBJECTS OF POWER HAS BEEN CLEANSED BY OUR ALLIES.
"ALLIES"?
I THOUGHT WE WERE ON OUR OWN.
NOT AT ALL. THERE ARE OTHER QUESTS HAPPENING NOW. HAPPENING ALWAYS...
...OTHER TIMES AND PLACES...
I HAVE NO MOOD FOR RIDDLES, DEAD MAN.
SPEAK PLAINLY OR I'LL THROW YOU TO THE FIRE AND BE DONE WITH THIS HERETIC MAGIC THAT VOMITS WORDS FROM A DEAD MAN'S MOUTH.
OUR NEXT OBJECTIVE IS CLOSE, PALADIN.
THAT'S BASSO'S SHIP, THE SHANDY! HE'S HERE EVEN SOONER THAN EXPECTED...

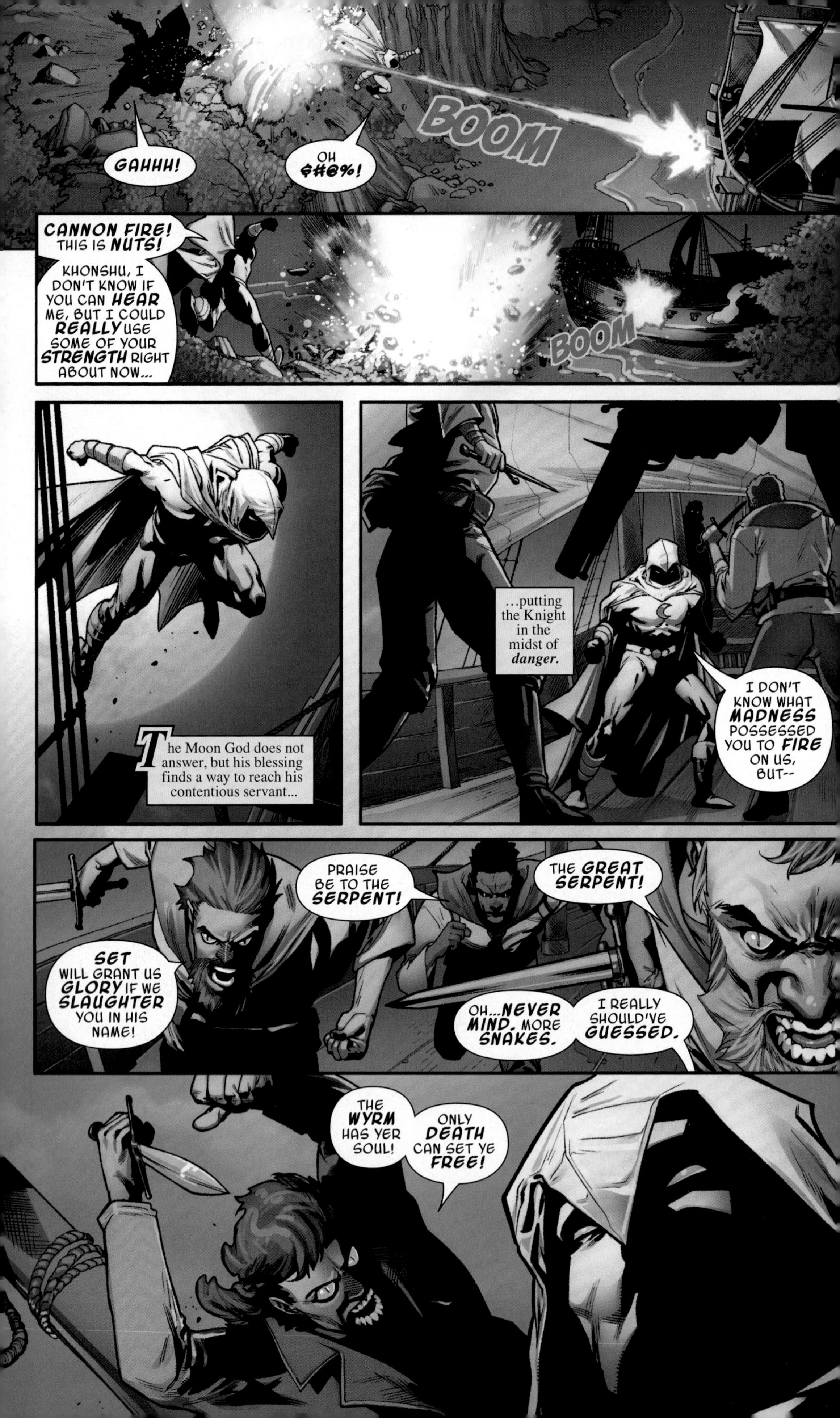
GAHHH!
OH $#@%!
BOOM
CANNON FIRE! THIS IS NUTS!
KHONSHU, I DON'T KNOW IF YOU CAN HEAR ME, BUT I COULD REALLY USE SOME OF YOUR STRENGTH RIGHT ABOUT NOW...
BOOM
The Moon God does not answer, but his blessing finds a way to reach his contentious servant...
...putting the Knight in the midst of danger.
I DON'T KNOW WHAT MADNESS POSSESSED YOU TO FIRE ON US, BUT--
PRAISE BE TO THE SERPENT!
THE GREAT SERPENT!
SET WILL GRANT US GLORY IF WE SLAUGHTER YOU IN HIS NAME!
OH...NEVER MIND. MORE SNAKES.
I REALLY SHOULD'VE GUESSED.
THE WYRM HAS YER SOUL!
ONLY DEATH CAN SET YE FREE!

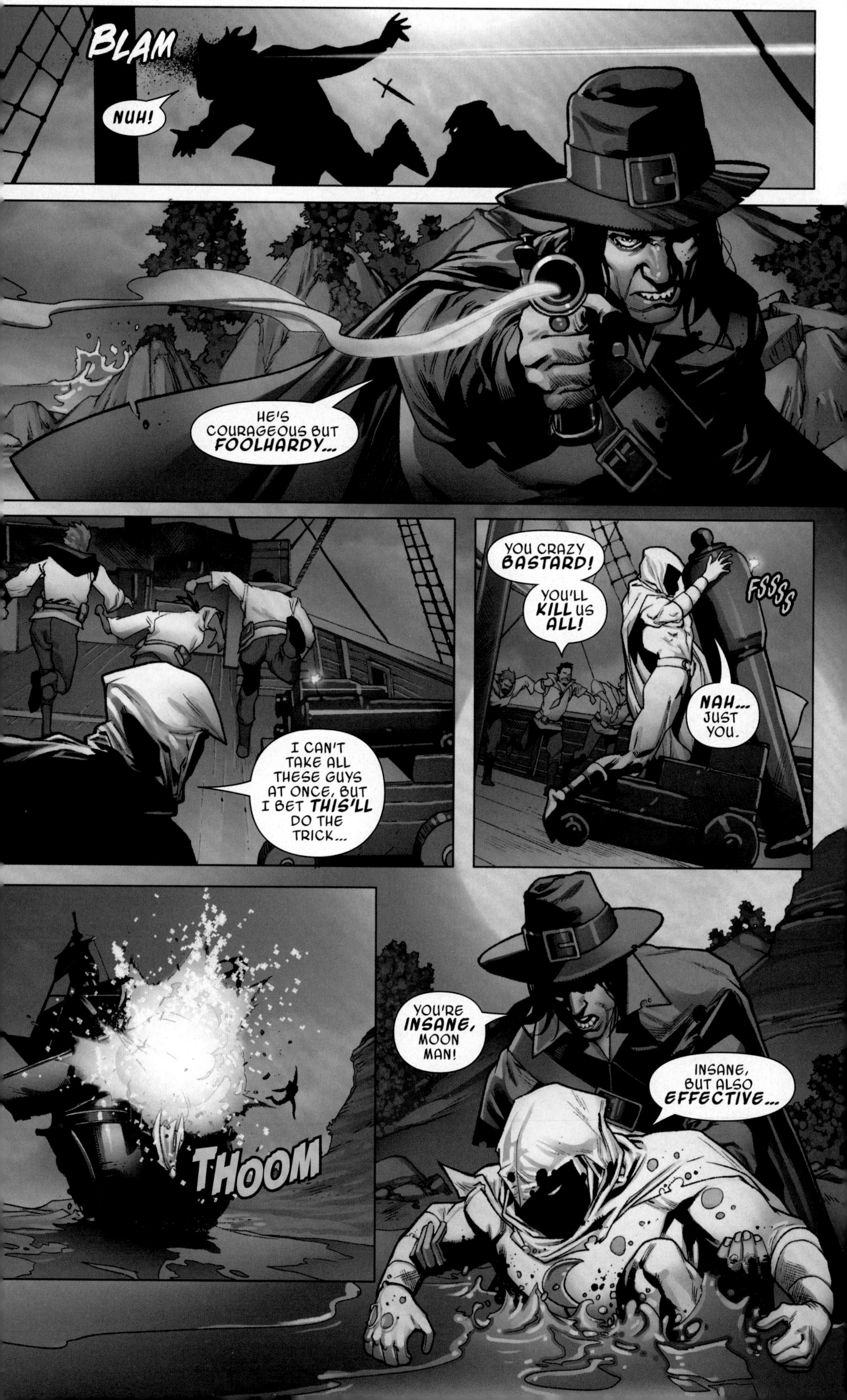
BLAM
NUH!
HE'S COURAGEOUS BUT FOOLHARDY...
I CAN'T TAKE ALL THESE GUYS AT ONCE, BUT I BET THIS'LL DO THE TRICK...
YOU CRAZY BASTARD!
YOU'LL KILL US ALL!
FSSSS
NAH... JUST YOU.
THOOM
YOU'RE INSANE, MOON MAN!
INSANE, BUT ALSO EFFECTIVE...

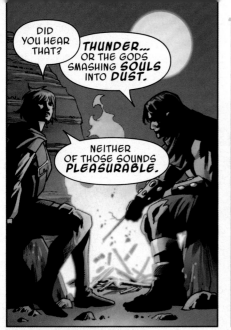

DID YOU HEAR THAT?

THUNDER... OR THE GODS SMASHING SOULS INTO DUST.

NEITHER OF THOSE SOUNDS PLEASURABLE.

I DON'T RELISH THE THOUGHT OF BEING DRAGGED ACROSS THIS LAND BY THE WHIMS OF A MASK SPOUTING PROPHECY.

IF IT'S TOO MUCH TO BEAR, THEN YOU SHOULD LEAVE, RED HAIR.

QUIT CALLING ME THAT, YOU SULLEN APE OF A MAN! BESIDES, WHERE WOULD I GO?

WHEREVER COWARDS TRAVEL...

TAKE THAT BACK, YOU OAF, OR I'LL CUT YOUR HEAD FREE AND LEAVE IT ROTTING ON THE SAND!

KILL ME IF YOU MUST, BUT YOU'LL DIE WITHIN A DAY IF I DON'T GUIDE US THROUGH THE KHARAMUN DESERT.

DAMN YOU, CONAN.

BOTH OF US ARE DAMNED ON THIS SNAKE-TAINTED JOURNEY, WOMAN. AND IF WE FAIL, WE'LL HAVE PLENTY OF OTHER DAMNED FOOLS ALONG TO KEEP US COMPANY...

NEWCASTLE ISN'T FAR. WE'LL FIND ANOTHER SHIP THERE AND HEAD TO ROTTERDAM, THEN HIRE A CARAVAN TO TAKE US SOUTH THROUGH GERMANY...THEN ON TO ITALY...

YOU MAKE IT SOUND SO SIMPLE.

I HAVE FAITH IN THE TASK AT HAND...DO YOU NOT?

SURE...

YOUR PAL, THE SHIP CAPTAIN...BEFORE I TORCHED HIS SHIP, HE SAID SOMETHING REALLY WEIRD...

"THE WORM HAS YOUR SOUL..."

DOES THAT MAKE ANY SENSE TO YOU?

NO.

"The Worm"...

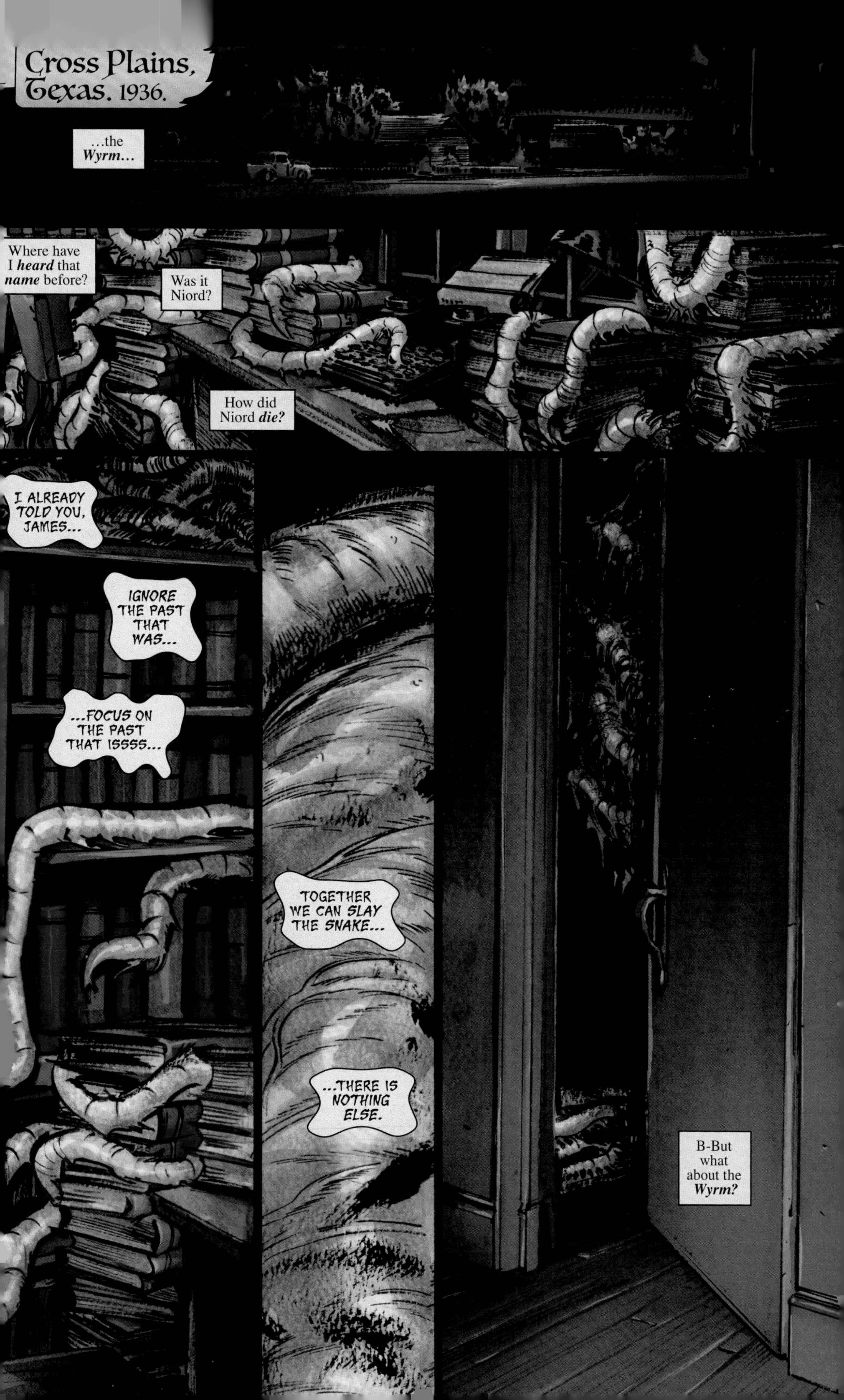
Cross Plains, Texas. 1936.
...the *Wyrm*...
Where have I ***heard*** that ***name*** before?
Was it Niord?
How did Niord ***die?***
I ALREADY TOLD YOU, JAMES...
IGNORE THE PAST THAT WAS...
...FOCUS ON THE PAST THAT ISSSS...
TOGETHER WE CAN *SLAY* THE *SNAKE*...
...THERE IS *NOTHING ELSE.*
B-But what about the ***Wyrm?***

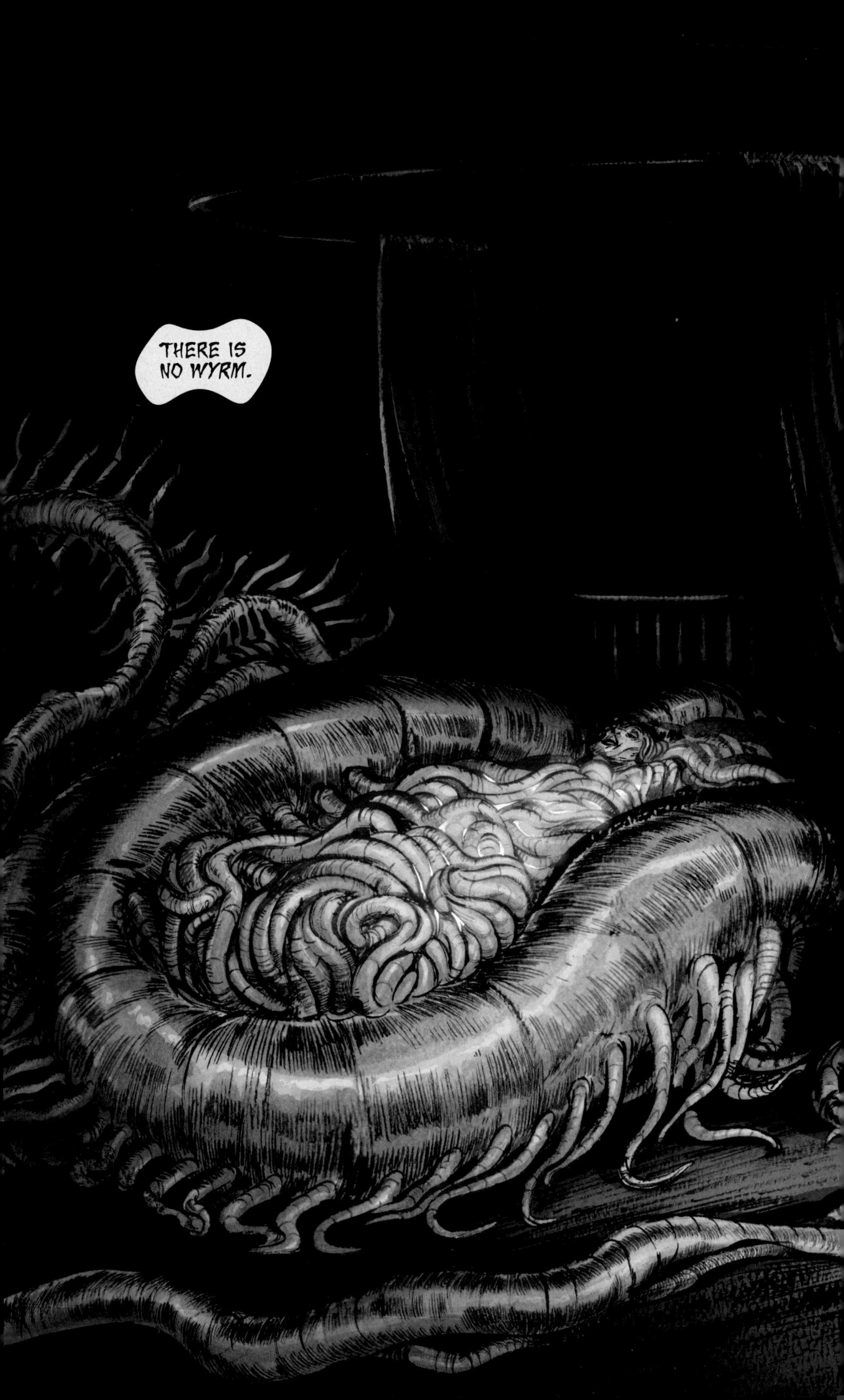
THERE IS NO WYRM.

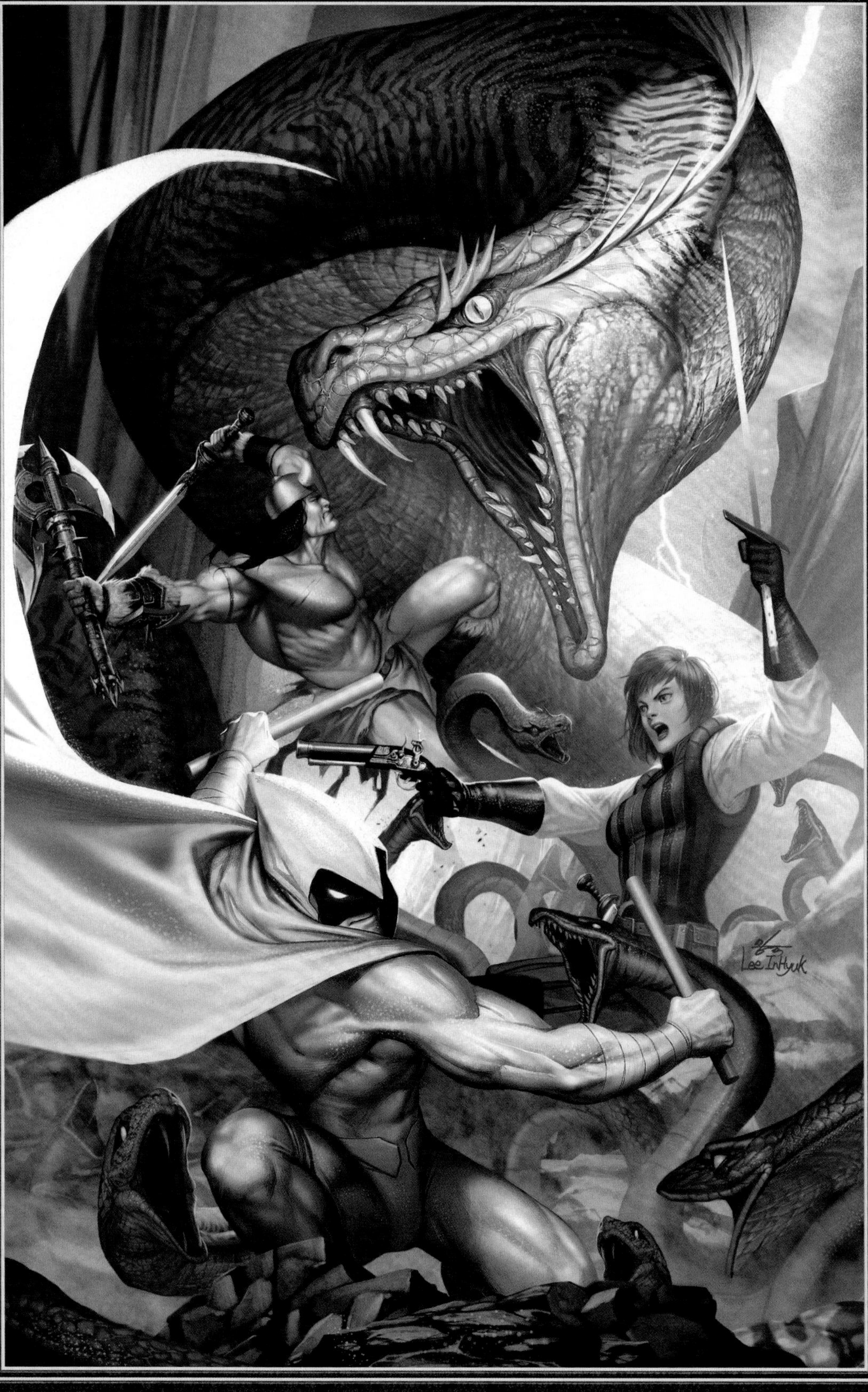
Lee InHyuk

#1 VARIANT BY INHYUK LEE

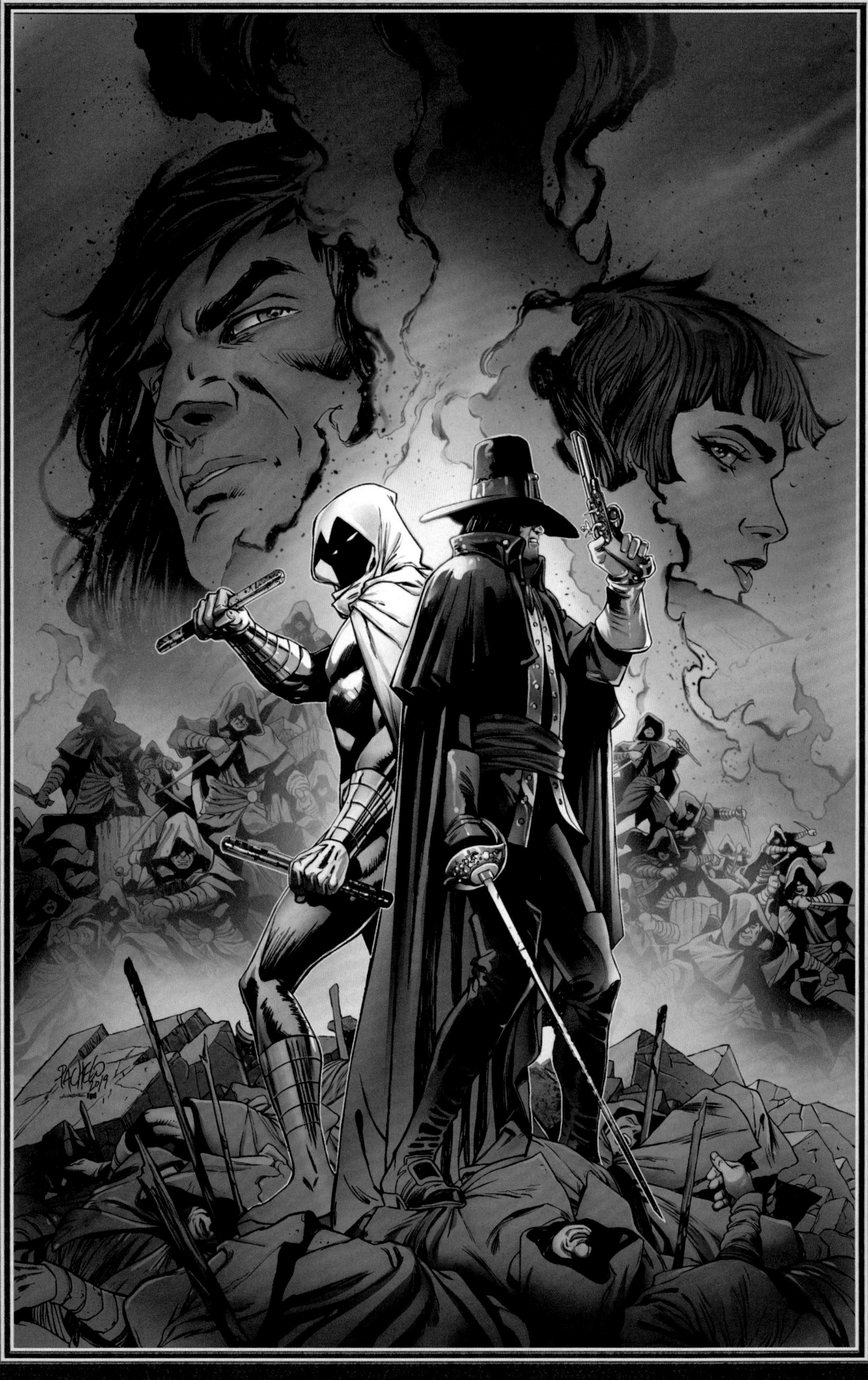

CHAPTER III: THE FAITHFUL AND THE FALLEN

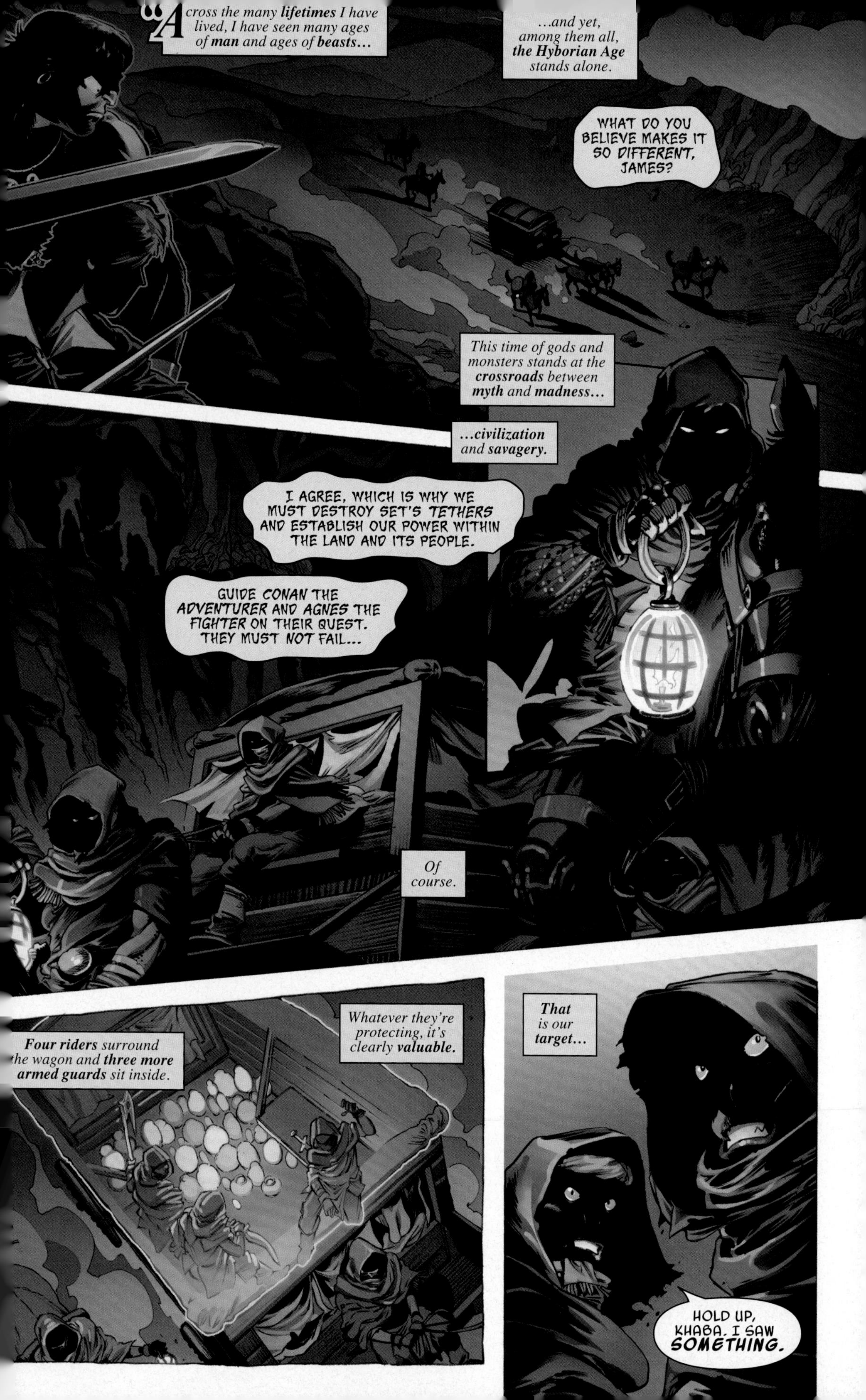

Across the many lifetimes I have lived, I have seen many ages of man and ages of beasts...
...and yet, among them all, the Hyborian Age stands alone.
WHAT DO YOU BELIEVE MAKES IT SO DIFFERENT, JAMES?
This time of gods and monsters stands at the crossroads between myth and madness...
...civilization and savagery.
I AGREE, WHICH IS WHY WE MUST DESTROY SET'S TETHERS AND ESTABLISH OUR POWER WITHIN THE LAND AND ITS PEOPLE.
GUIDE CONAN THE ADVENTURER AND AGNES THE FIGHTER ON THEIR QUEST. THEY MUST NOT FAIL...
Of course.
Four riders surround the wagon and three more armed guards sit inside.
Whatever they're protecting, it's clearly valuable.
That is our target...
HOLD UP, KHABA. I SAW SOMETHING.

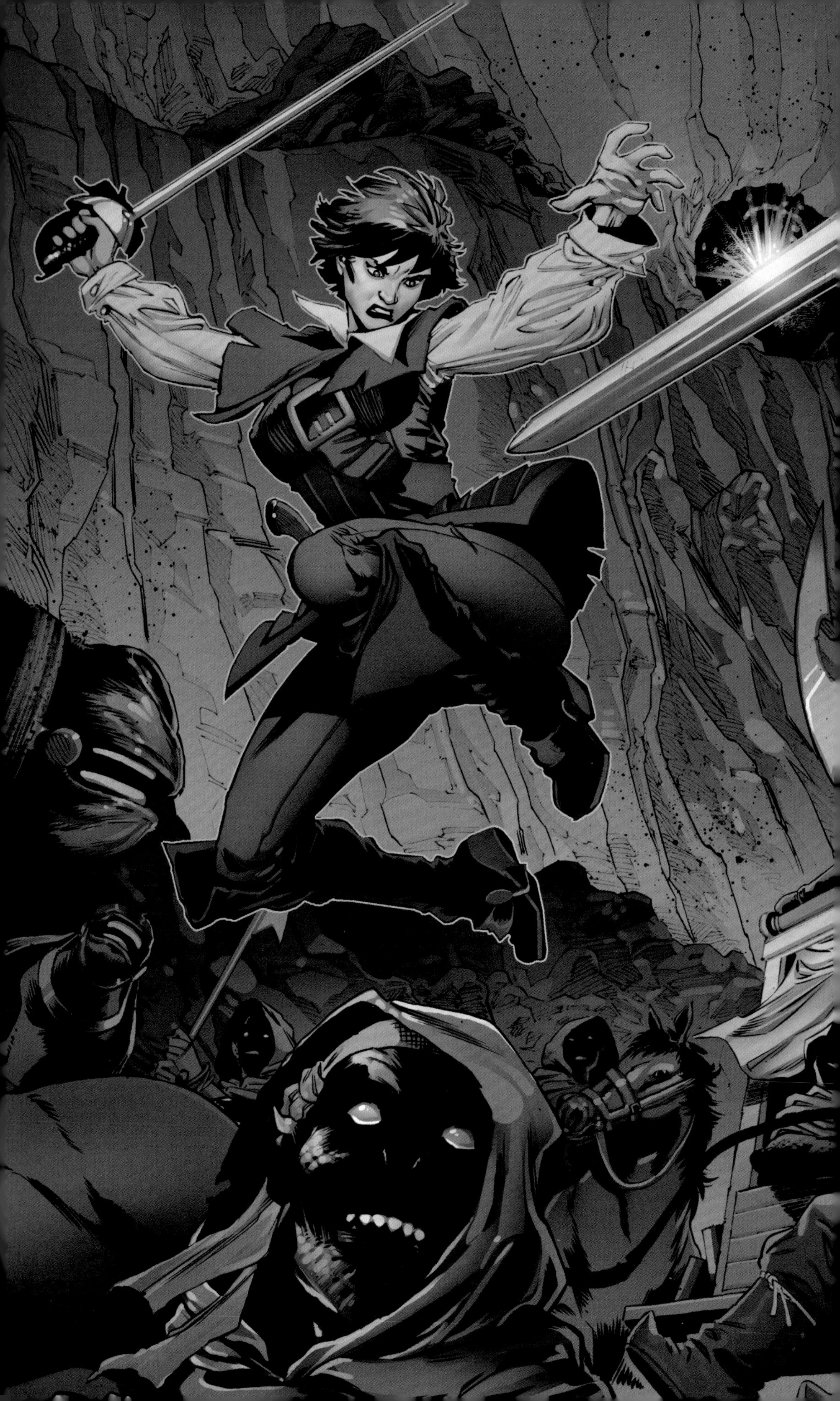

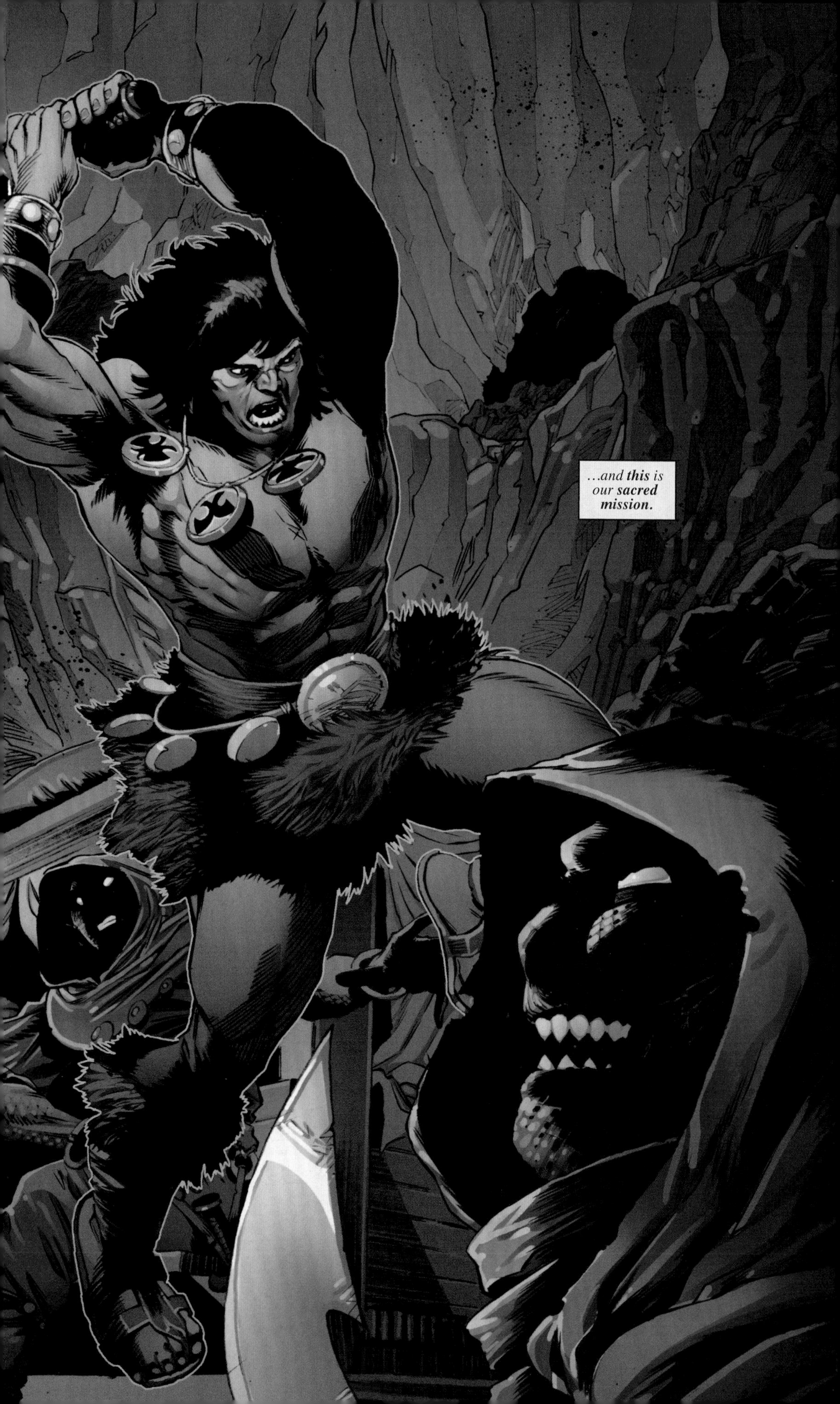
...and *this* is our *sacred mission.*

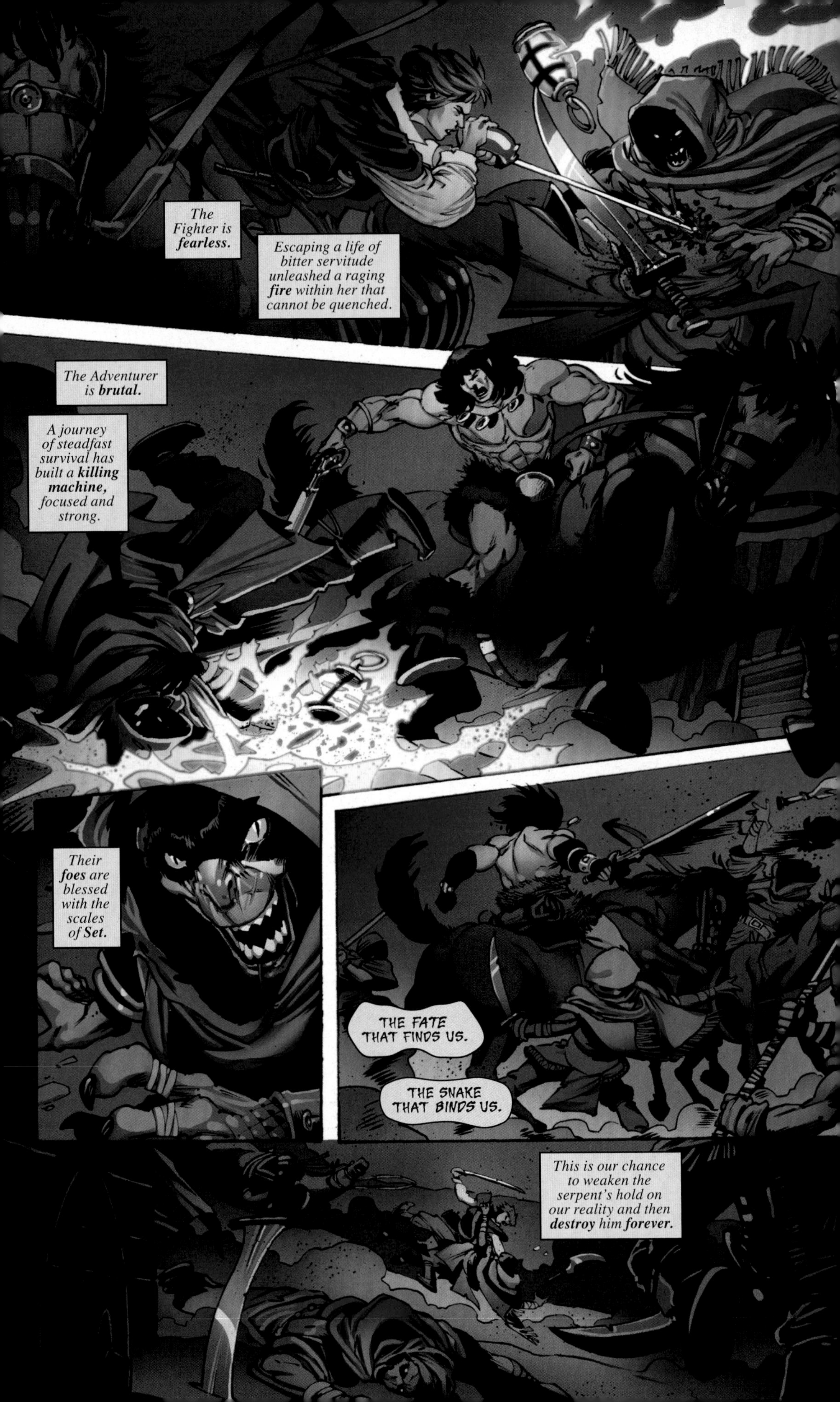
The Fighter is **fearless.**
*Escaping a life of bitter servitude unleashed a raging **fire** within her that cannot be quenched.*
The Adventurer is **brutal.**
*A journey of steadfast survival has built a **killing machine,** focused and strong.*
*Their **foes** are blessed with the scales of **Set.***
THE FATE THAT FINDS US.
THE SNAKE THAT BINDS US.
*This is our chance to weaken the serpent's hold on our reality and then **destroy** him **forever.***

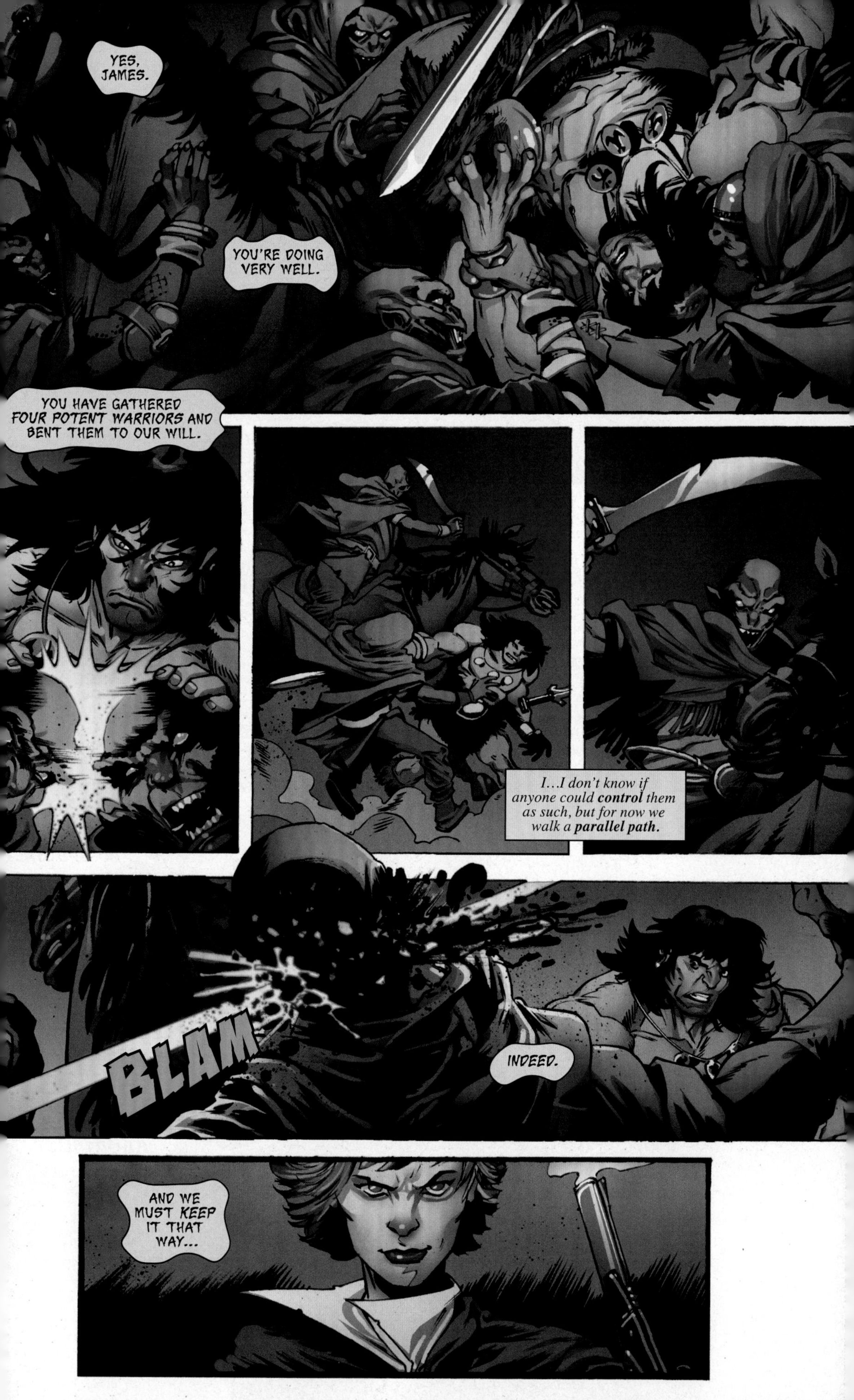
YES, JAMES.
YOU'RE DOING VERY WELL.
YOU HAVE GATHERED FOUR POTENT WARRIORS AND BENT THEM TO OUR WILL.
I...I don't know if anyone could control them as such, but for now we walk a parallel path.
BLAM
INDEED.
AND WE MUST KEEP IT THAT WAY...

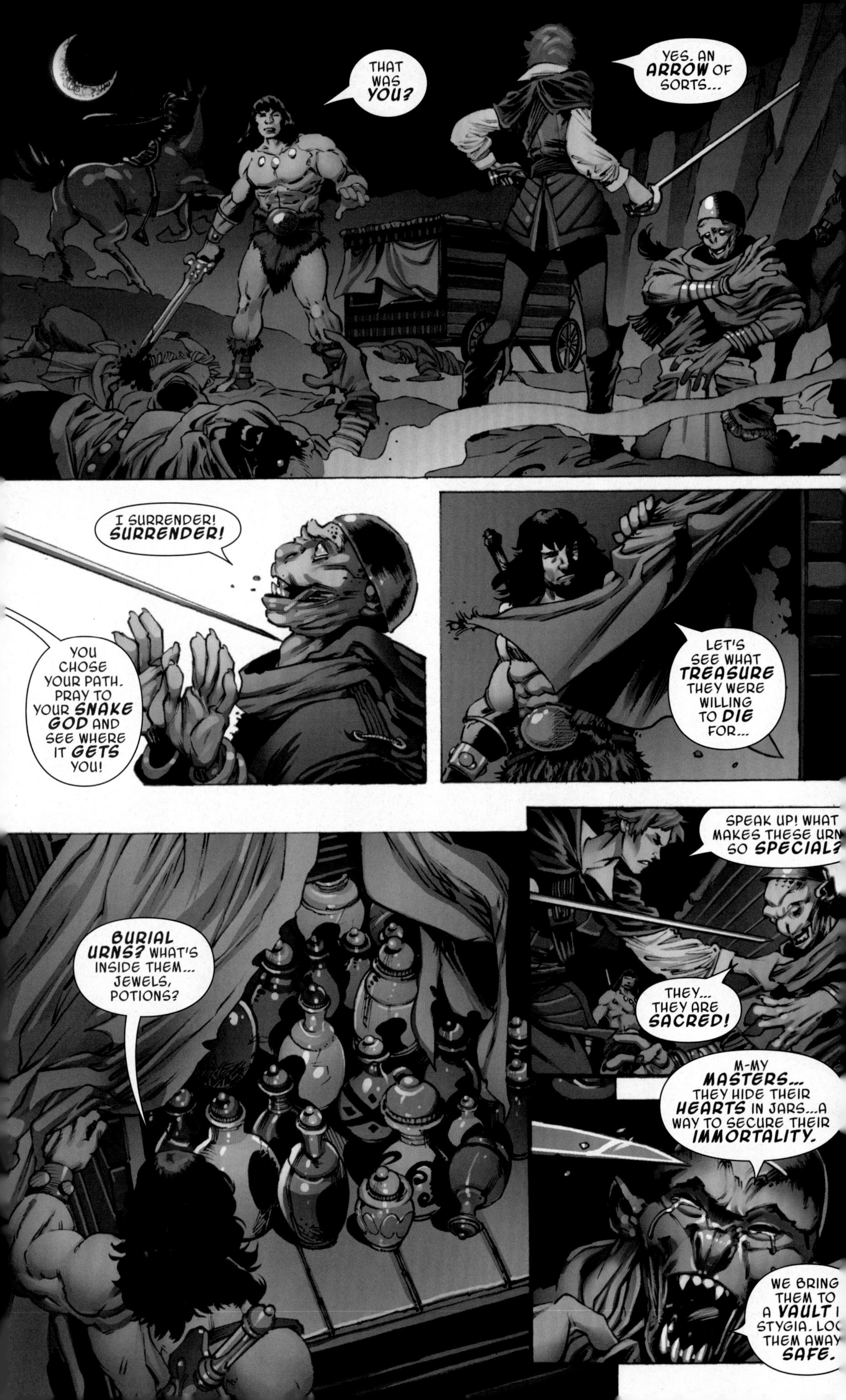
THAT WAS YOU?
YES. AN ARROW OF SORTS...
I SURRENDER! SURRENDER!
YOU CHOSE YOUR PATH. PRAY TO YOUR SNAKE GOD AND SEE WHERE IT GETS YOU!
LET'S SEE WHAT TREASURE THEY WERE WILLING TO DIE FOR...
BURIAL URNS? WHAT'S INSIDE THEM... JEWELS, POTIONS?
SPEAK UP! WHAT MAKES THESE URN SO SPECIAL?
THEY... THEY ARE SACRED!
M-MY MASTERS... THEY HIDE THEIR HEARTS IN JARS...A WAY TO SECURE THEIR IMMORTALITY.
WE BRING THEM TO A VAULT STYGIA. LO THEM AWAY SAFE.

WELL THEN, THAT'S EITHER **FOUL MAGIC** OR YOU'RE **INSANE.**

EITHER WAY, IT DESERVES TO **BURN**...

NO, **PLEASE!**

TH-TH-THE **GREAT SERPENT** WILL **CURSE** YOU FOR THIS!

OH, WE'RE **WELL** PAST THAT, LITTLE MAN.

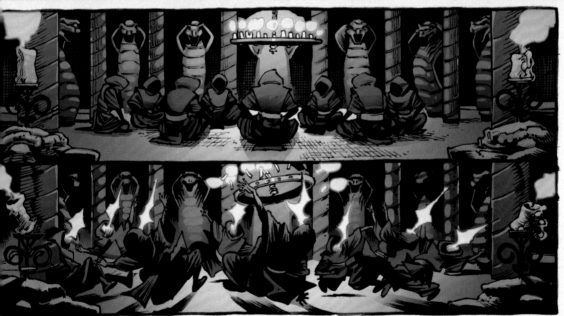

WE COULD HAVE SED THAT **WAGON,** YOU **OAF.**

FOR WHAT? WE'RE NOT **MERCHANTS.**

BETTER TO MOVE **SWIFTLY** AND STAY AHEAD OF THESE **VENGEFUL REPTILES.**

I--I TOLD YOU THE **SECRET!** LET ME **GO!**

NOT YET.

IF YOU WANT TO SEE THE **SUN RISE** ON YOUR **SNAKISH SKIN,** YOU'LL SHOW US WHERE THIS **VAULT** OF YOURS CAN BE FOUND...

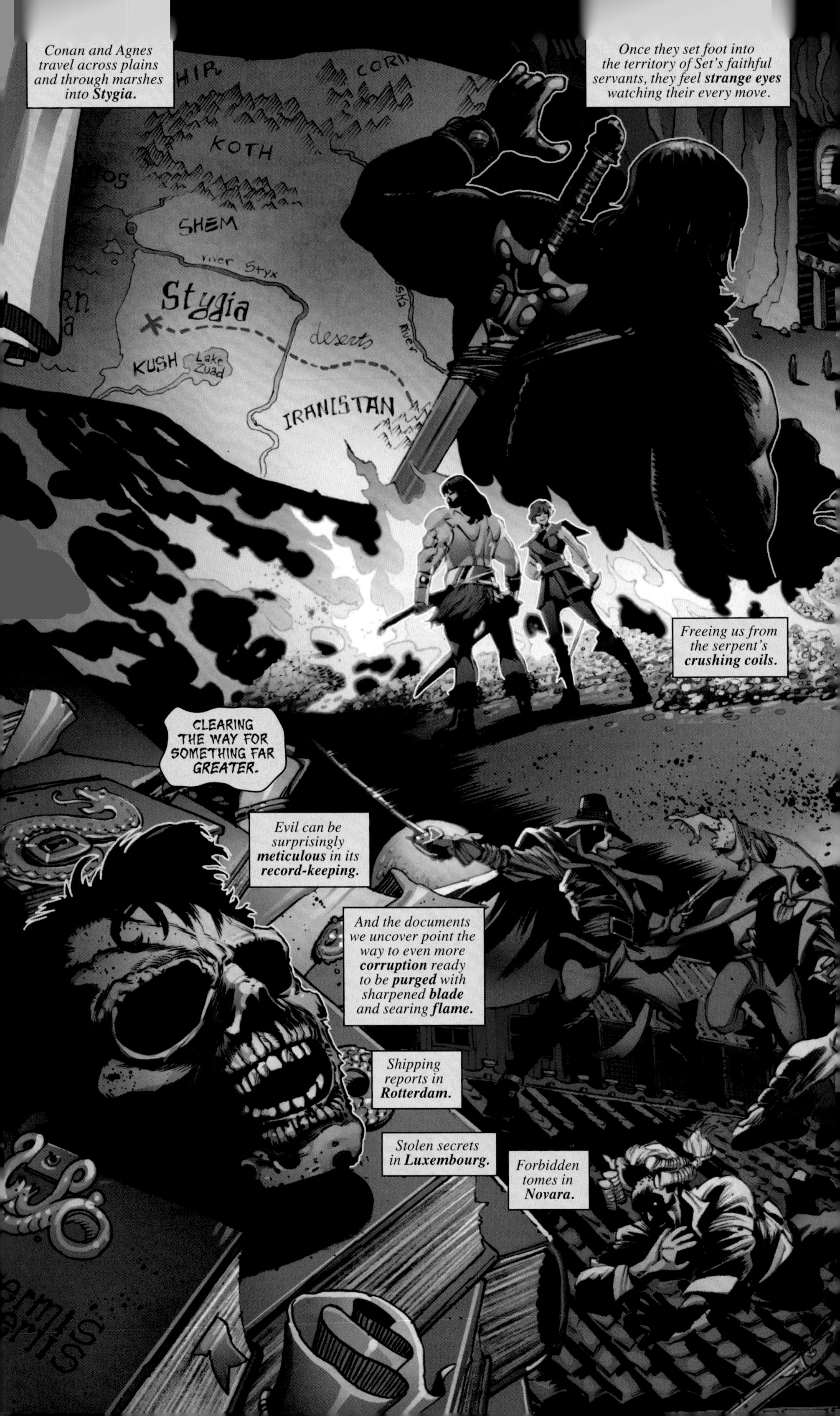
Conan and Agnes travel across plains and through marshes into **Stygia.**
Once they set foot into the territory of Set's faithful servants, they feel **strange eyes** watching their every move.
KOTH
SHEM
River Styx
Stygia
deserts
KUSH
Lake Zuad
IRANISTAN
Freeing us from the serpent's **crushing coils.**
CLEARING THE WAY FOR SOMETHING FAR GREATER.
Evil can be surprisingly **meticulous** in its **record-keeping.**
And the documents we uncover point the way to even more **corruption** ready to be **purged** with sharpened **blade** and searing **flame.**
Shipping reports in **Rotterdam.**
Stolen secrets in **Luxembourg.**
Forbidden tomes in **Novara.**

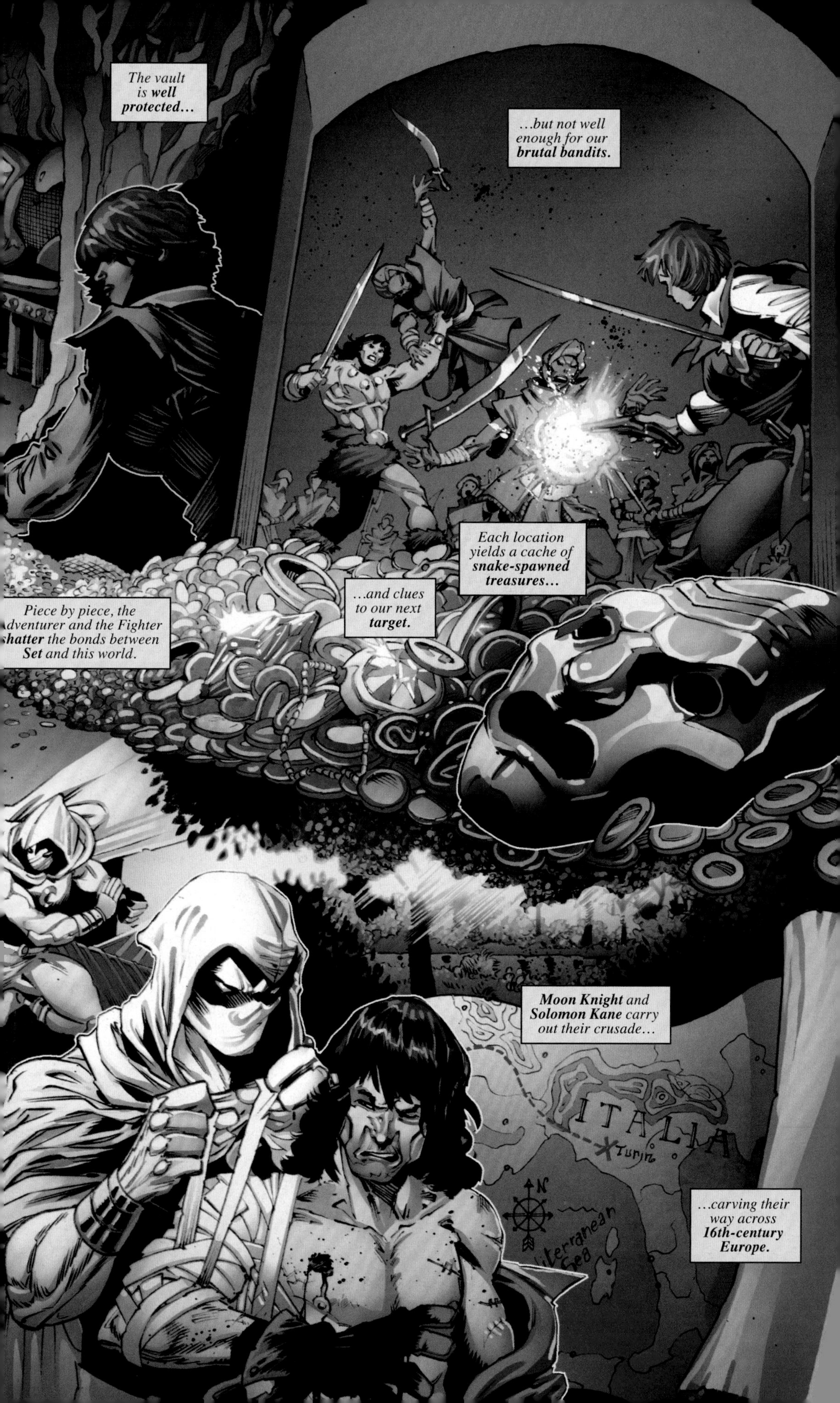

The vault is well protected...
...but not well enough for our brutal bandits.
Each location yields a cache of snake-spawned treasures...
...and clues to our next target.
Piece by piece, the Adventurer and the Fighter shatter the bonds between Set and this world.
Moon Knight and Solomon Kane carry out their crusade...
ITALIA
Turin
N
...carving their way across 16th-century Europe.

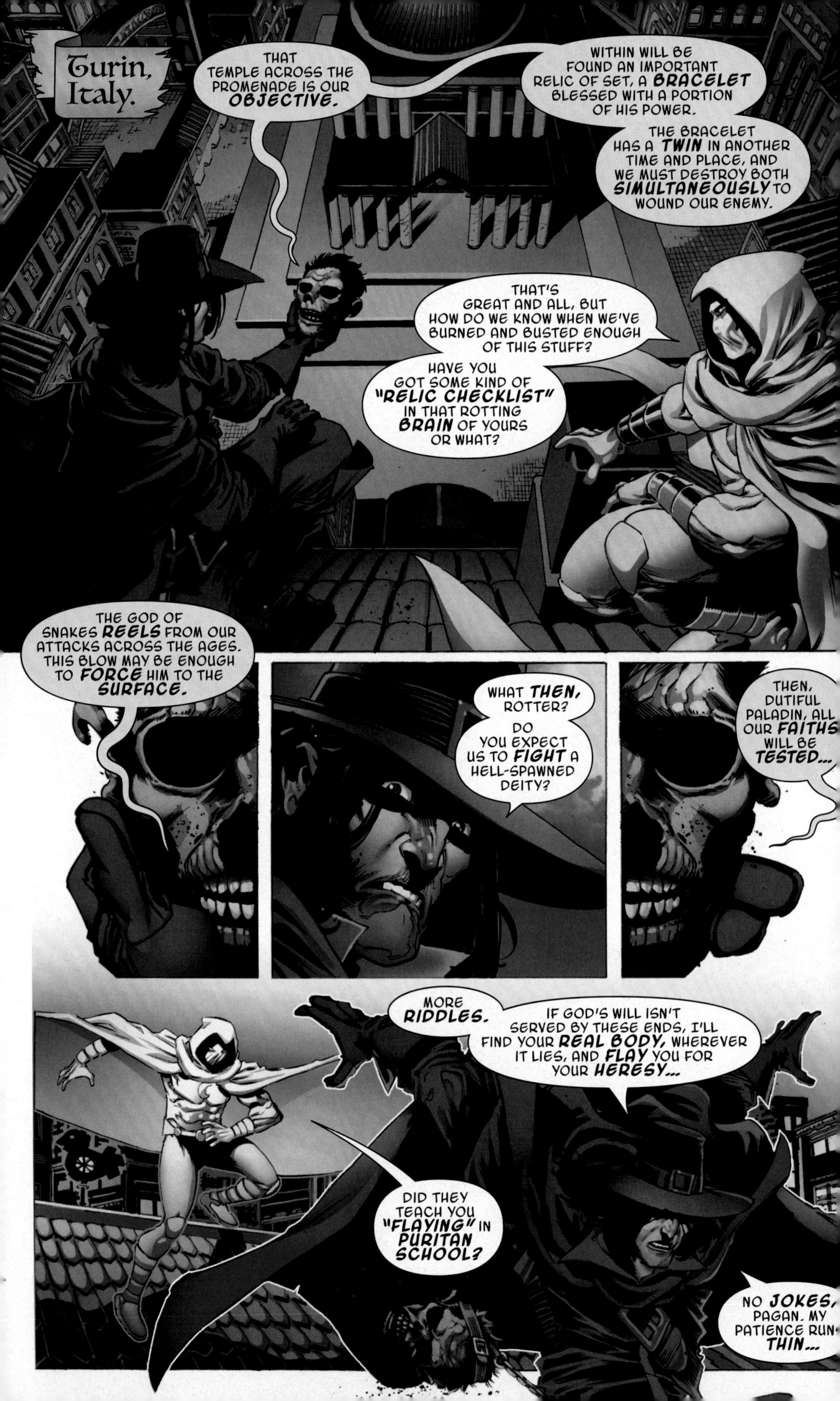
Turin, Italy.
THAT TEMPLE ACROSS THE PROMENADE IS OUR OBJECTIVE.
WITHIN WILL BE FOUND AN IMPORTANT RELIC OF SET, A BRACELET BLESSED WITH A PORTION OF HIS POWER.
THE BRACELET HAS A TWIN IN ANOTHER TIME AND PLACE, AND WE MUST DESTROY BOTH SIMULTANEOUSLY TO WOUND OUR ENEMY.
THAT'S GREAT AND ALL, BUT HOW DO WE KNOW WHEN WE'VE BURNED AND BUSTED ENOUGH OF THIS STUFF?
HAVE YOU GOT SOME KIND OF "RELIC CHECKLIST" IN THAT ROTTING BRAIN OF YOURS OR WHAT?
THE GOD OF SNAKES REELS FROM OUR ATTACKS ACROSS THE AGES. THIS BLOW MAY BE ENOUGH TO FORCE HIM TO THE SURFACE.
WHAT THEN, ROTTER?
DO YOU EXPECT US TO FIGHT A HELL-SPAWNED DEITY?
THEN, DUTIFUL PALADIN, ALL OUR FAITHS WILL BE TESTED...
MORE RIDDLES.
IF GOD'S WILL ISN'T SERVED BY THESE ENDS, I'LL FIND YOUR REAL BODY, WHEREVER IT LIES, AND FLAY YOU FOR YOUR HERESY...
DID THEY TEACH YOU "FLAYING" IN PURITAN SCHOOL?
NO JOKES, PAGAN. MY PATIENCE RUN THIN...

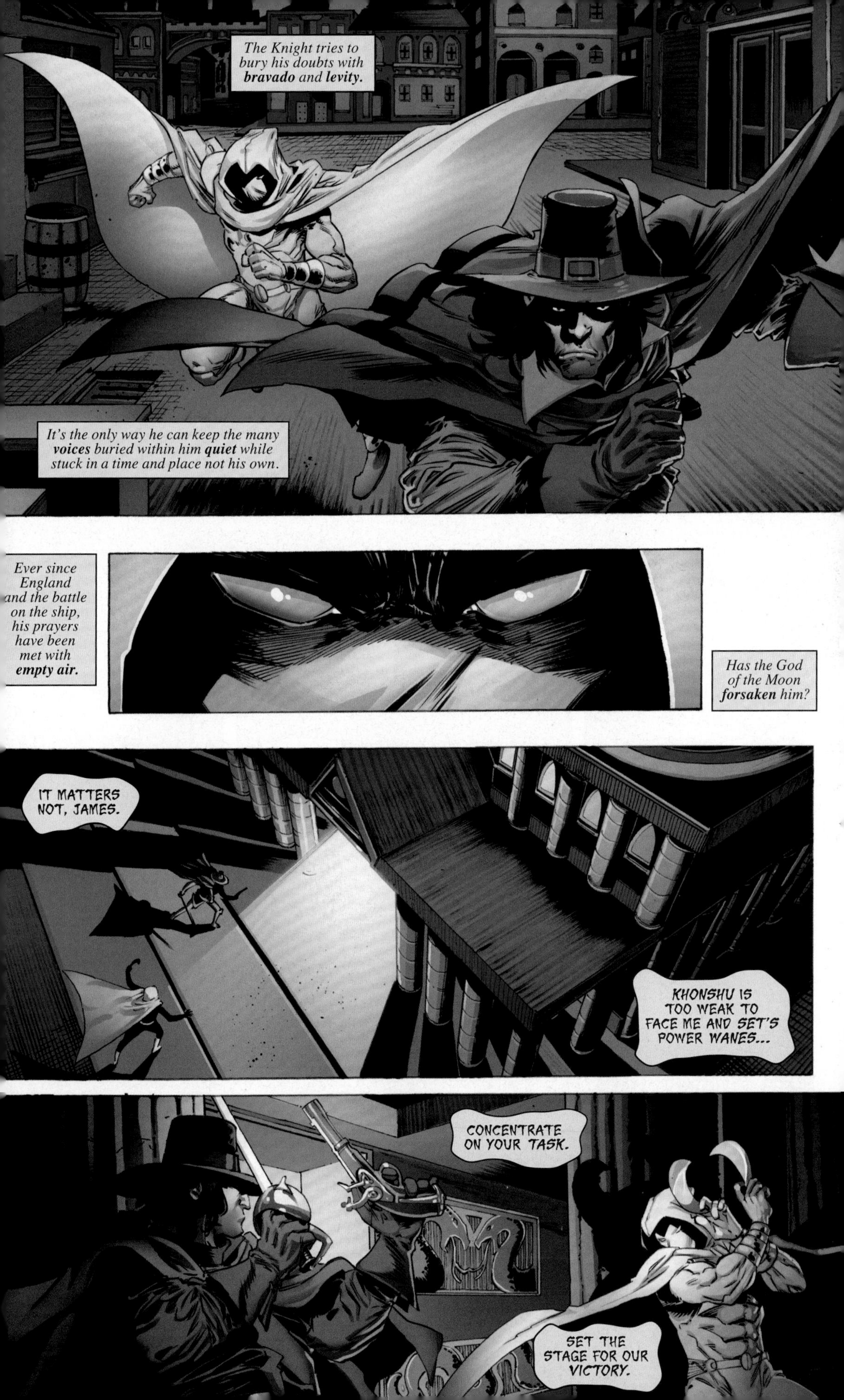
The Knight tries to bury his doubts with bravado and levity.
It's the only way he can keep the many voices buried within him quiet while stuck in a time and place not his own.
Ever since England and the battle on the ship, his prayers have been met with empty air.
Has the God of the Moon forsaken him?
IT MATTERS NOT, JAMES.
KHONSHU IS TOO WEAK TO FACE ME AND SET'S POWER WANES...
CONCENTRATE ON YOUR TASK.
SET THE STAGE FOR OUR VICTORY.

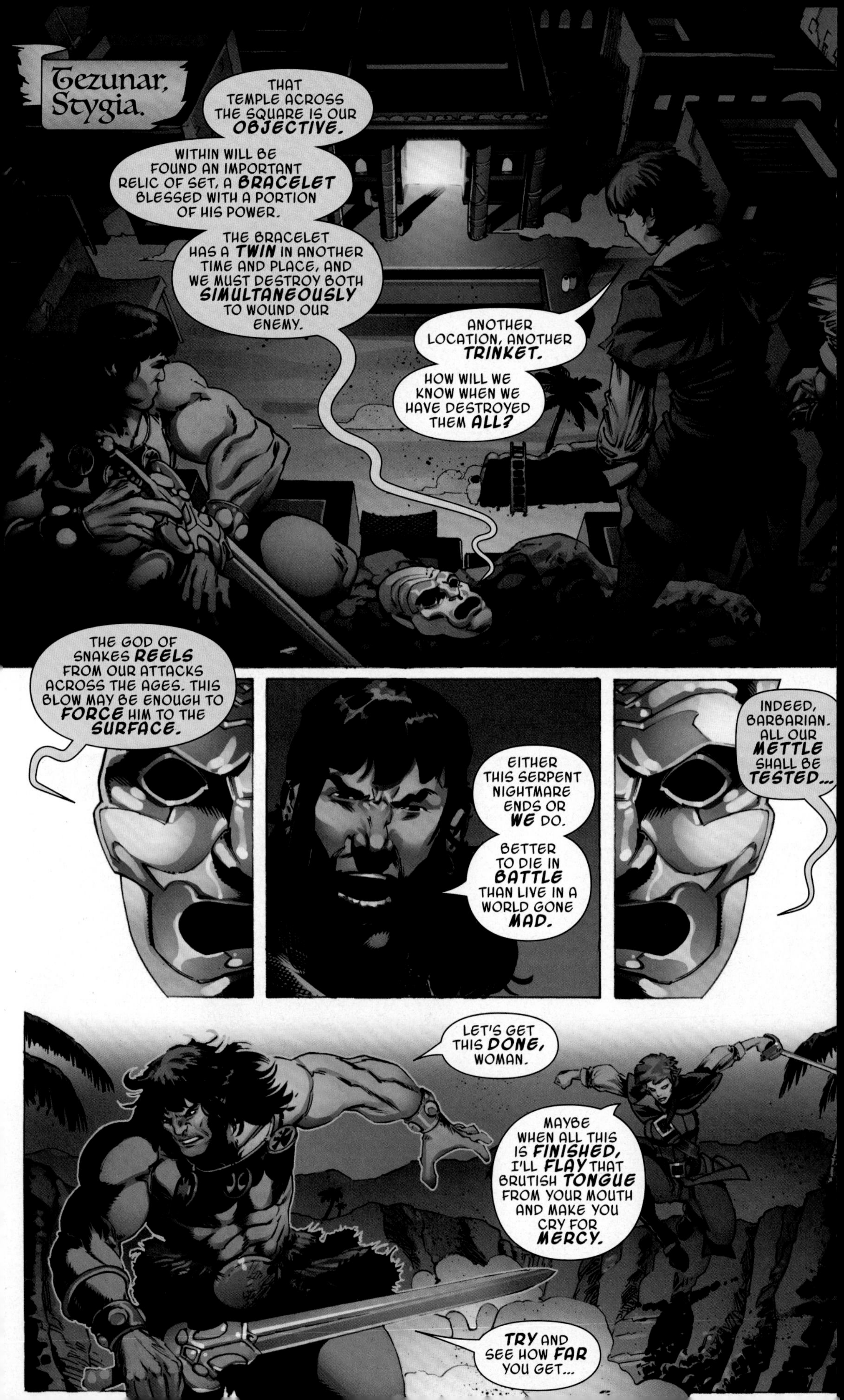
Tezunar, Stygia.
THAT TEMPLE ACROSS THE SQUARE IS OUR OBJECTIVE.
WITHIN WILL BE FOUND AN IMPORTANT RELIC OF SET, A BRACELET BLESSED WITH A PORTION OF HIS POWER.
THE BRACELET HAS A TWIN IN ANOTHER TIME AND PLACE, AND WE MUST DESTROY BOTH SIMULTANEOUSLY TO WOUND OUR ENEMY.
ANOTHER LOCATION, ANOTHER TRINKET.
HOW WILL WE KNOW WHEN WE HAVE DESTROYED THEM ALL?
THE GOD OF SNAKES REELS FROM OUR ATTACKS ACROSS THE AGES. THIS BLOW MAY BE ENOUGH TO FORCE HIM TO THE SURFACE.
EITHER THIS SERPENT NIGHTMARE ENDS OR WE DO.
BETTER TO DIE IN BATTLE THAN LIVE IN A WORLD GONE MAD.
INDEED, BARBARIAN. ALL OUR METTLE SHALL BE TESTED...
LET'S GET THIS DONE, WOMAN.
MAYBE WHEN ALL THIS IS FINISHED, I'LL FLAY THAT BRUTISH TONGUE FROM YOUR MOUTH AND MAKE YOU CRY FOR MERCY.
TRY AND SEE HOW FAR YOU GET...

The **Fighter** will not let her thoughts linger on the past.

Her **anger** keeps her grounded, no matter how **insane** this all seems.

She used to wonder if there was a god at all. Now she has seen proof of **magic**, spirits, and the demonic.

Will she be **punished** in the afterlife for the **bloody** trail she leaves in her wake?

HER FAITH DOES NOT CONCERN US.

ALL GODS AND CREATURES SHALL BOW TO THE WYRM...

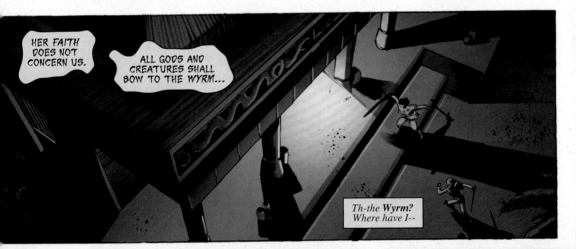

Th-the **Wyrm?** Where have I--

FOCUS HERE.

THE SNAKE IS OUR ENEMY...

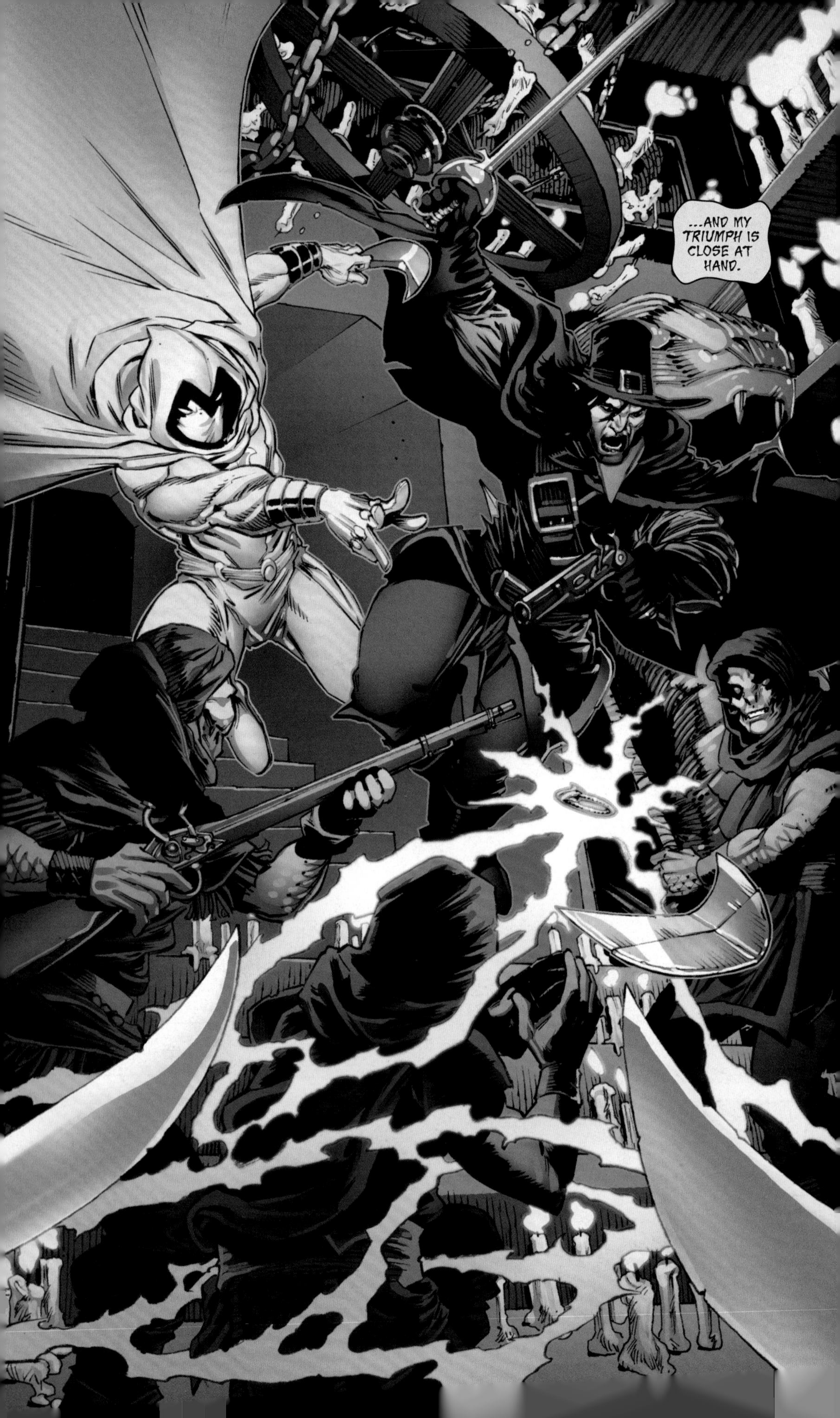
...AND MY TRIUMPH IS CLOSE AT HAND.

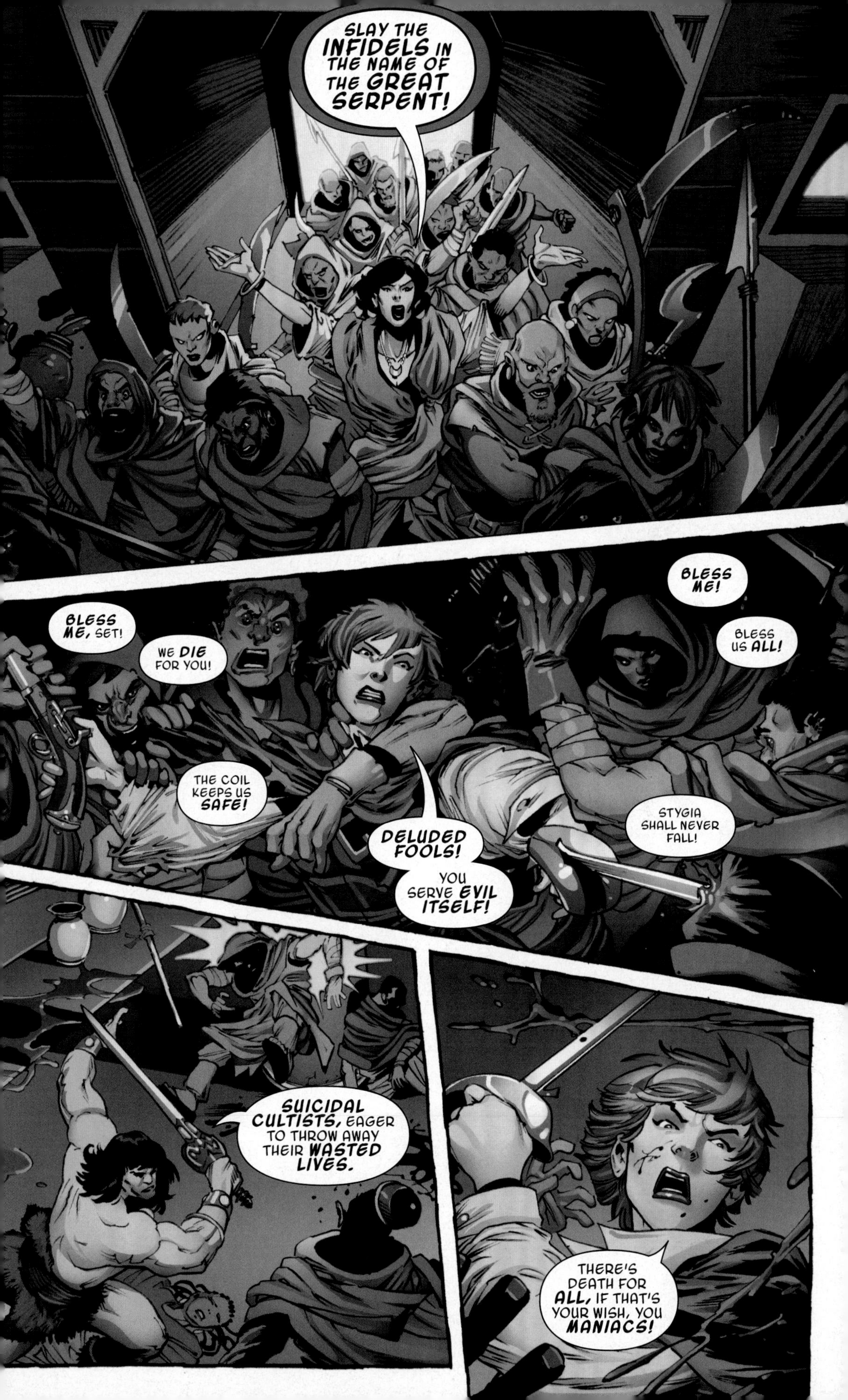
SLAY THE INFIDELS IN THE NAME OF THE GREAT SERPENT!
BLESS ME, SET!
WE DIE FOR YOU!
BLESS ME!
BLESS US ALL!
THE COIL KEEPS US SAFE!
DELUDED FOOLS!
YOU SERVE EVIL ITSELF!
STYGIA SHALL NEVER FALL!
SUICIDAL CULTISTS, EAGER TO THROW AWAY THEIR WASTED LIVES.
THERE'S DEATH FOR ALL, IF THAT'S YOUR WISH, YOU MANIACS!

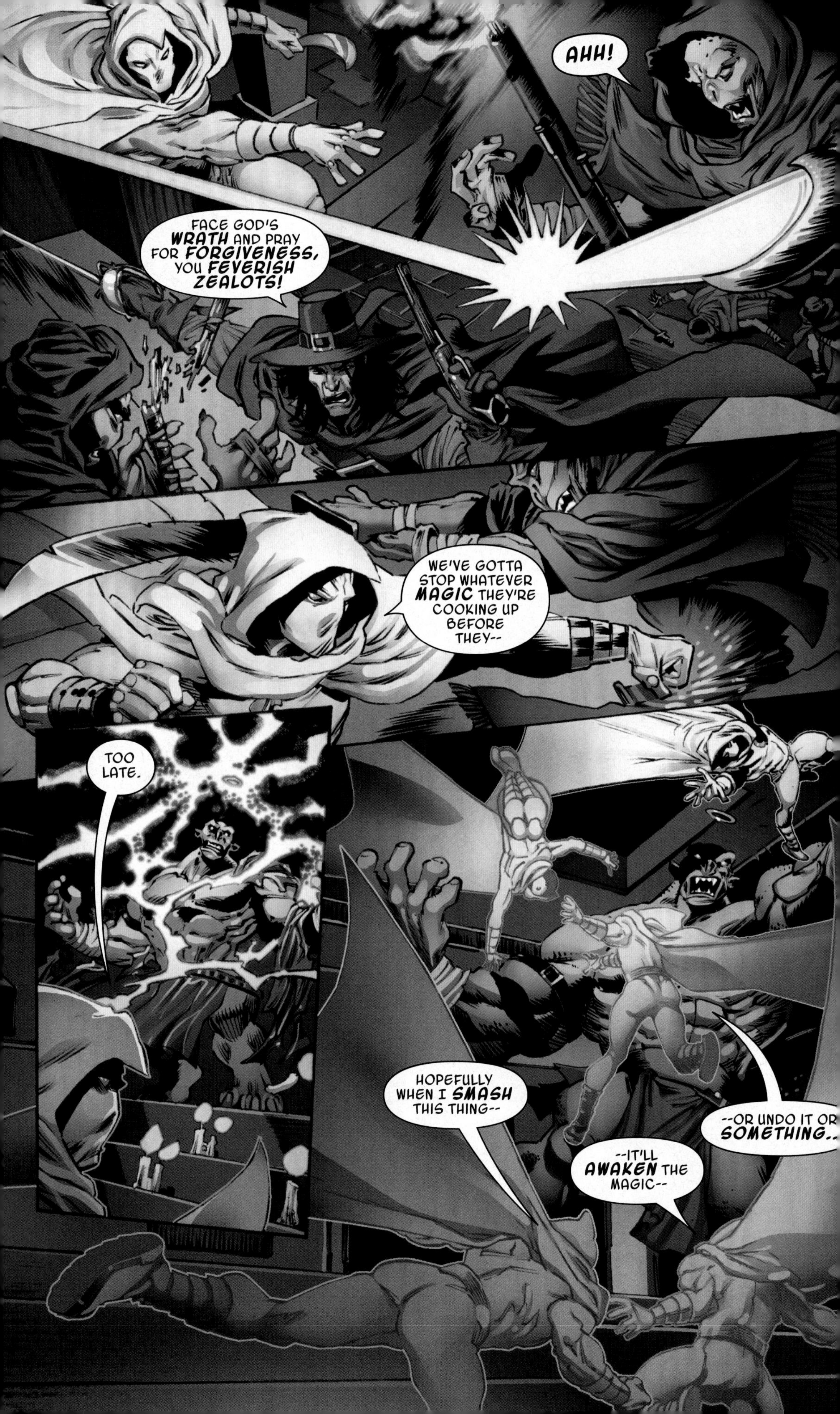
AHH!
FACE GOD'S WRATH AND PRAY FOR FORGIVENESS, YOU FEVERISH ZEALOTS!
WE'VE GOTTA STOP WHATEVER MAGIC THEY'RE COOKING UP BEFORE THEY--
TOO LATE.
HOPEFULLY WHEN I SMASH THIS THING--
--IT'LL AWAKEN THE MAGIC--
--OR UNDO IT OR SOMETHING..

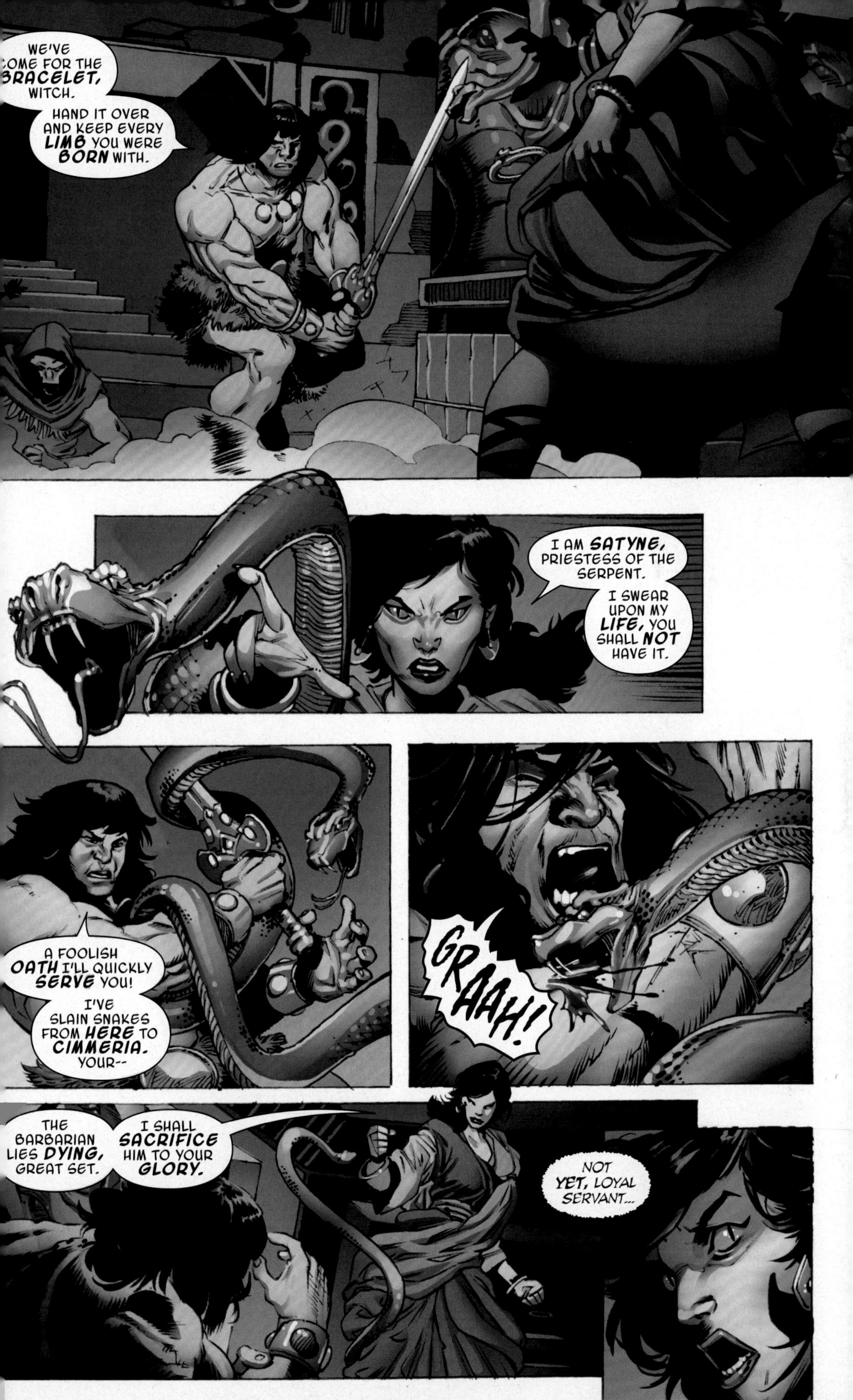
WE'VE COME FOR THE BRACELET, WITCH.
HAND IT OVER AND KEEP EVERY LIMB YOU WERE BORN WITH.
I AM SATYNE, PRIESTESS OF THE SERPENT.
I SWEAR UPON MY LIFE, YOU SHALL NOT HAVE IT.
A FOOLISH OATH I'LL QUICKLY SERVE YOU!
I'VE SLAIN SNAKES FROM HERE TO CIMMERIA. YOUR--
GRAAAH!
THE BARBARIAN LIES DYING, GREAT SET.
I SHALL SACRIFICE HIM TO YOUR GLORY.
NOT YET, LOYAL SERVANT...

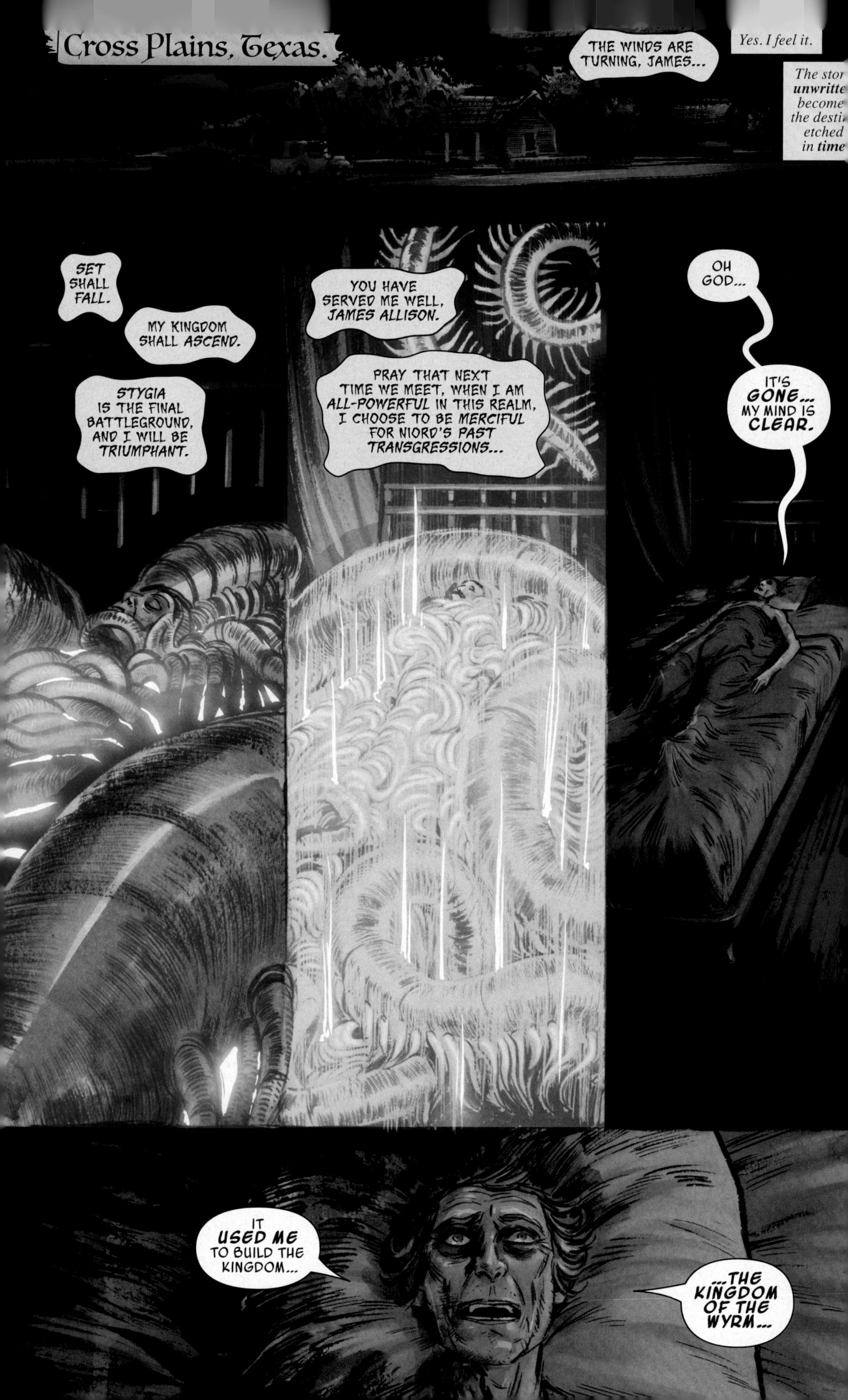
Cross Plains, Texas.
THE WINDS ARE TURNING, JAMES...
Yes. I feel it.
The stor unwritte become the desti etched in time
SET SHALL FALL.
MY KINGDOM SHALL ASCEND.
STYGIA IS THE FINAL BATTLEGROUND, AND I WILL BE TRIUMPHANT.
YOU HAVE SERVED ME WELL, JAMES ALLISON.
PRAY THAT NEXT TIME WE MEET, WHEN I AM ALL-POWERFUL IN THIS REALM, I CHOOSE TO BE MERCIFUL FOR NIORD'S PAST TRANSGRESSIONS...
OH GOD...
IT'S GONE... MY MIND IS CLEAR.
IT USED ME TO BUILD THE KINGDOM...
...THE KINGDOM OF THE WYRM...

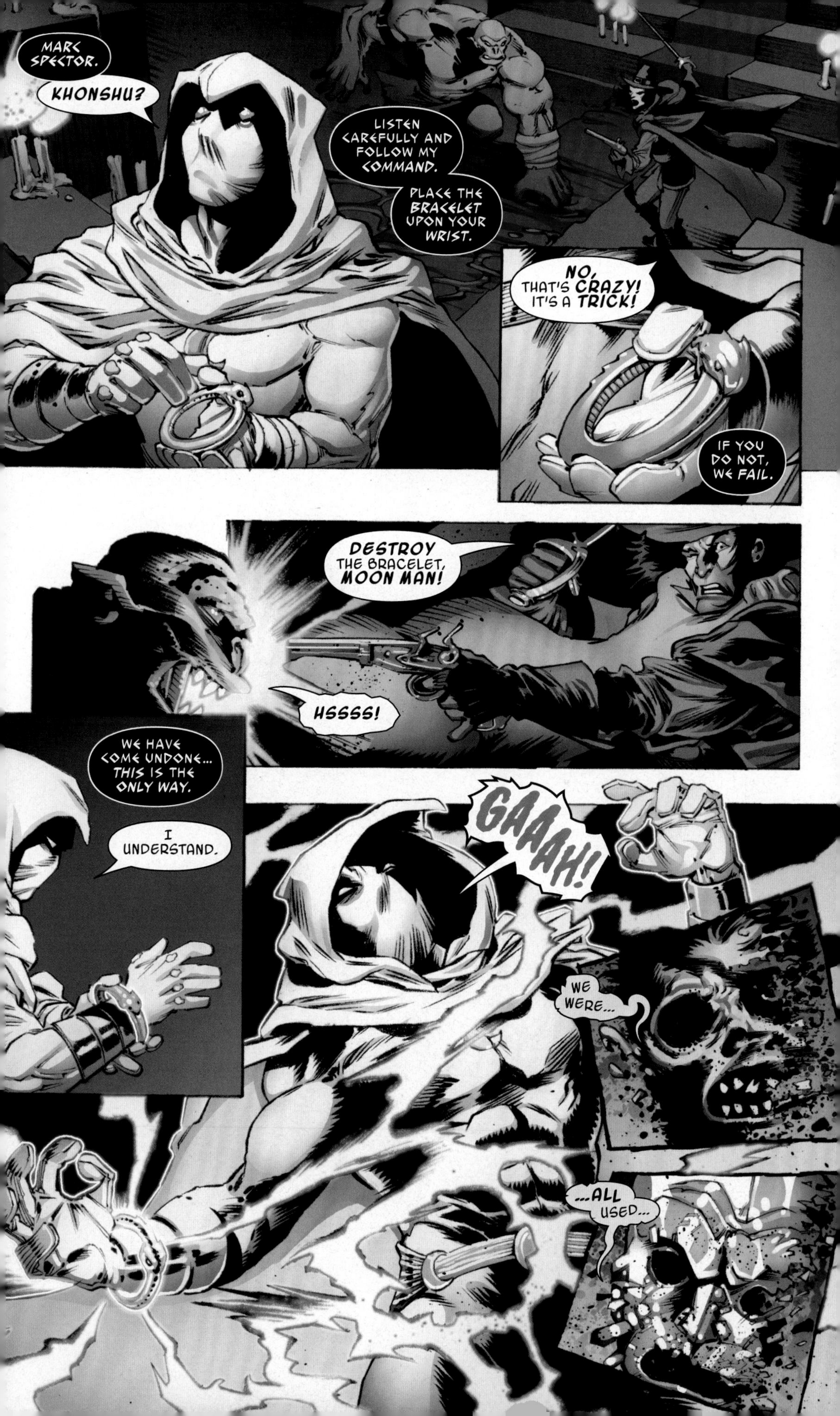
MARC SPECTOR.
KHONSHU?
LISTEN CAREFULLY AND FOLLOW MY COMMAND.
PLACE THE BRACELET UPON YOUR WRIST.
NO, THAT'S CRAZY! IT'S A TRICK!
IF YOU DO NOT, WE FAIL.
DESTROY THE BRACELET, MOON MAN!
HSSSS!
WE HAVE COME UNDONE... THIS IS THE ONLY WAY.
I UNDERSTAND.
GAAAH!
WE WERE...
...ALL USED...

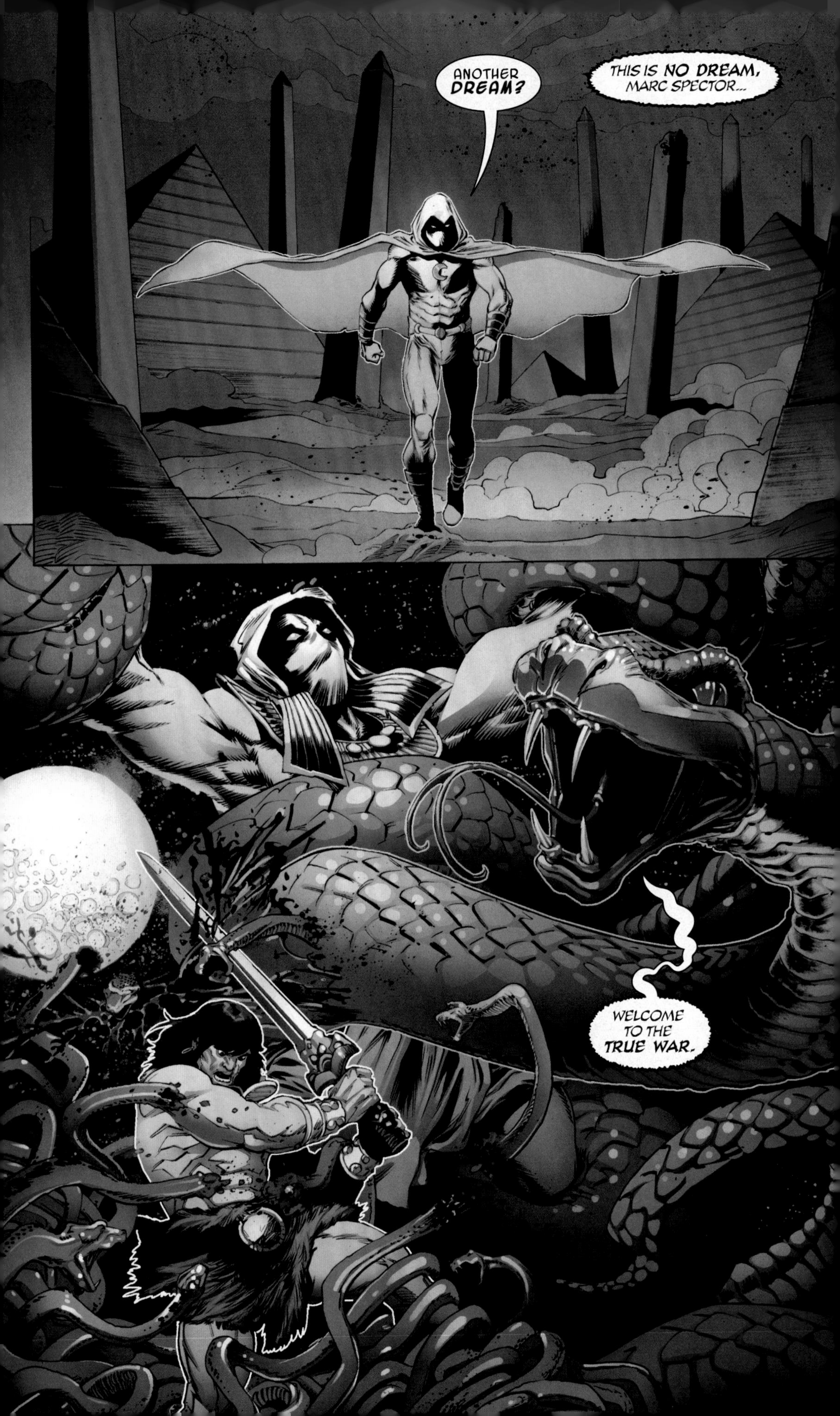
ANOTHER DREAM?
THIS IS NO DREAM, MARC SPECTOR...
WELCOME TO THE TRUE WAR.

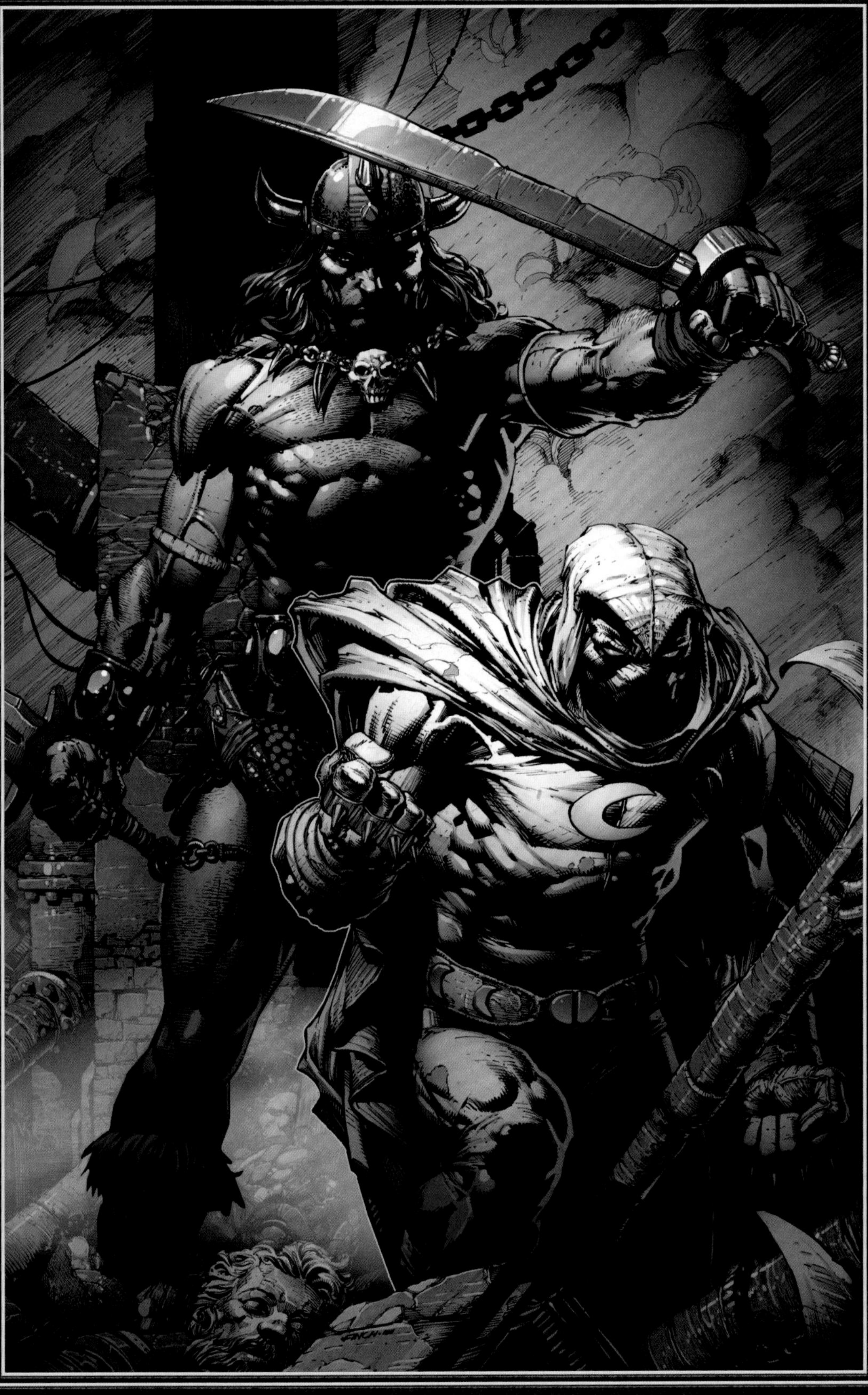

#1 VARIANT BY DAVID FINCH & FRANK D'ARMATA

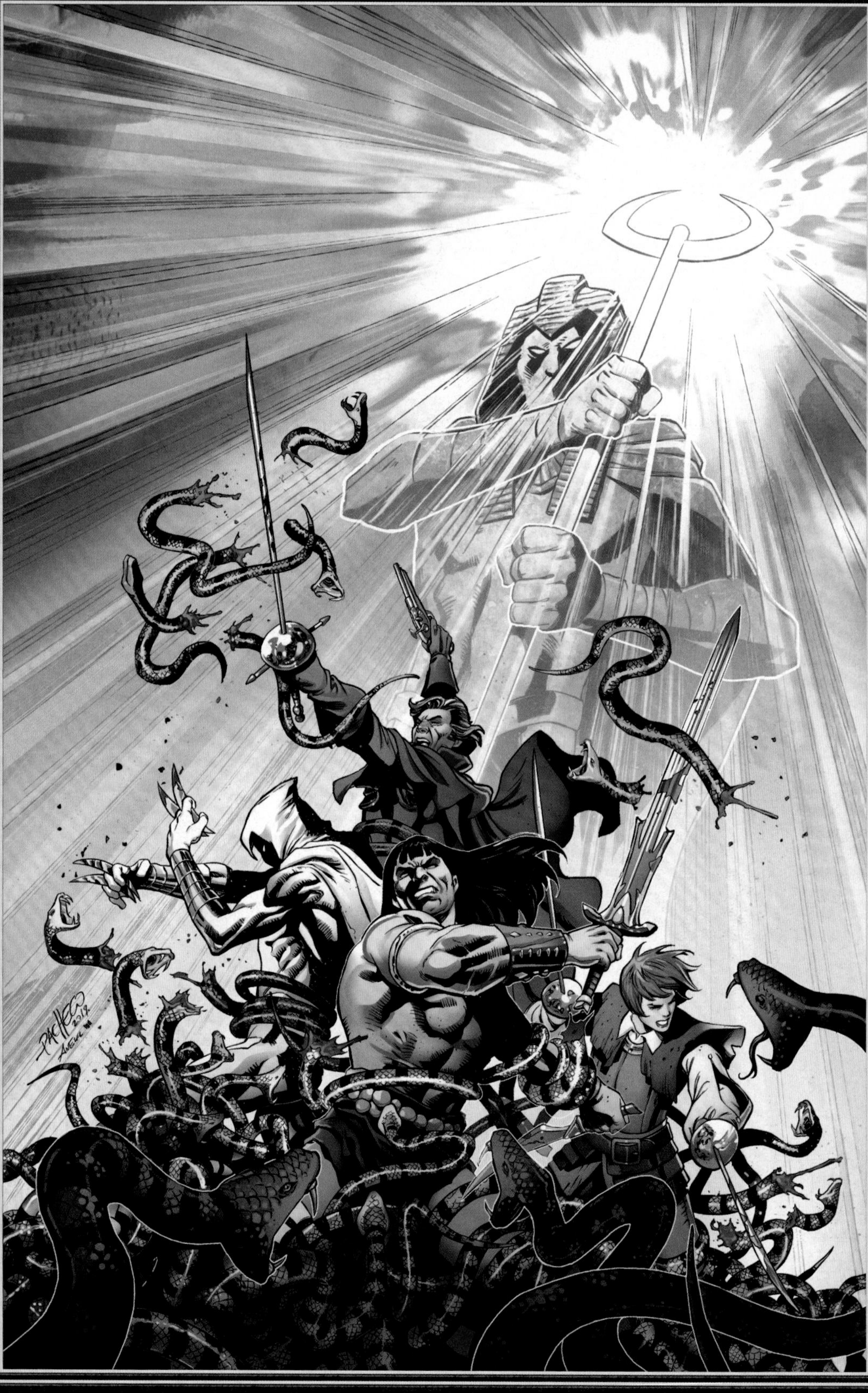

CHAPTER IV: KINGDON OF THE WYRM

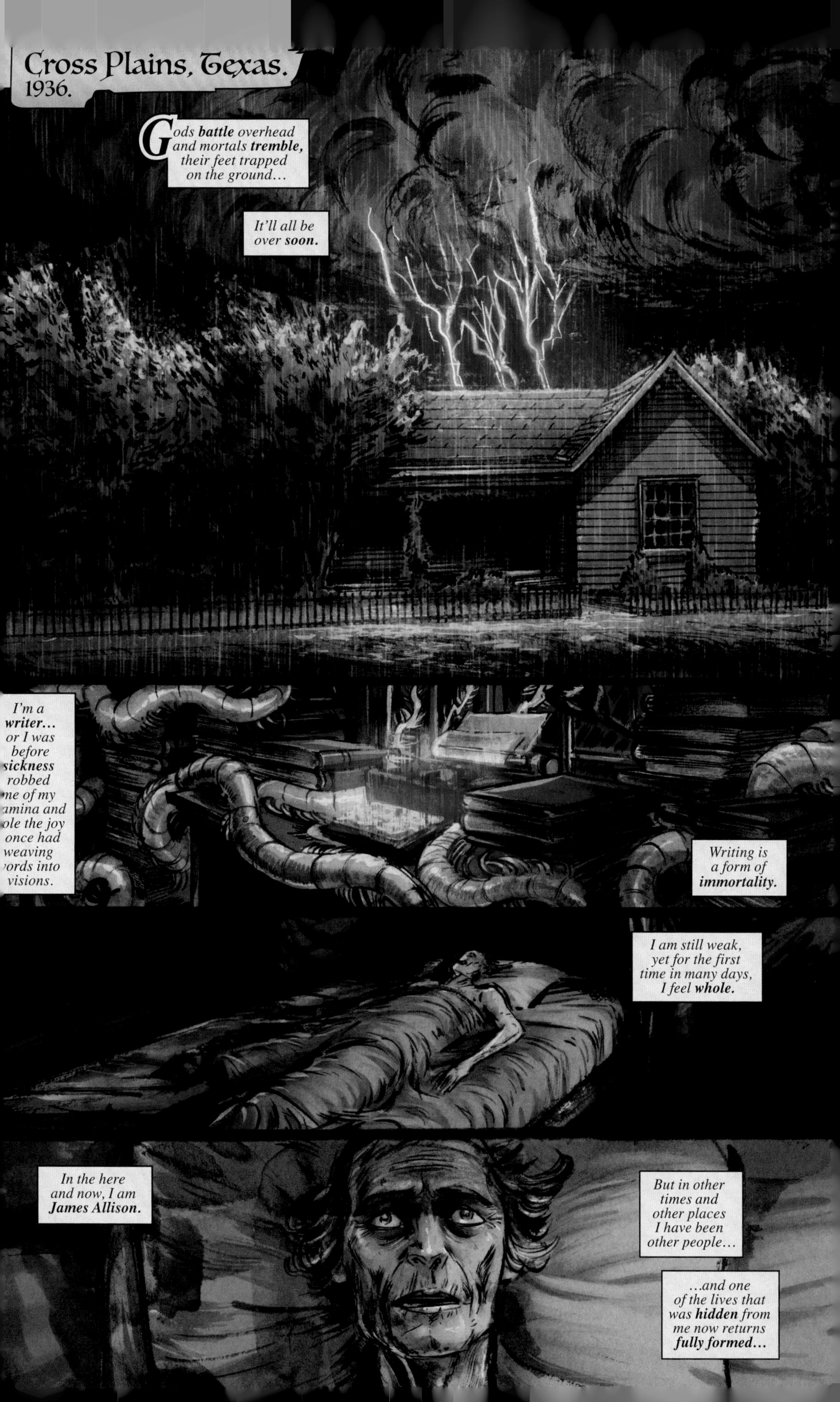
Cross Plains, Texas.
1936.
Gods battle overhead and mortals tremble, their feet trapped on the ground…
It'll all be over soon.
I'm a writer… or I was before sickness robbed me of my stamina and stole the joy I once had weaving words into visions.
Writing is a form of immortality.
I am still weak, yet for the first time in many days, I feel whole.
In the here and now, I am James Allison.
But in other times and other places I have been other people…
…and one of the lives that was hidden from me now returns fully formed…

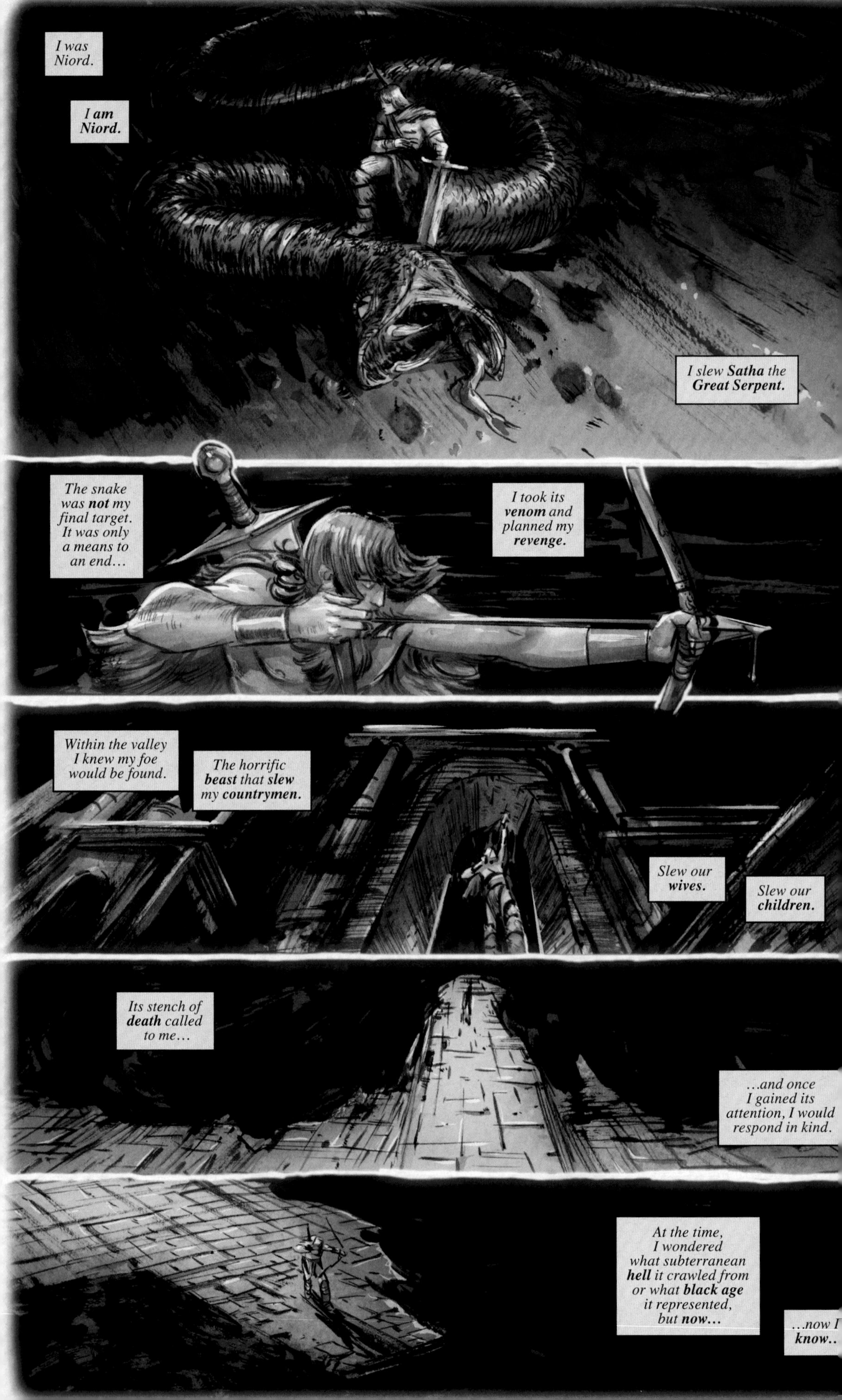
I was Niord.
I am Niord.
I slew Satha the Great Serpent.
The snake was not my final target. It was only a means to an end…
I took its venom and planned my revenge.
Within the valley I knew my foe would be found.
The horrific beast that slew my countrymen.
Slew our wives.
Slew our children.
Its stench of death called to me…
…and once I gained its attention, I would respond in kind.
At the time, I wondered what subterranean hell it crawled from or what black age it represented, but now…
…now I know..

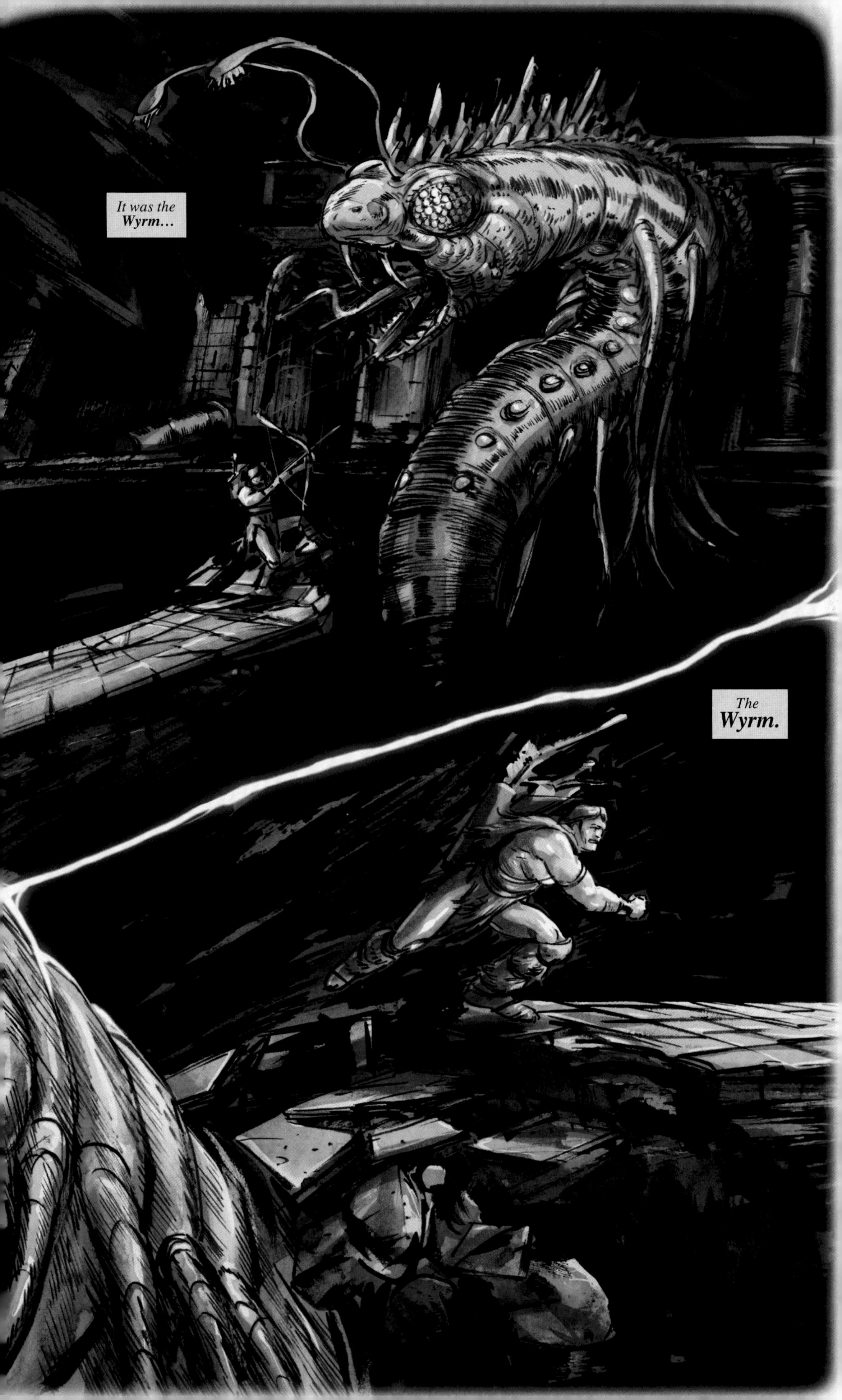

It was the *Wyrm...*
The *Wyrm.*

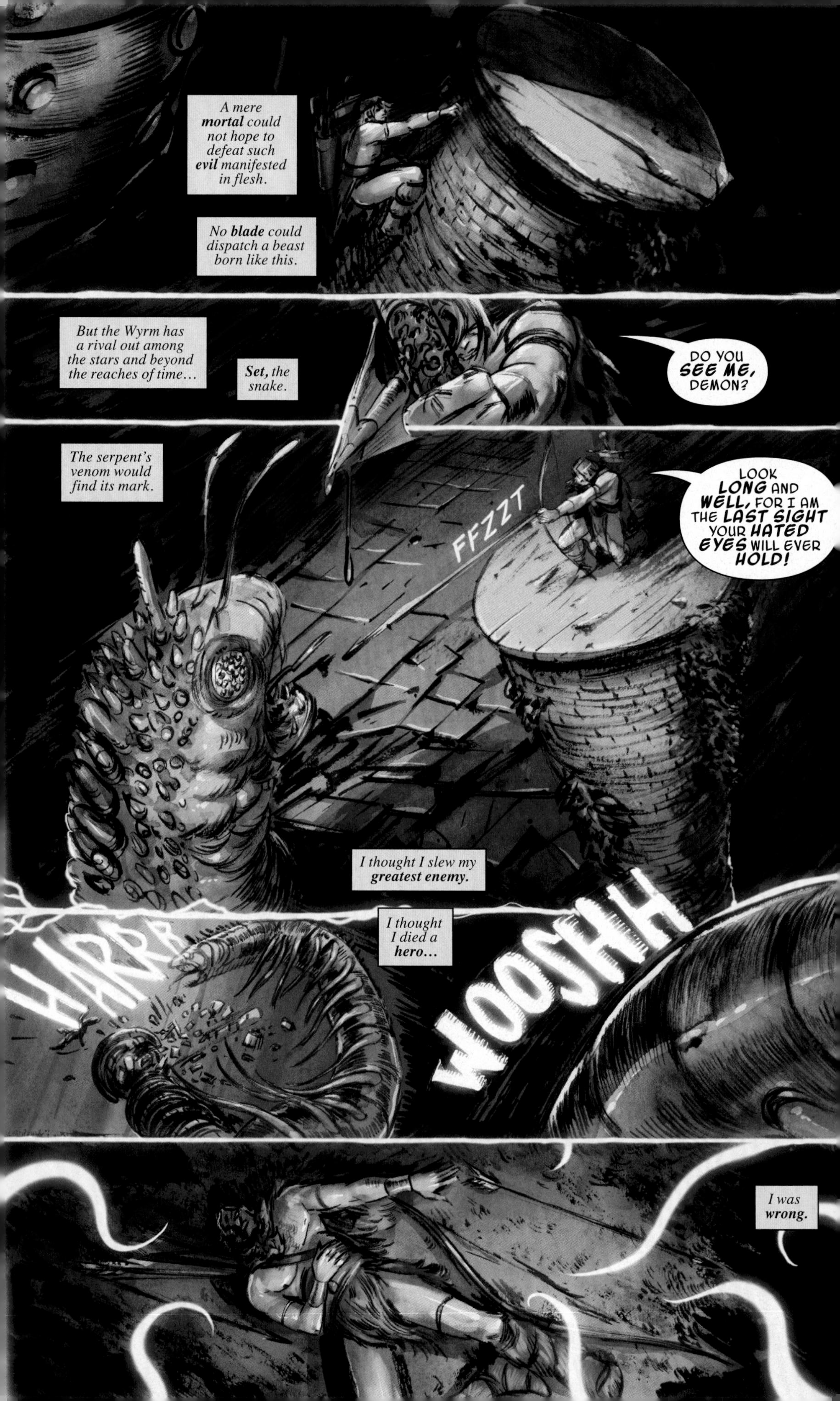

A mere **mortal** could not hope to defeat such **evil** manifested in flesh.
No **blade** could dispatch a beast born like this.
But the Wyrm has a rival out among the stars and beyond the reaches of time...
Set, the snake.
DO YOU **SEE ME,** DEMON?
The serpent's venom would find its mark.
LOOK **LONG** AND **WELL,** FOR I AM THE **LAST SIGHT** YOUR **HATED EYES** WILL EVER **HOLD!**
FFZZT
I thought I slew my **greatest enemy.**
I thought I died a **hero...**
WOOSHH
I was **wrong.**

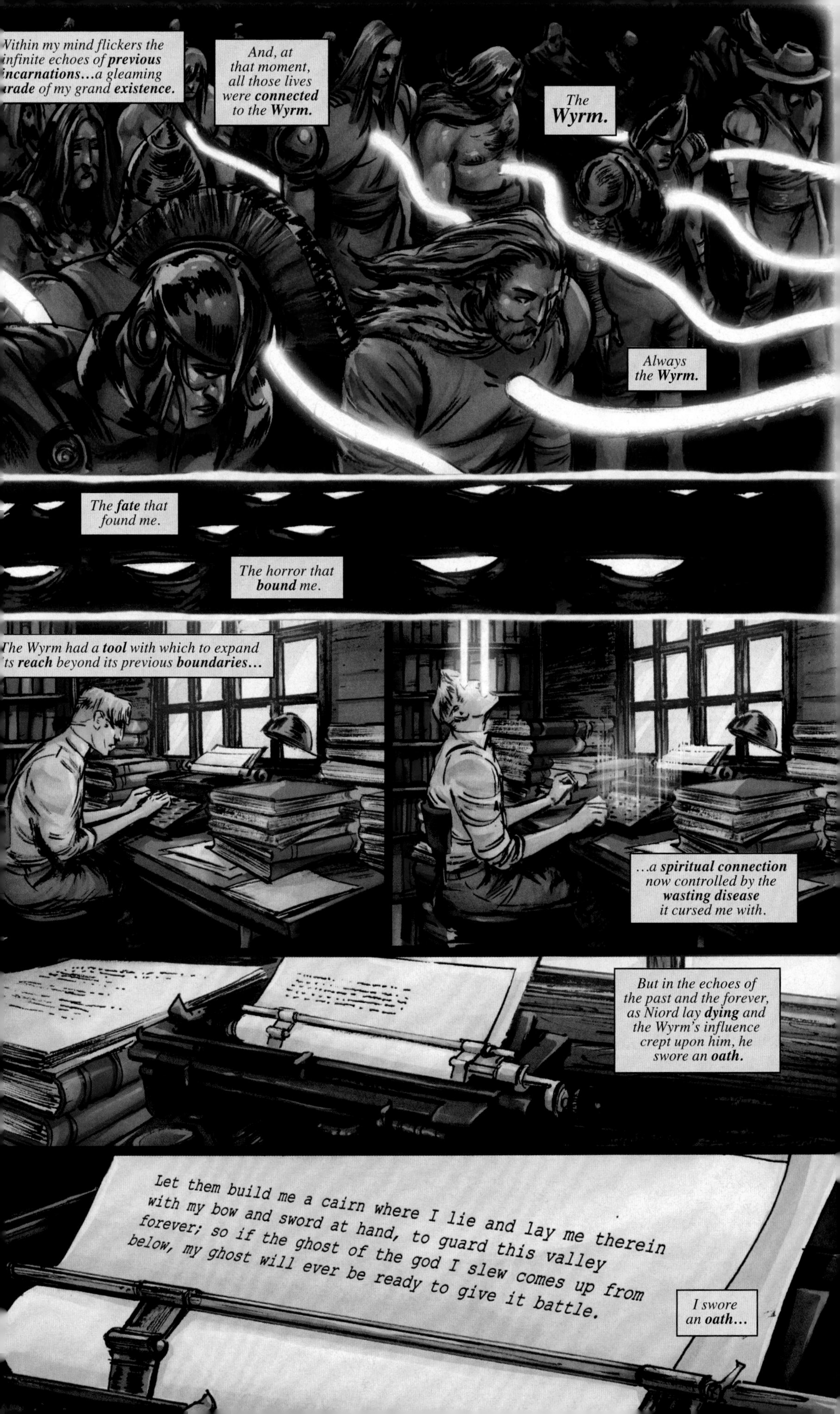
Within my mind flickers the infinite echoes of previous incarnations...a gleaming parade of my grand existence.
And, at that moment, all those lives were connected to the Wyrm.
The Wyrm.
Always the Wyrm.
The fate that found me.
The horror that bound me.
The Wyrm had a tool with which to expand its reach beyond its previous boundaries...
...a spiritual connection now controlled by the wasting disease it cursed me with.
But in the echoes of the past and the forever, as Niord lay dying and the Wyrm's influence crept upon him, he swore an oath.
Let them build me a cairn where I lie and lay me therein with my bow and sword at hand, to guard this valley forever; so if the ghost of the god I slew comes up from below, my ghost will ever be ready to give it battle.
I swore an oath...

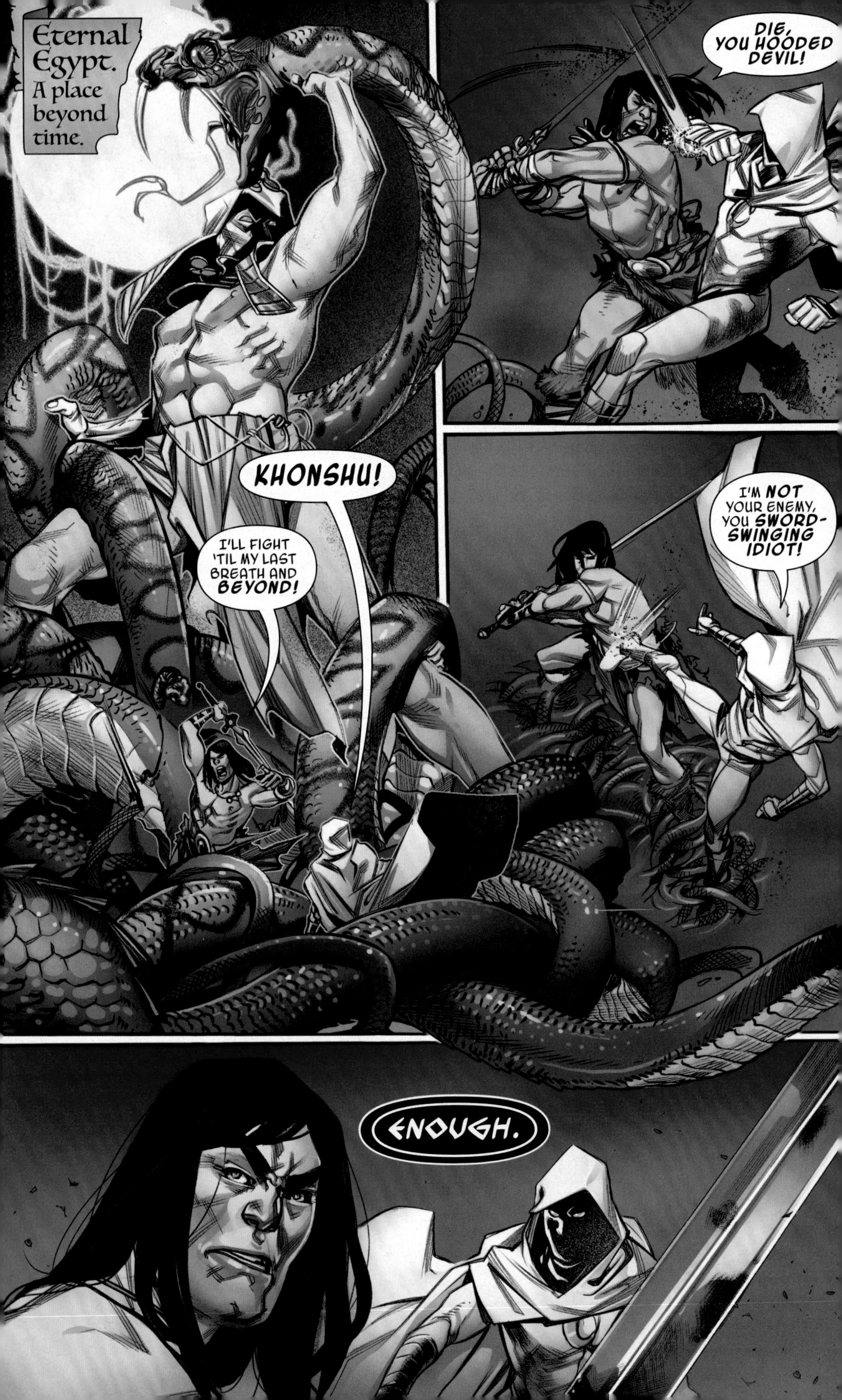

Eternal Egypt. A place beyond time.
DIE, YOU HOODED DEVIL!
KHONSHU!
I'LL FIGHT 'TIL MY LAST BREATH AND BEYOND!
I'M NOT YOUR ENEMY, YOU SWORD-SWINGING IDIOT!
ENOUGH.

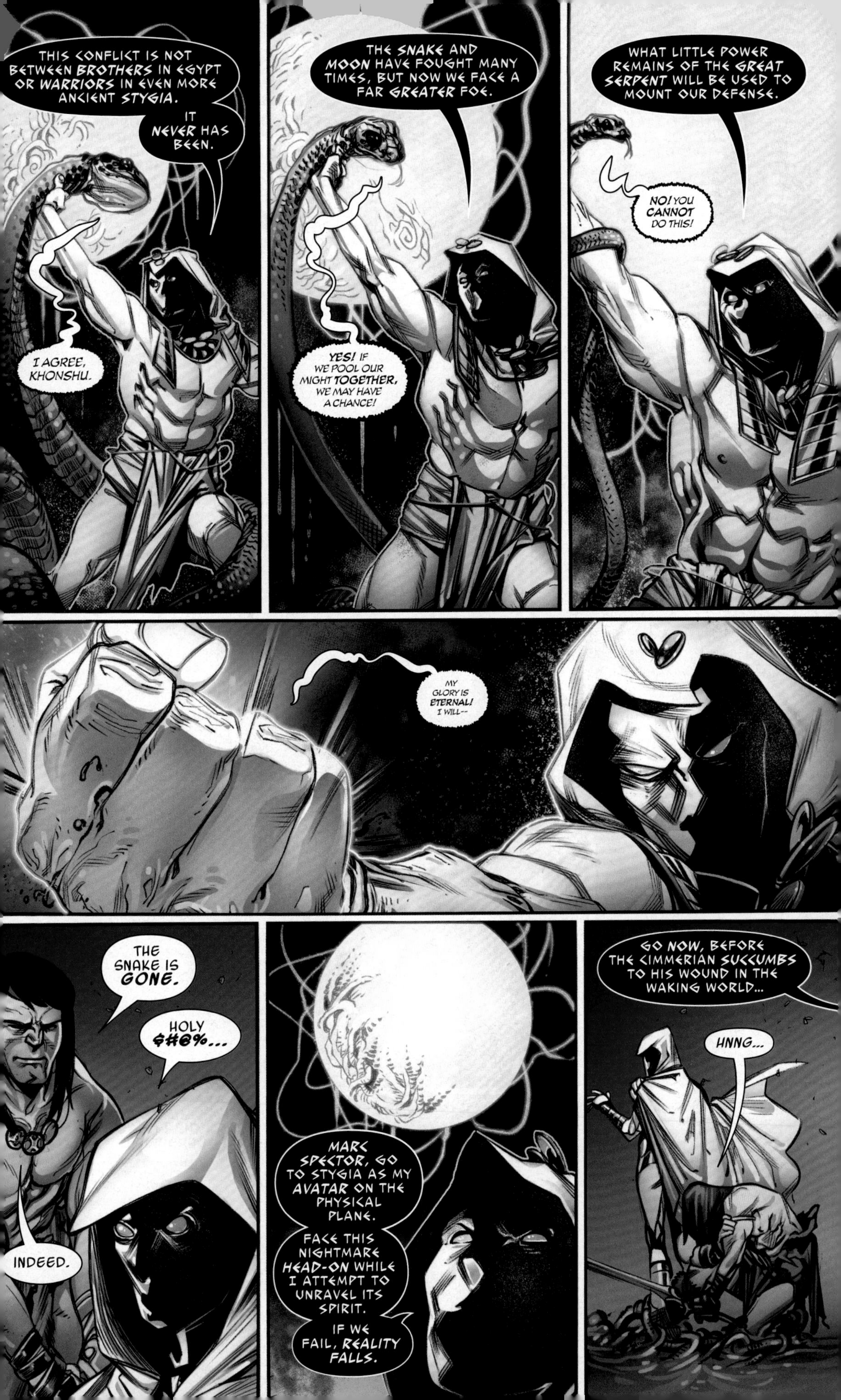
THIS CONFLICT IS NOT BETWEEN BROTHERS IN EGYPT OR WARRIORS IN EVEN MORE ANCIENT STYGIA.
IT NEVER HAS BEEN.
I AGREE, KHONSHU.
THE SNAKE AND MOON HAVE FOUGHT MANY TIMES, BUT NOW WE FACE A FAR GREATER FOE.
YES! IF WE POOL OUR MIGHT TOGETHER, WE MAY HAVE A CHANCE!
WHAT LITTLE POWER REMAINS OF THE GREAT SERPENT WILL BE USED TO MOUNT OUR DEFENSE.
NO! YOU CANNOT DO THIS!
MY GLORY IS ETERNAL! I WILL--
THE SNAKE IS GONE.
HOLY $#@%...
INDEED.
MARC SPECTOR, GO TO STYGIA AS MY AVATAR ON THE PHYSICAL PLANE.
FACE THIS NIGHTMARE HEAD-ON WHILE I ATTEMPT TO UNRAVEL ITS SPIRIT.
IF WE FAIL, REALITY FALLS.
GO NOW, BEFORE THE CIMMERIAN SUCCUMBS TO HIS WOUND IN THE WAKING WORLD...
HNNG...

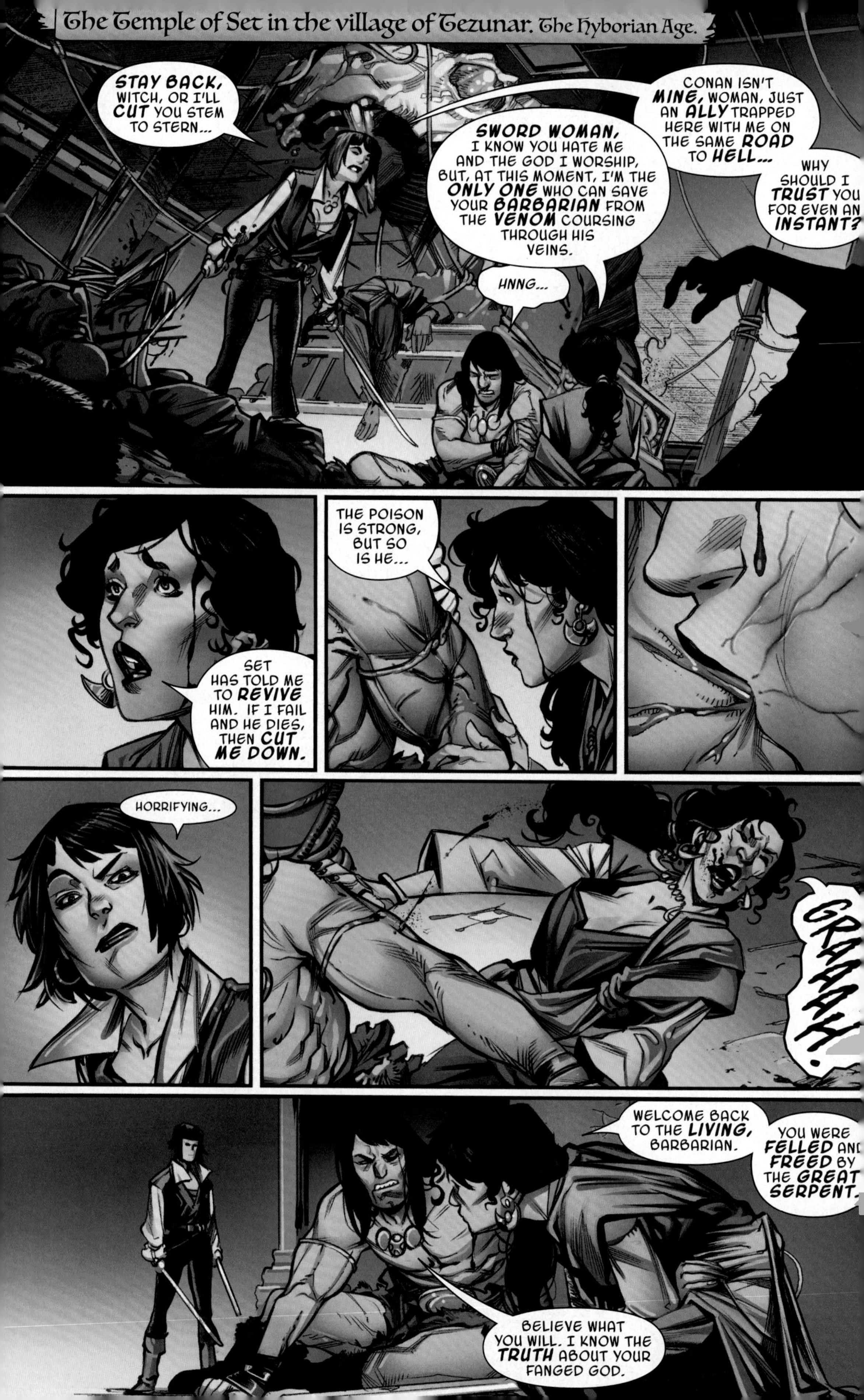
The Temple of Set in the village of Tezunar. The Hyborian Age.
STAY BACK, WITCH, OR I'LL CUT YOU STEM TO STERN...
SWORD WOMAN, I KNOW YOU HATE ME AND THE GOD I WORSHIP, BUT, AT THIS MOMENT, I'M THE ONLY ONE WHO CAN SAVE YOUR BARBARIAN FROM THE VENOM COURSING THROUGH HIS VEINS.
CONAN ISN'T MINE, WOMAN, JUST AN ALLY TRAPPED HERE WITH ME ON THE SAME ROAD TO HELL...
WHY SHOULD I TRUST YOU FOR EVEN AN INSTANT?
HNNG...
SET HAS TOLD ME TO REVIVE HIM. IF I FAIL AND HE DIES, THEN CUT ME DOWN.
THE POISON IS STRONG, BUT SO IS HE...
HORRIFYING...
GRAAAAH!
WELCOME BACK TO THE LIVING, BARBARIAN.
YOU WERE FELLED AND FREED BY THE GREAT SERPENT.
BELIEVE WHAT YOU WILL. I KNOW THE TRUTH ABOUT YOUR FANGED GOD.

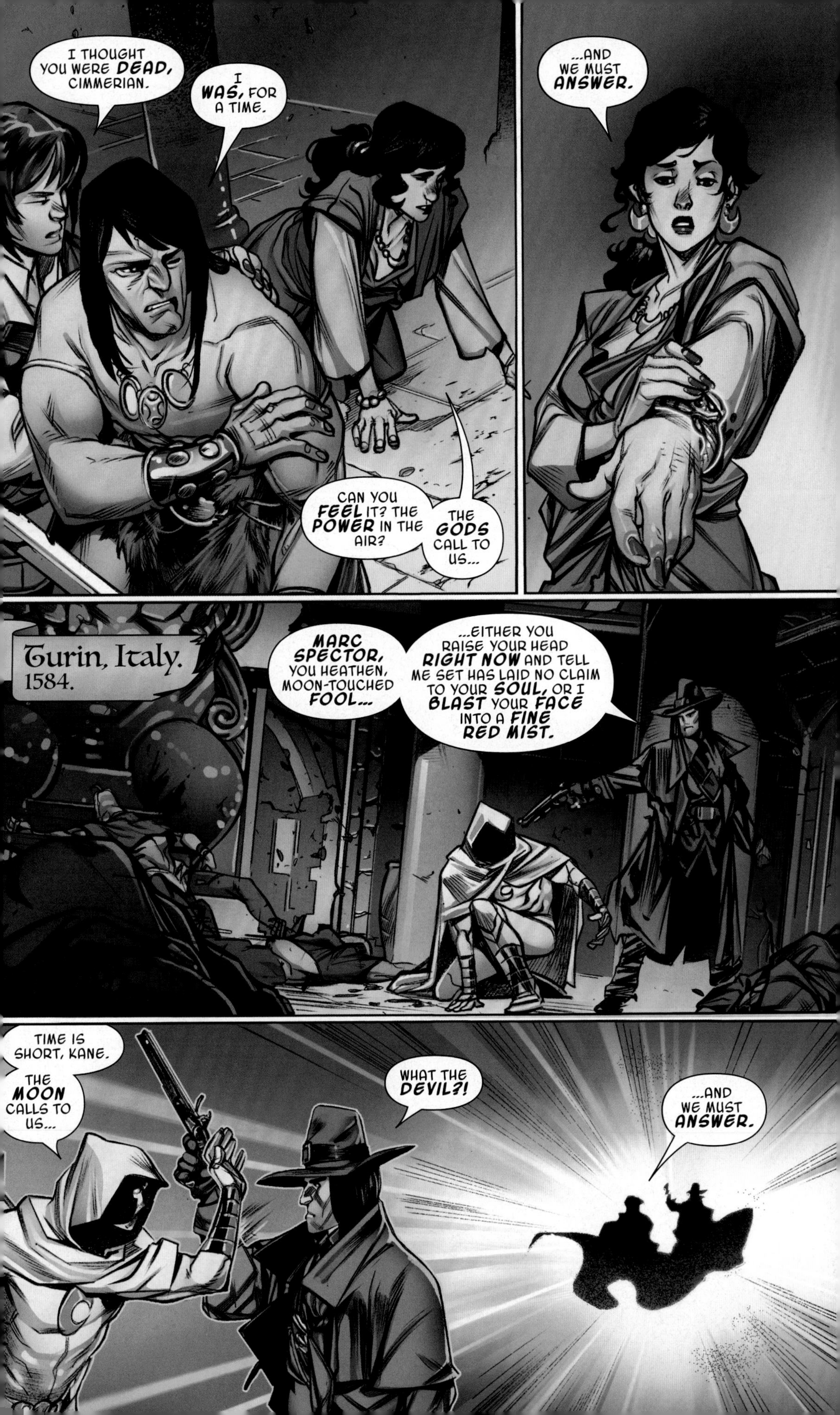
I THOUGHT YOU WERE DEAD, CIMMERIAN.
I WAS, FOR A TIME.
CAN YOU FEEL IT? THE POWER IN THE AIR?
THE GODS CALL TO US...
...AND WE MUST ANSWER.
Turin, Italy. 1584.
MARC SPECTOR, YOU HEATHEN, MOON-TOUCHED FOOL...
...EITHER YOU RAISE YOUR HEAD RIGHT NOW AND TELL ME SET HAS LAID NO CLAIM TO YOUR SOUL, OR I BLAST YOUR FACE INTO A FINE RED MIST.
TIME IS SHORT, KANE.
THE MOON CALLS TO US...
WHAT THE DEVIL?!
...AND WE MUST ANSWER.

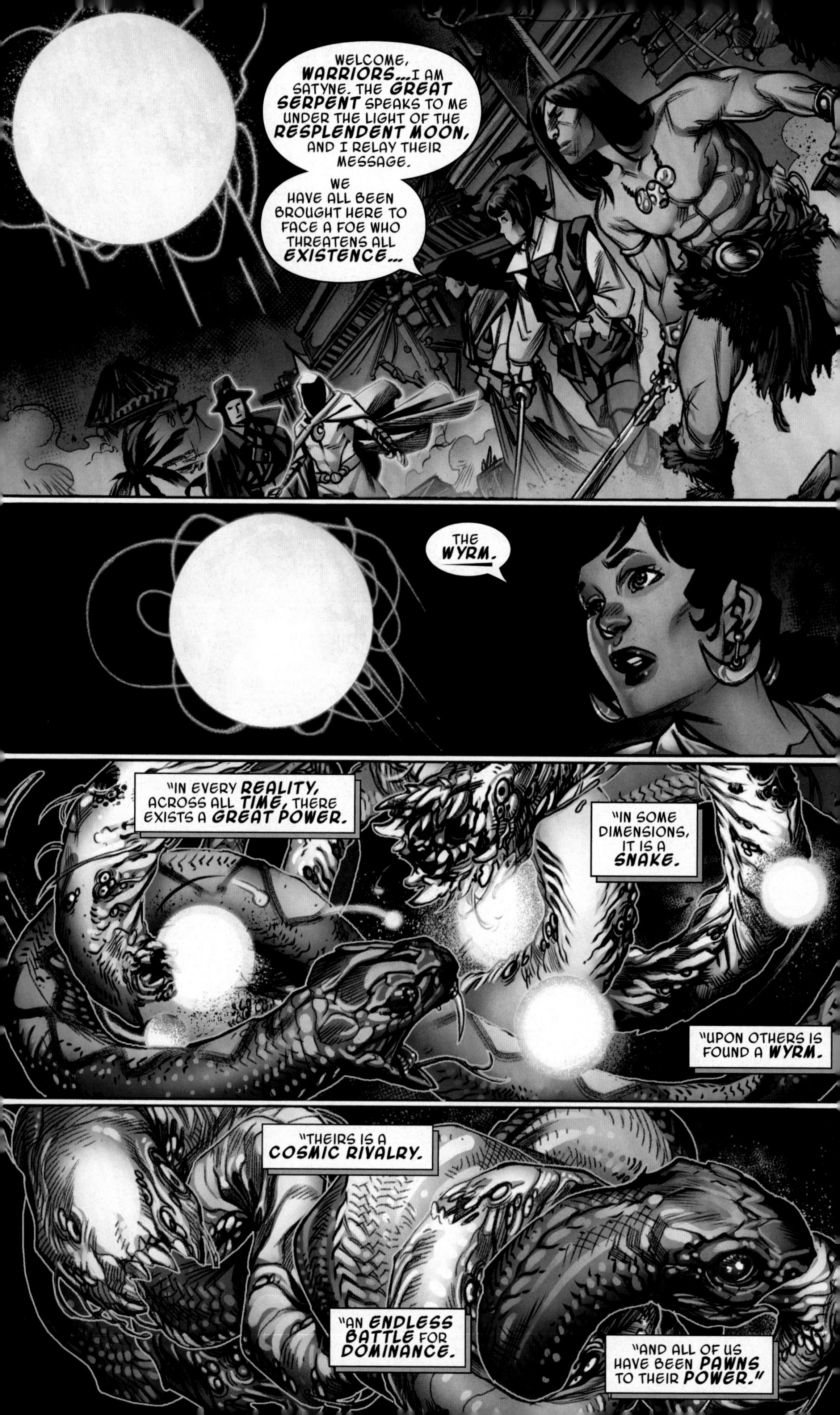

WELCOME, WARRIORS...I AM SATYNE. THE GREAT SERPENT SPEAKS TO ME UNDER THE LIGHT OF THE RESPLENDENT MOON, AND I RELAY THEIR MESSAGE.
WE HAVE ALL BEEN BROUGHT HERE TO FACE A FOE WHO THREATENS ALL EXISTENCE...
THE WYRM.
"IN EVERY REALITY, ACROSS ALL TIME, THERE EXISTS A GREAT POWER.
"IN SOME DIMENSIONS, IT IS A SNAKE.
"UPON OTHERS IS FOUND A WYRM.
"THEIRS IS A COSMIC RIVALRY.
"AN ENDLESS BATTLE FOR DOMINANCE.
"AND ALL OF US HAVE BEEN PAWNS TO THEIR POWER."

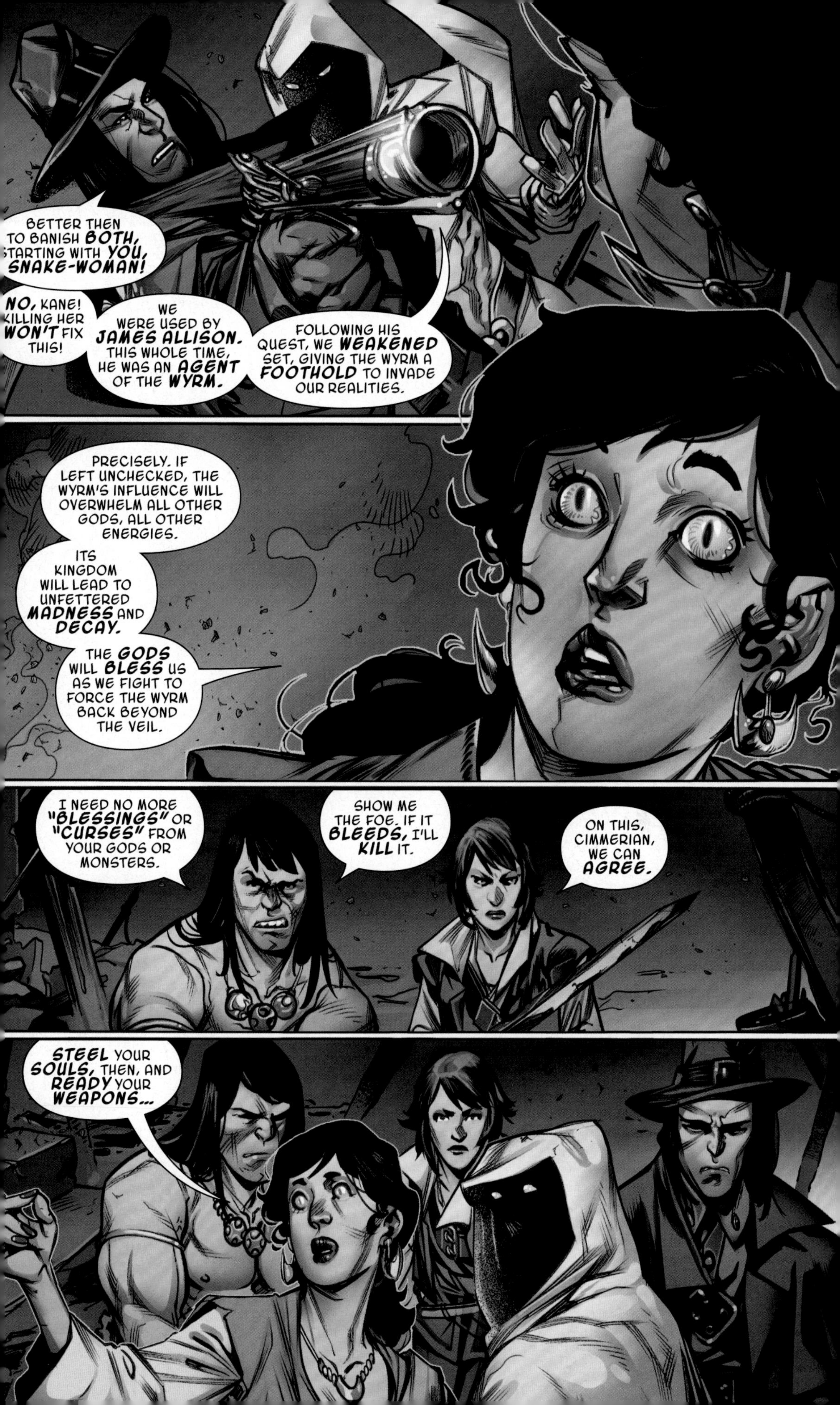

BETTER THEN TO BANISH BOTH, STARTING WITH YOU, SNAKE-WOMAN!
NO, KANE! KILLING HER WON'T FIX THIS!
WE WERE USED BY JAMES ALLISON. THIS WHOLE TIME, HE WAS AN AGENT OF THE WYRM.
FOLLOWING HIS QUEST, WE WEAKENED SET, GIVING THE WYRM A FOOTHOLD TO INVADE OUR REALITIES.
PRECISELY. IF LEFT UNCHECKED, THE WYRM'S INFLUENCE WILL OVERWHELM ALL OTHER GODS, ALL OTHER ENERGIES.
ITS KINGDOM WILL LEAD TO UNFETTERED MADNESS AND DECAY.
THE GODS WILL BLESS US AS WE FIGHT TO FORCE THE WYRM BACK BEYOND THE VEIL.
I NEED NO MORE "BLESSINGS" OR "CURSES" FROM YOUR GODS OR MONSTERS.
SHOW ME THE FOE. IF IT BLEEDS, I'LL KILL IT.
ON THIS, CIMMERIAN, WE CAN AGREE.
STEEL YOUR SOULS, THEN, AND READY YOUR WEAPONS...

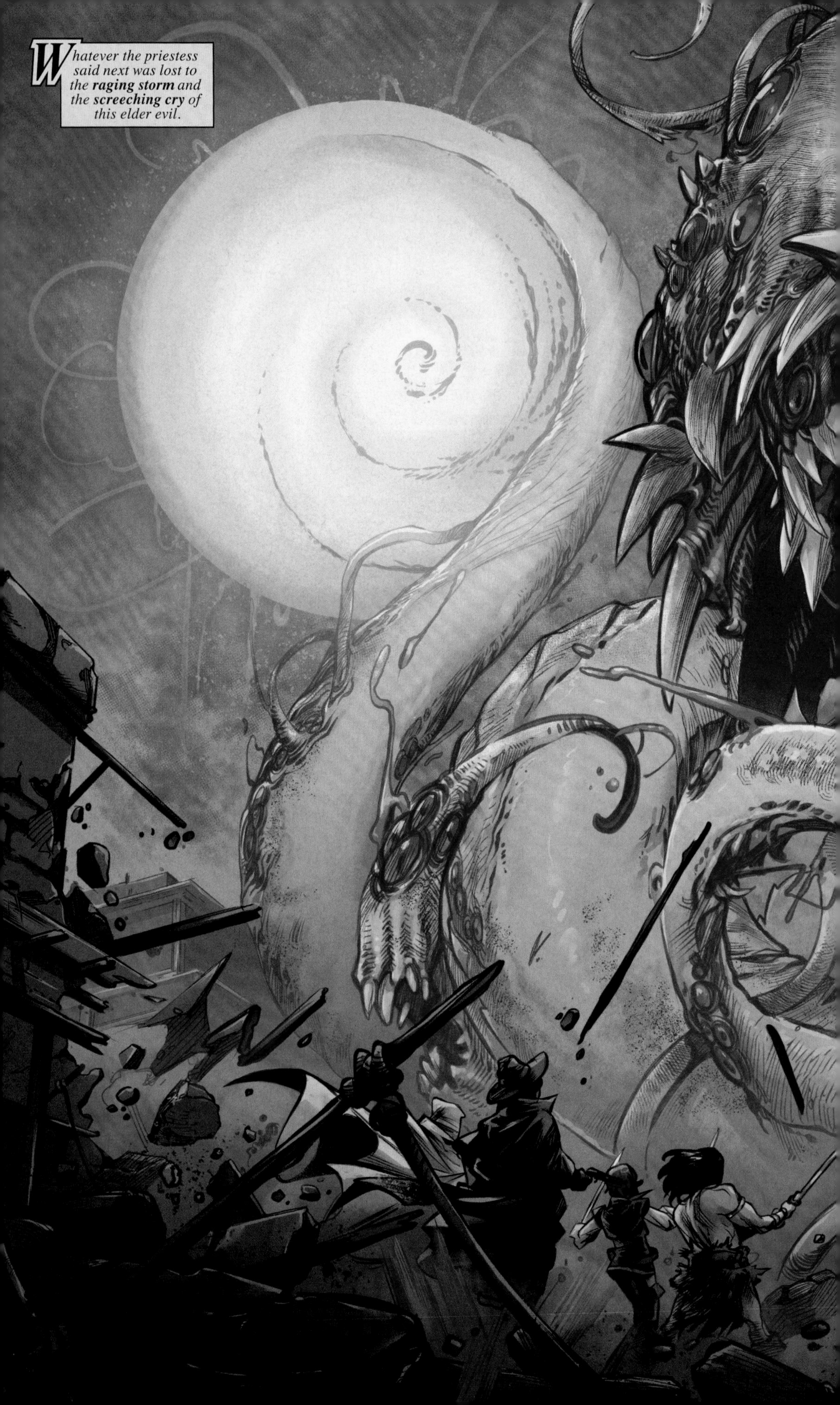
Whatever the priestess said next was lost to the raging storm and the screeching cry of this elder evil.

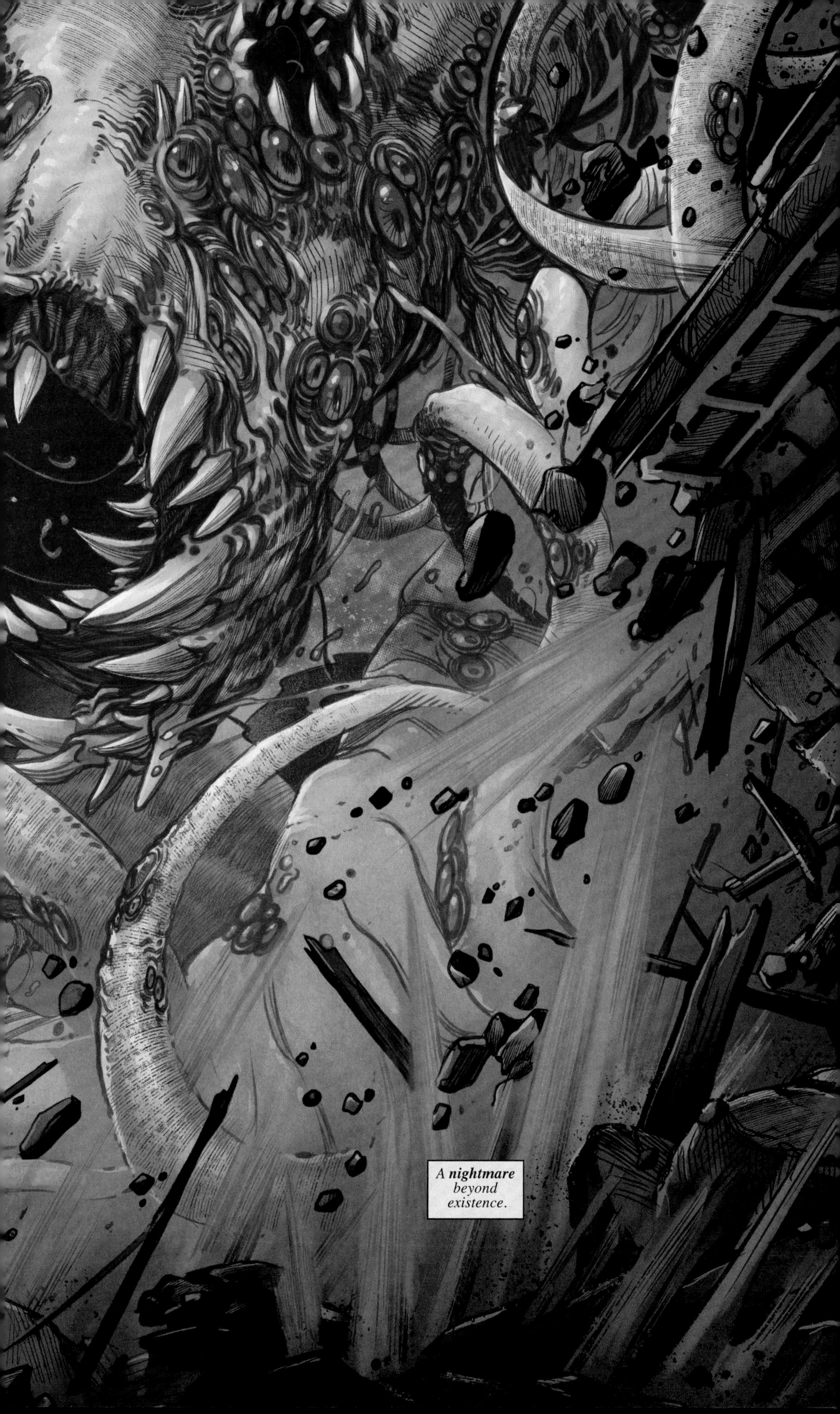
A **nightmare** beyond existence.

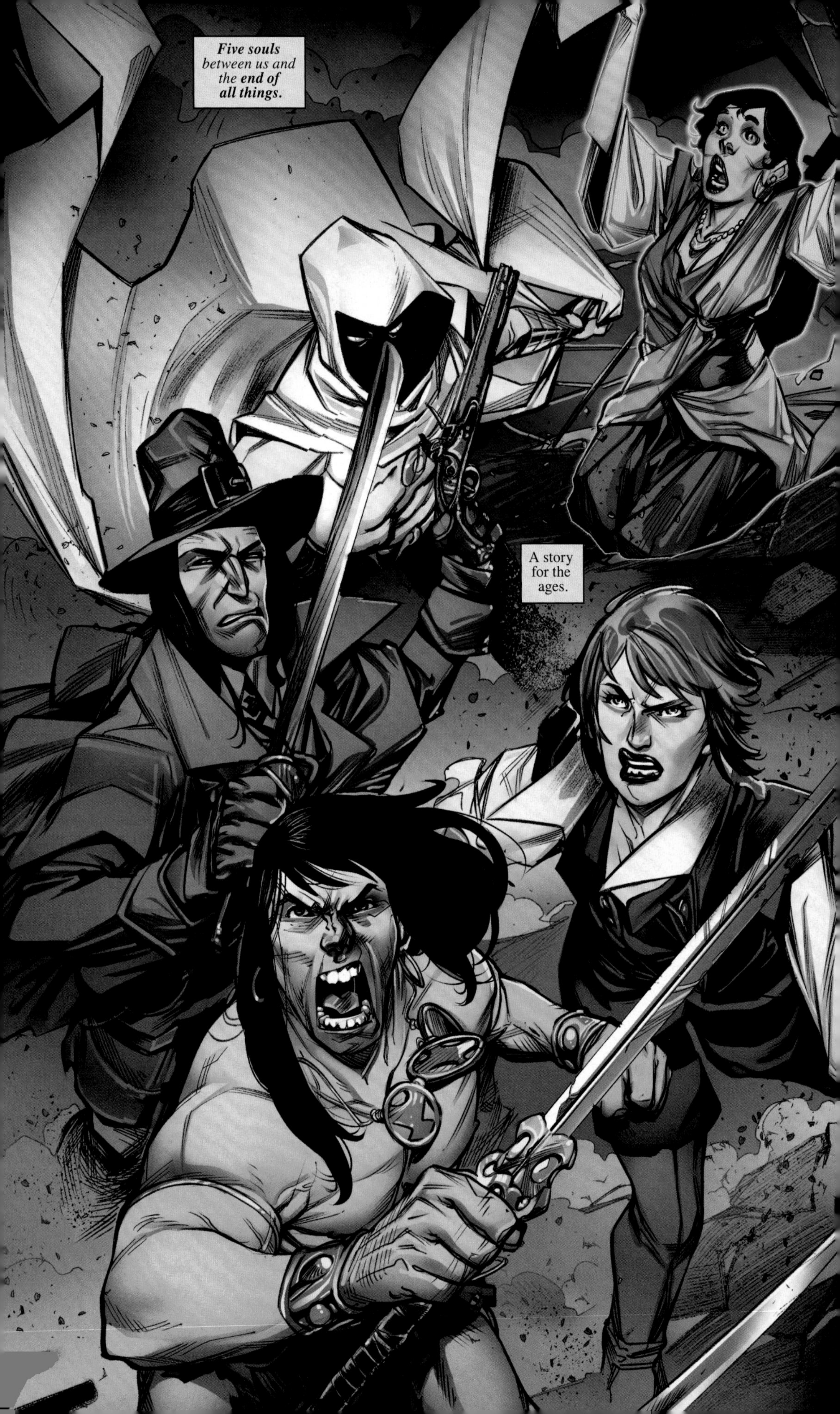

Five souls between us and the **end of all things.**
A story for the ages.

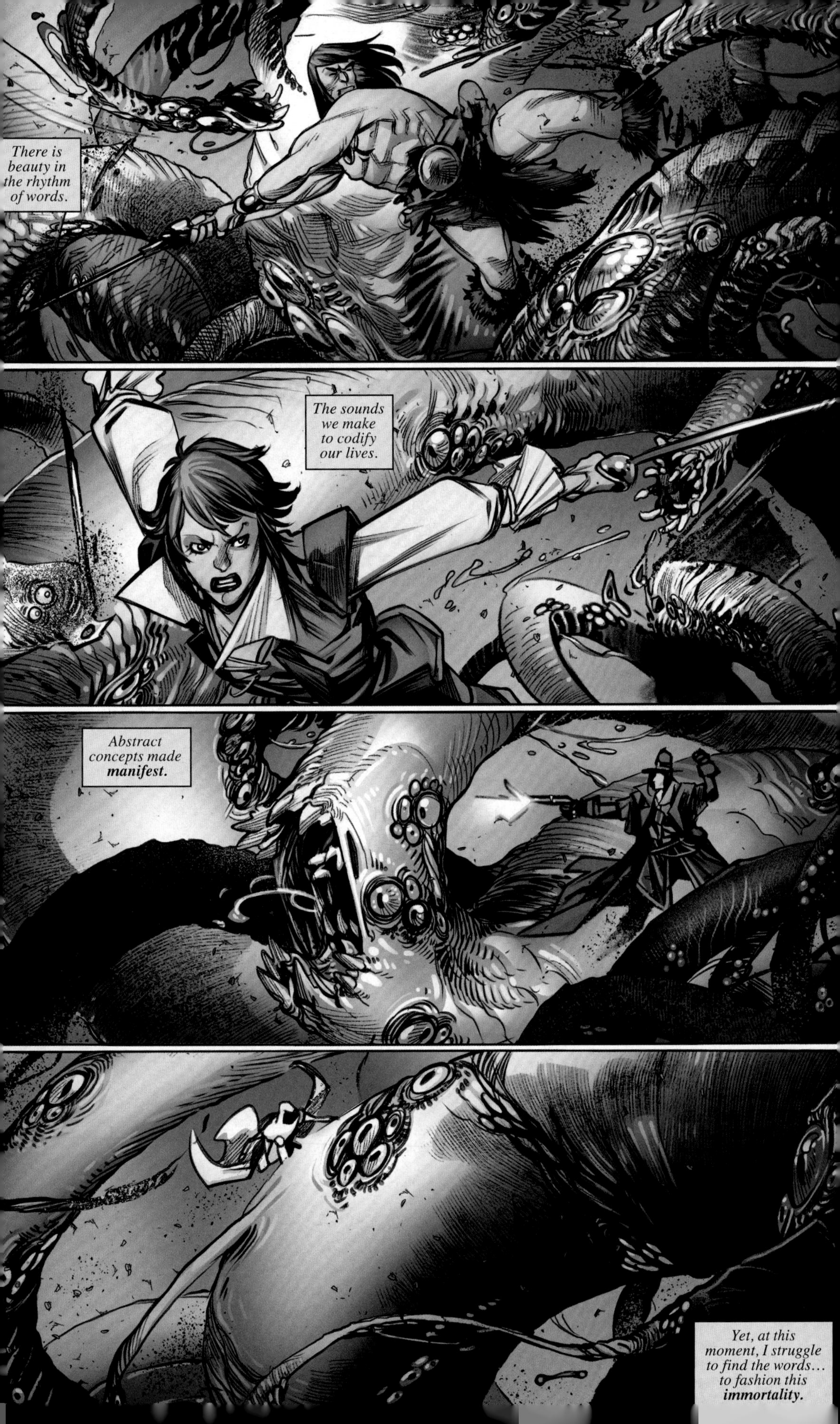
There is beauty in the rhythm of words.
The sounds we make to codify our lives.
Abstract concepts made **manifest.**
Yet, at this moment, I struggle to find the words… to fashion this **immortality.**

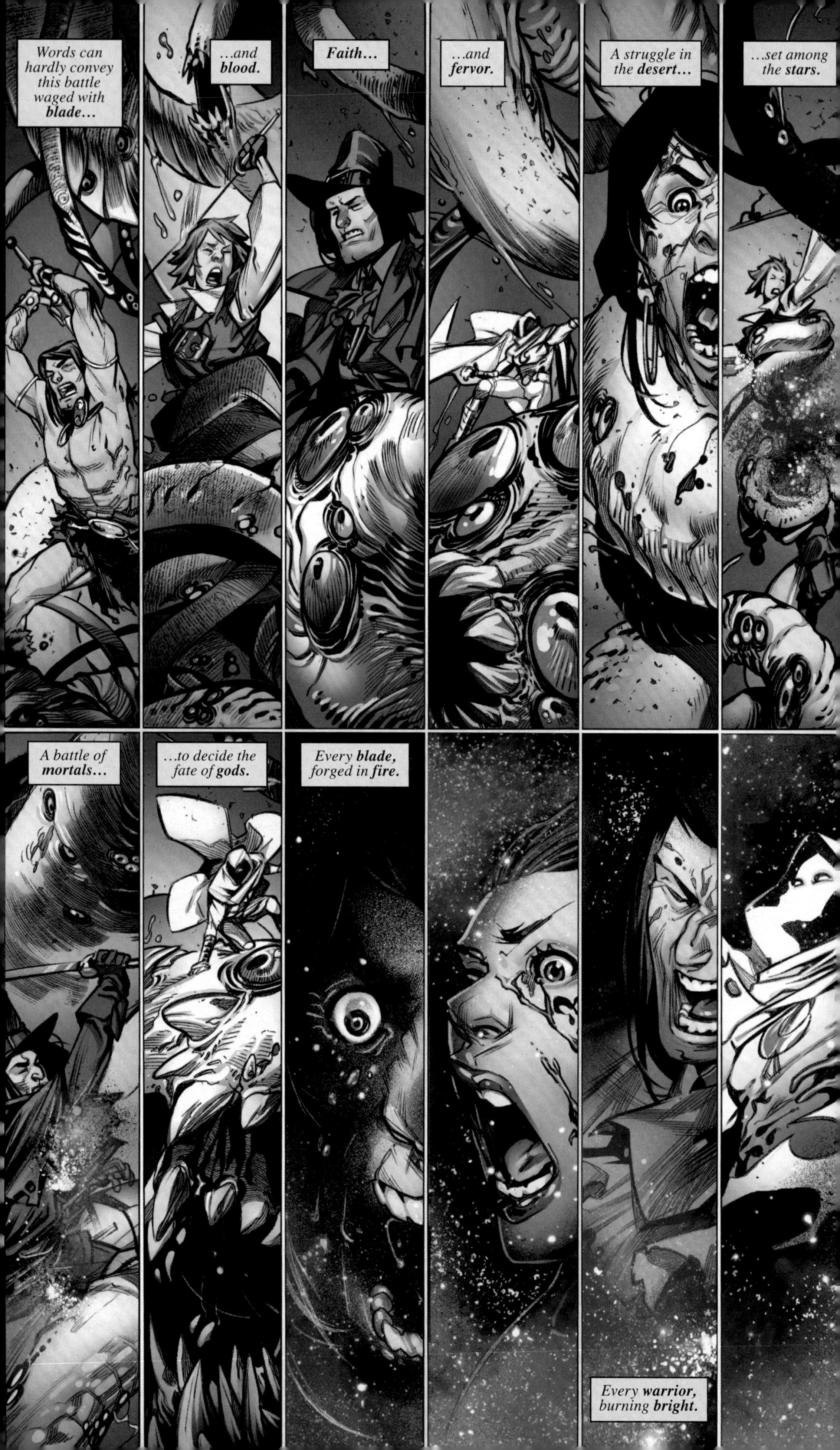
Words can hardly convey this battle waged with **blade...**
...and **blood.**
Faith...
...and **fervor.**
A struggle in the **desert...**
...set among the **stars.**
A battle of **mortals...**
...to decide the fate of **gods.**
Every **blade,** forged in **fire.**
Every **warrior,** burning **bright.**

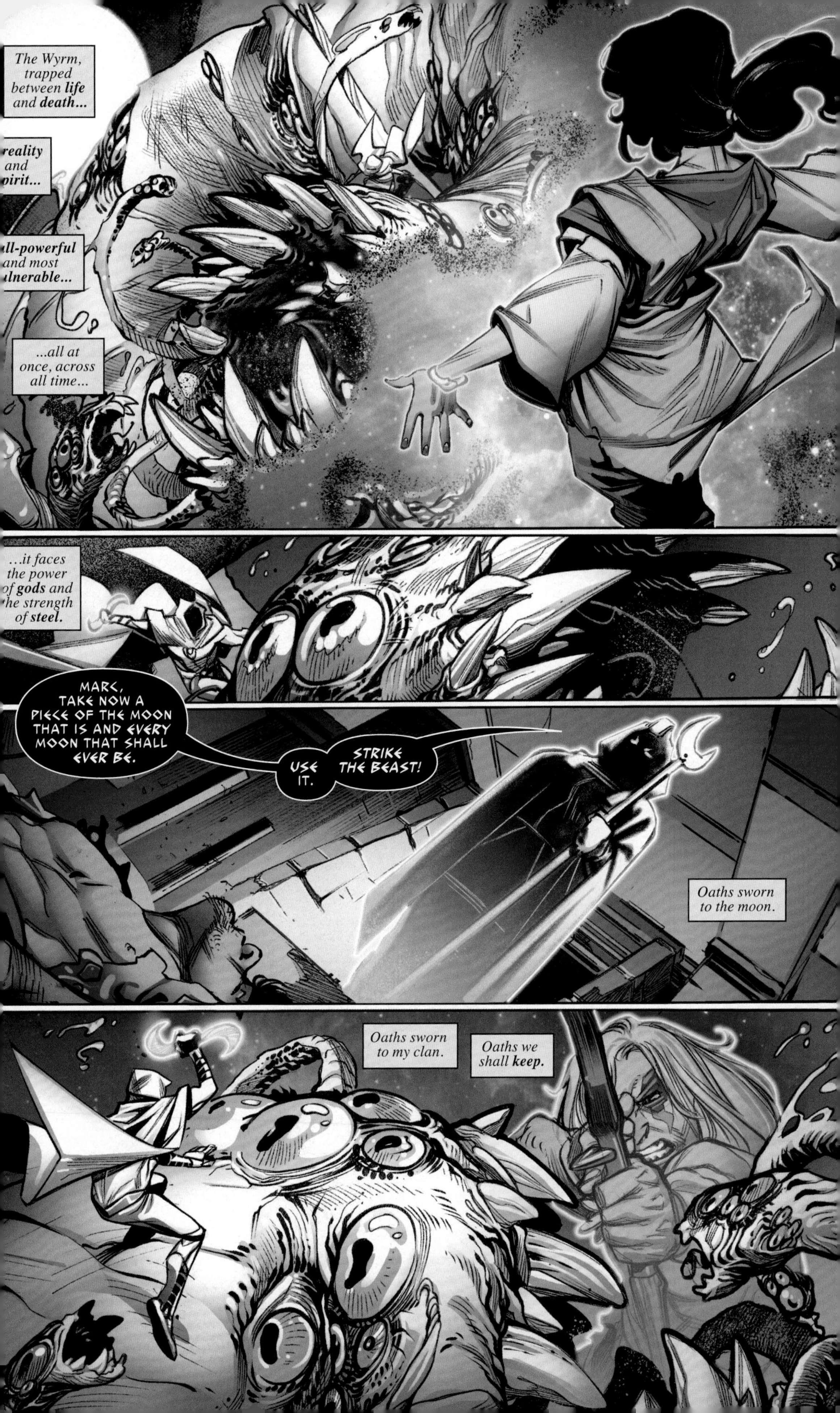
The Wyrm, trapped between **life** and **death...**
reality and pirit...
ll-powerful and most lnerable...
...all at once, across all time...
...it faces the power of **gods** and he strength of **steel.**
MARC, TAKE NOW A PIECE OF THE MOON THAT IS AND EVERY MOON THAT SHALL EVER BE.
USE IT.
STRIKE THE BEAST!
Oaths sworn to the moon.
Oaths sworn to my clan.
Oaths we shall **keep.**

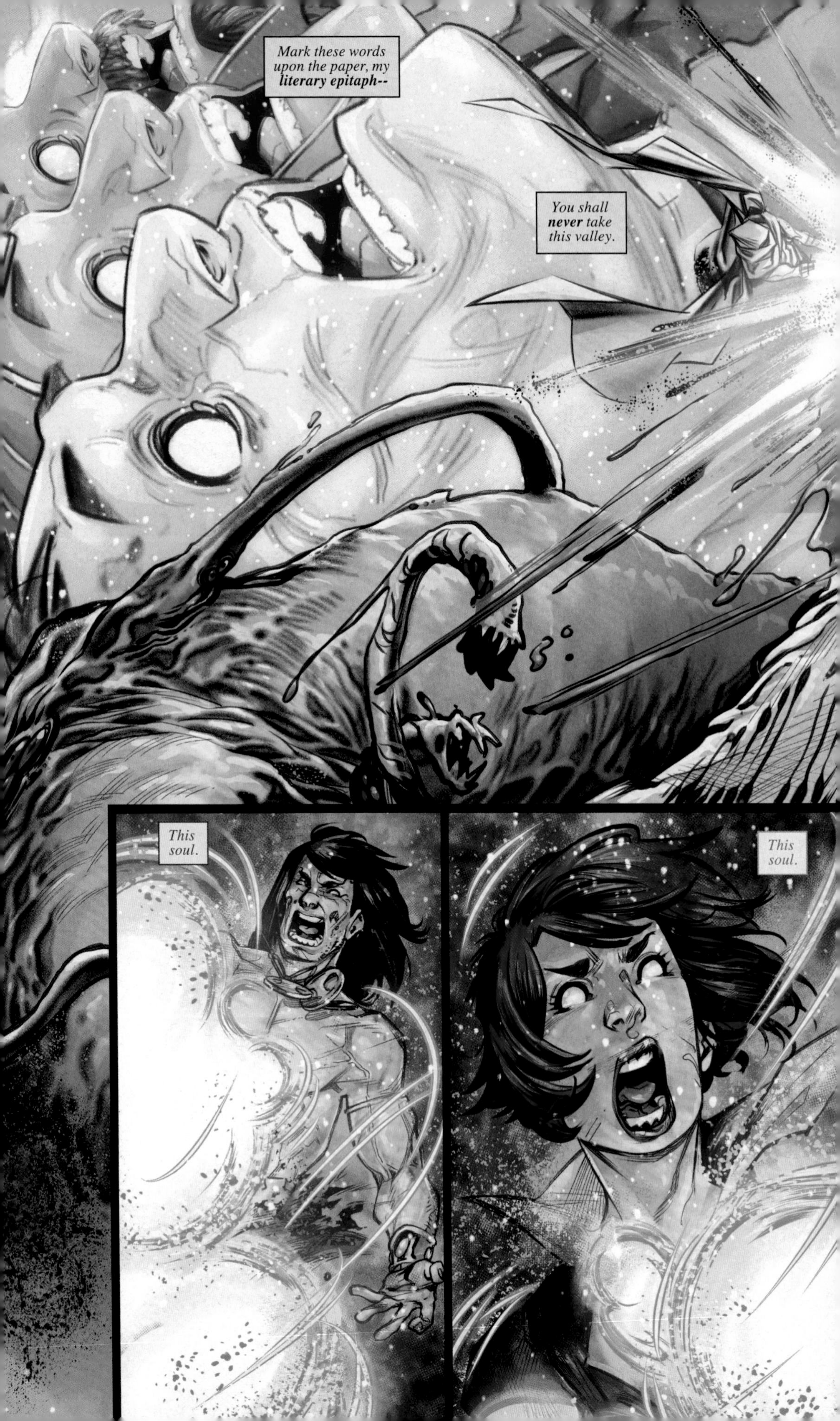
Mark these words upon the paper, my **literary epitaph--**
You shall **never** take this valley.
This soul.
This soul.

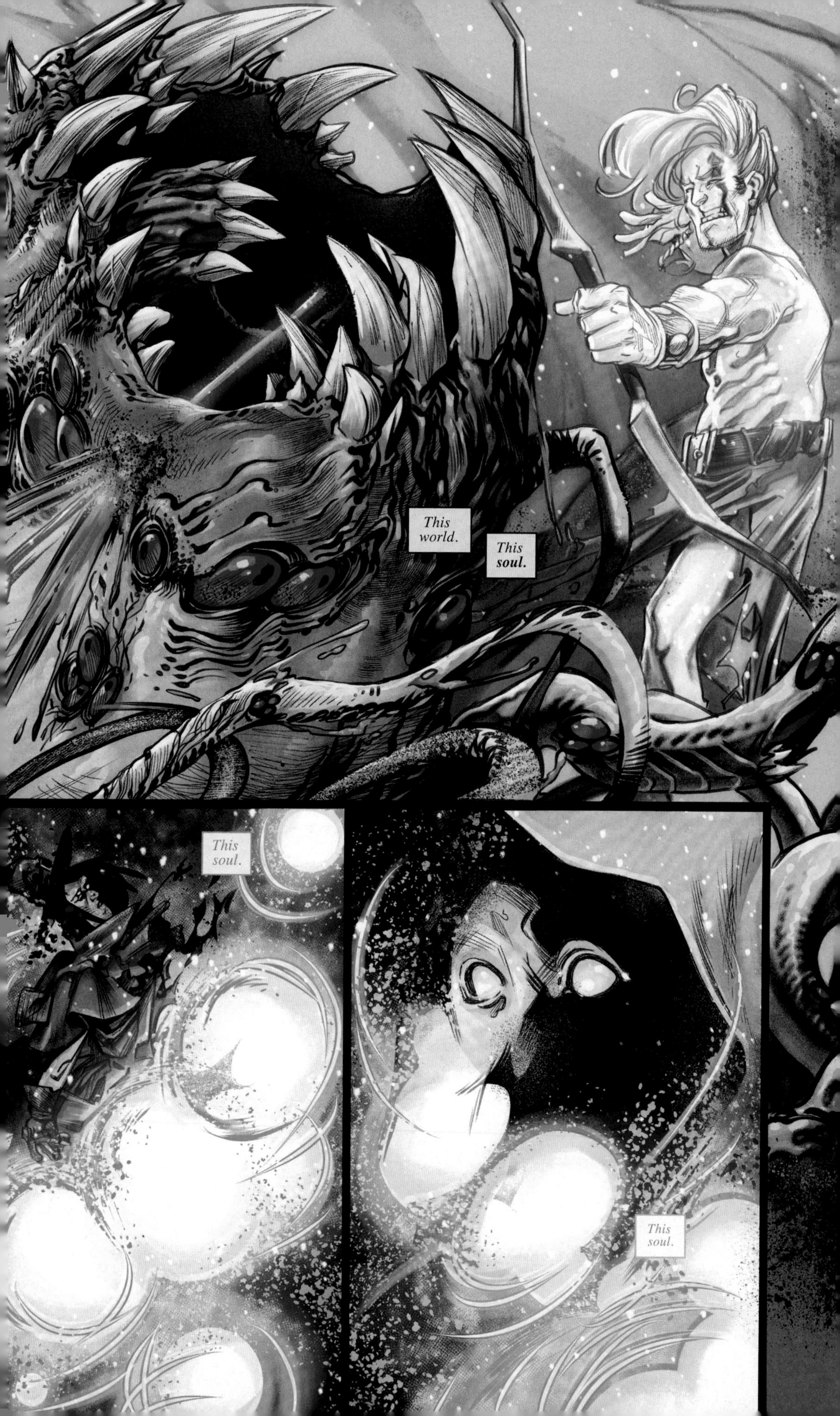
This world.
This **soul.**
This soul.
This soul.

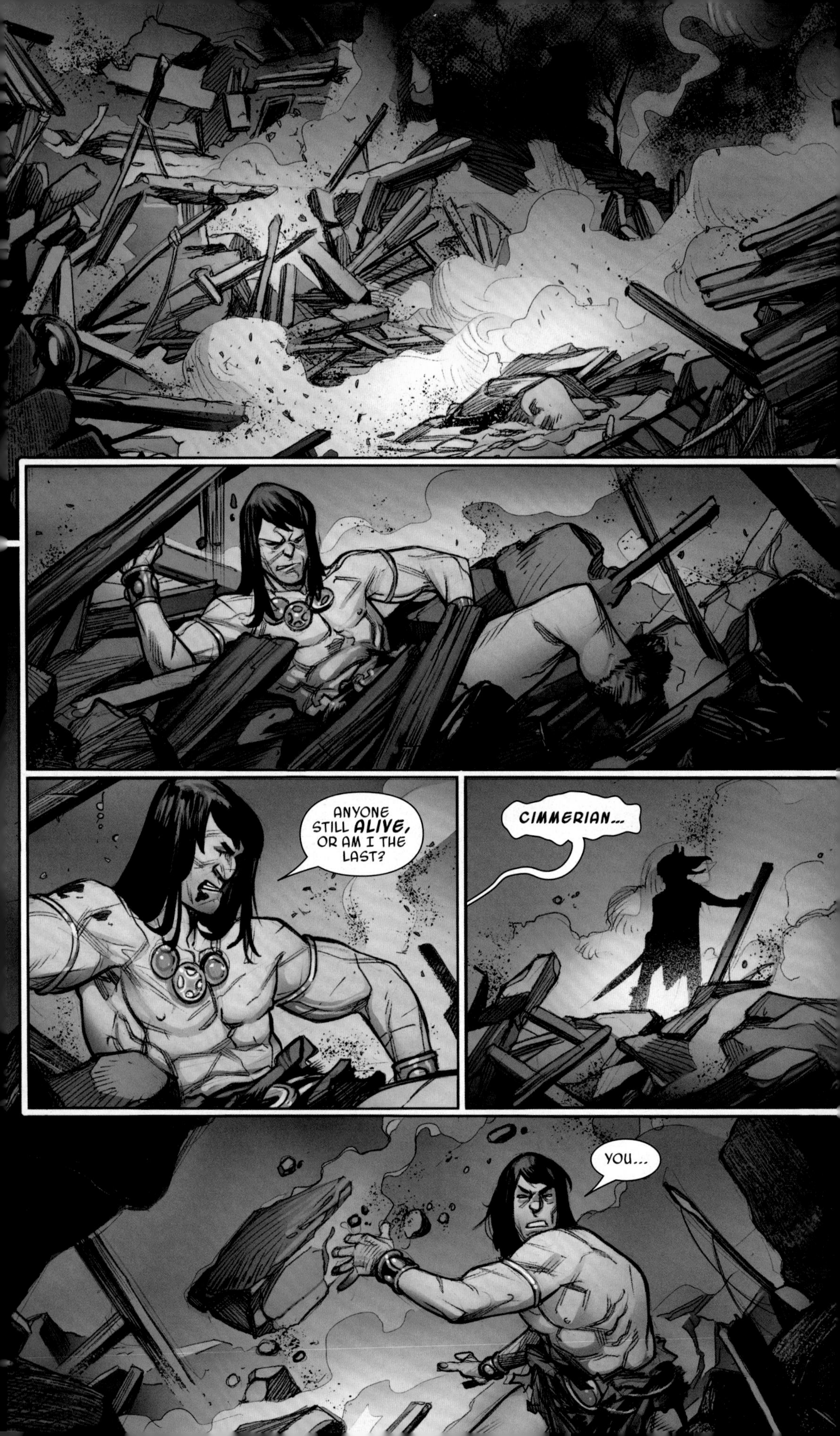
ANYONE STILL ALIVE, OR AM I THE LAST?
CIMMERIAN...
YOU...

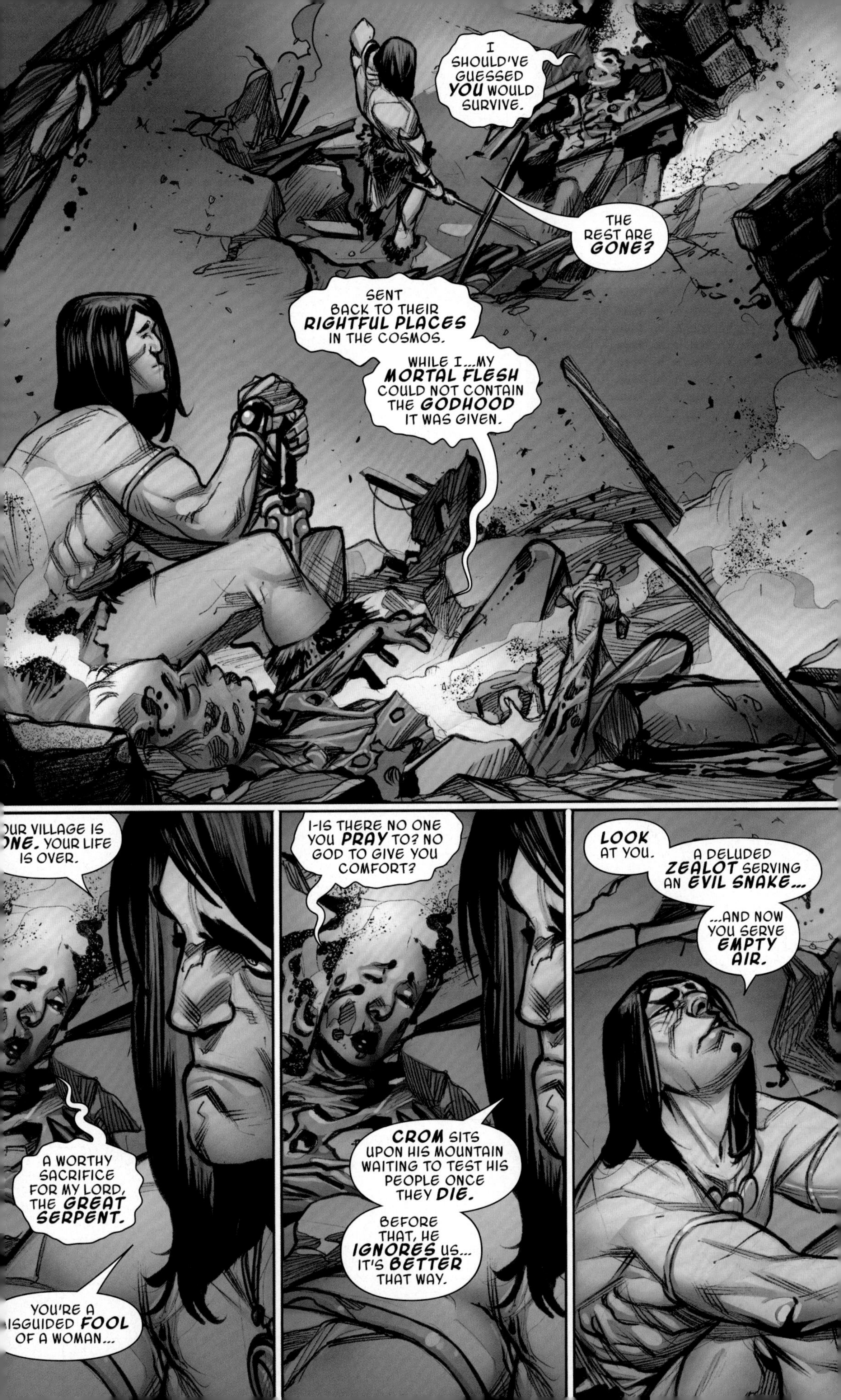

I SHOULD'VE GUESSED YOU WOULD SURVIVE.
THE REST ARE GONE?
SENT BACK TO THEIR RIGHTFUL PLACES IN THE COSMOS.
WHILE I...MY MORTAL FLESH COULD NOT CONTAIN THE GODHOOD IT WAS GIVEN.
OUR VILLAGE IS ONE. YOUR LIFE IS OVER.
A WORTHY SACRIFICE FOR MY LORD, THE GREAT SERPENT.
YOU'RE A ISGUIDED FOOL OF A WOMAN...
I-IS THERE NO ONE YOU PRAY TO? NO GOD TO GIVE YOU COMFORT?
CROM SITS UPON HIS MOUNTAIN WAITING TO TEST HIS PEOPLE ONCE THEY DIE.
BEFORE THAT, HE IGNORES US... IT'S BETTER THAT WAY.
LOOK AT YOU.
A DELUDED ZEALOT SERVING AN EVIL SNAKE...
...AND NOW YOU SERVE EMPTY AIR.

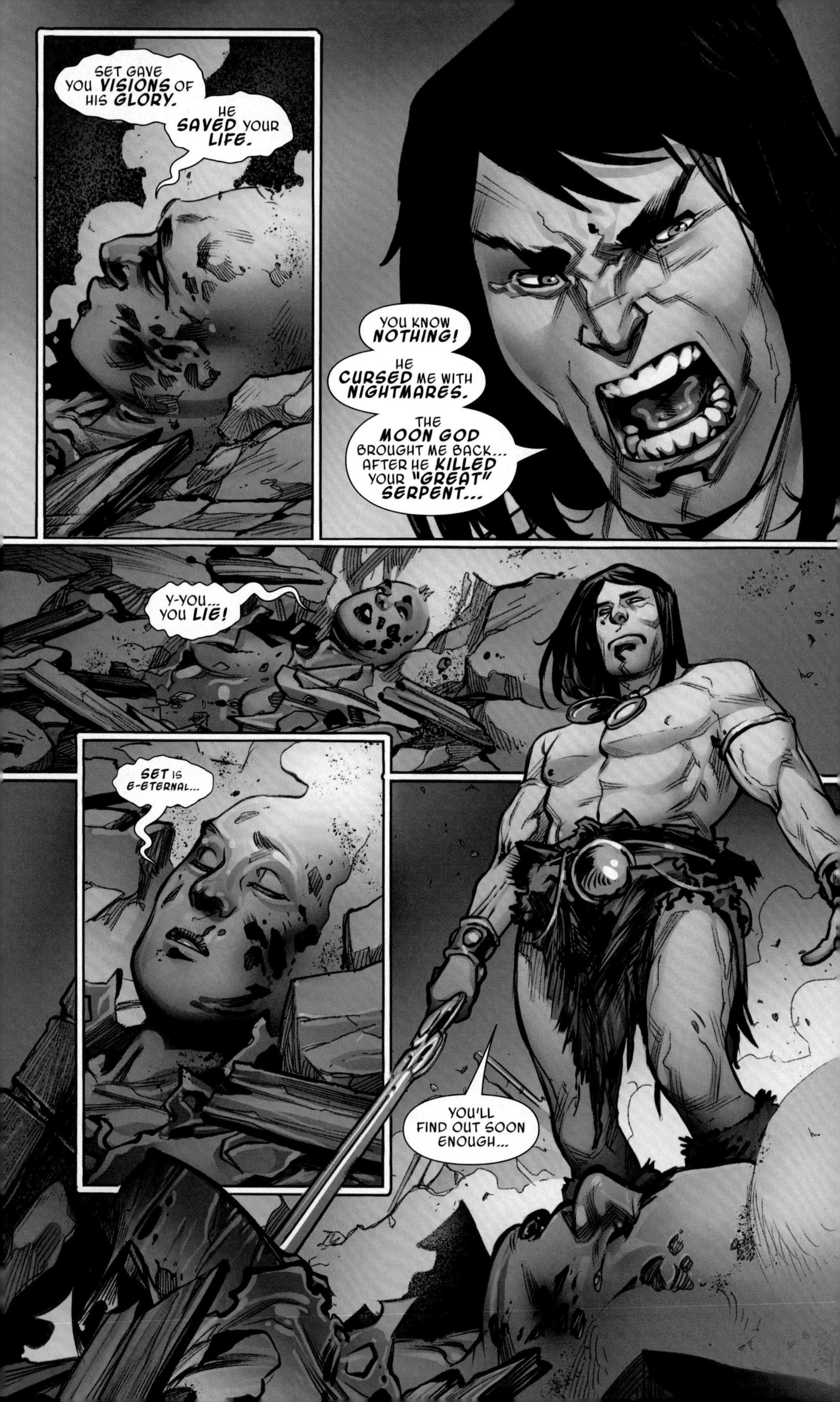
SET GAVE YOU VISIONS OF HIS GLORY.
HE SAVED YOUR LIFE.
YOU KNOW NOTHING!
HE CURSED ME WITH NIGHTMARES.
THE MOON GOD BROUGHT ME BACK... AFTER HE KILLED YOUR "GREAT" SERPENT...
Y-YOU... YOU LIE!
SET IS E-ETERNAL...
YOU'LL FIND OUT SOON ENOUGH...

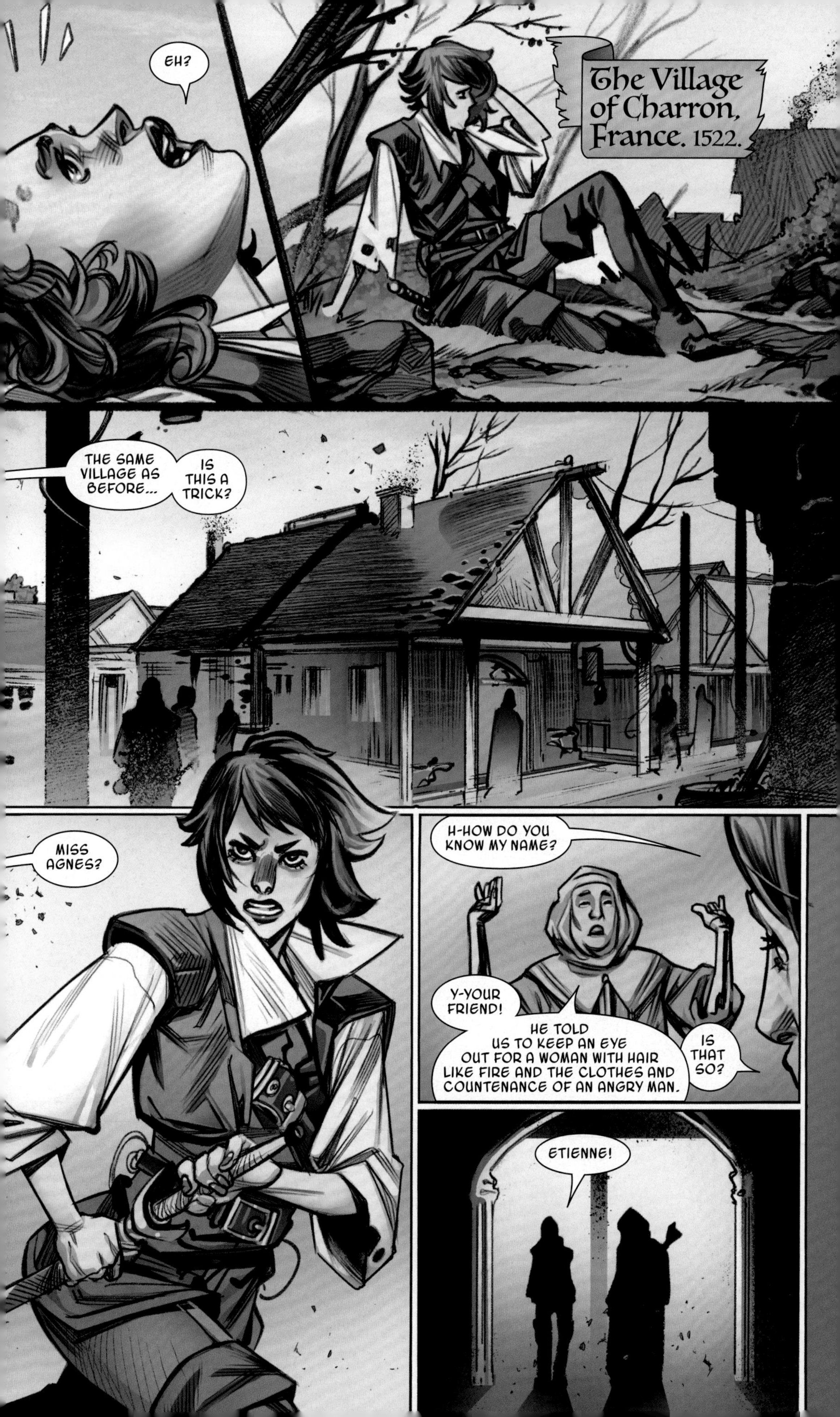
EH?
The Village of Charron, France. 1522.
THE SAME VILLAGE AS BEFORE...
IS THIS A TRICK?
MISS AGNES?
H-HOW DO YOU KNOW MY NAME?
Y-YOUR FRIEND!
HE TOLD US TO KEEP AN EYE OUT FOR A WOMAN WITH HAIR LIKE FIRE AND THE CLOTHES AND COUNTENANCE OF AN ANGRY MAN.
IS THAT SO?
ETIENNE!

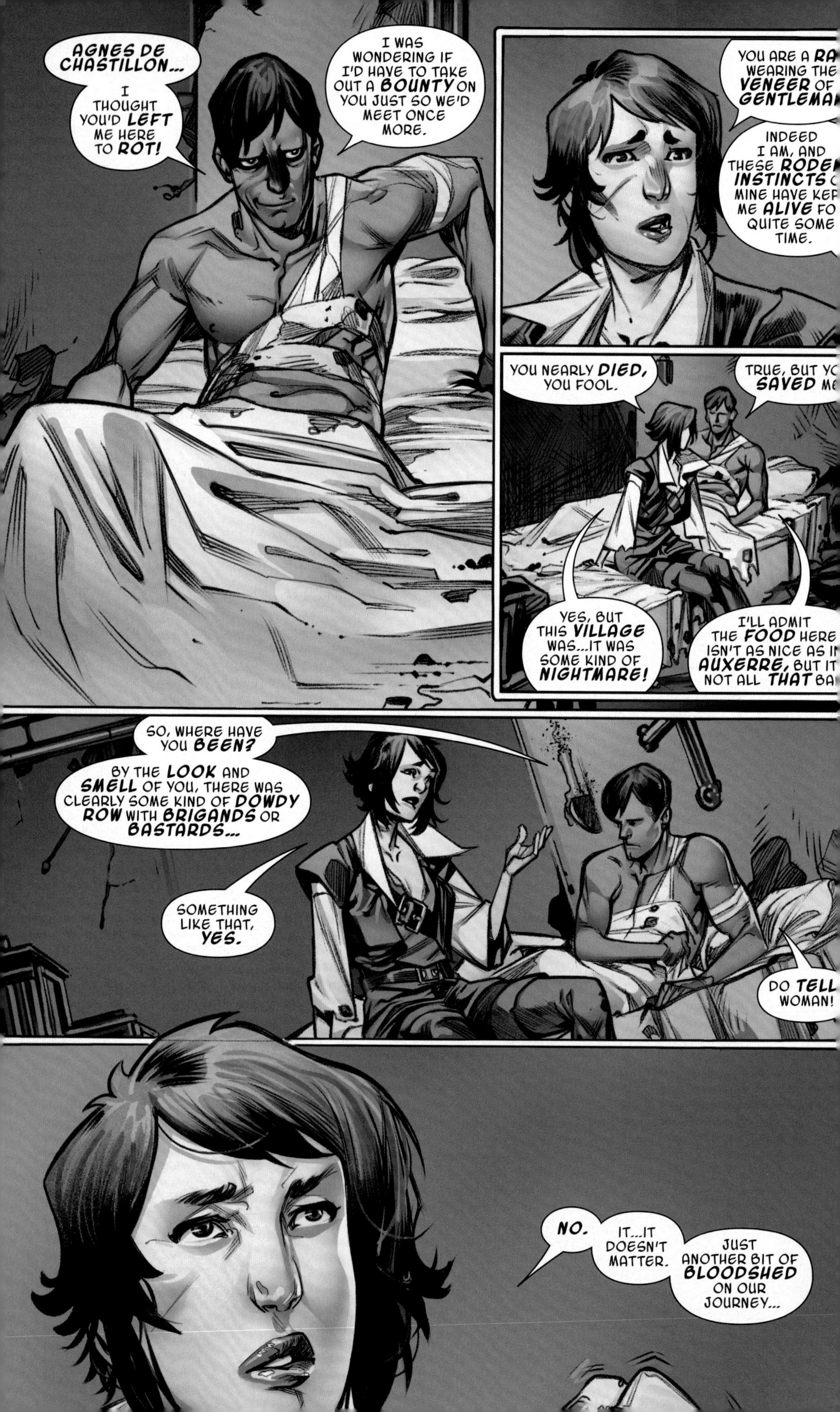
AGNES DE CHASTILLON...
I THOUGHT YOU'D LEFT ME HERE TO ROT!
I WAS WONDERING IF I'D HAVE TO TAKE OUT A BOUNTY ON YOU JUST SO WE'D MEET ONCE MORE.
YOU ARE A RA WEARING THE VENEER OF GENTLEMA
INDEED I AM, AND THESE RODE INSTINCTS MINE HAVE KEP ME ALIVE FO QUITE SOME TIME.
YOU NEARLY DIED, YOU FOOL.
TRUE, BUT YO SAVED M
YES, BUT THIS VILLAGE WAS...IT WAS SOME KIND OF NIGHTMARE!
I'LL ADMIT THE FOOD HERE ISN'T AS NICE AS I AUXERRE, BUT IT NOT ALL THAT BA
SO, WHERE HAVE YOU BEEN?
BY THE LOOK AND SMELL OF YOU, THERE WAS CLEARLY SOME KIND OF DOWDY ROW WITH BRIGANDS OR BASTARDS...
SOMETHING LIKE THAT, YES.
DO TELL WOMAN!
NO.
IT...IT DOESN'T MATTER.
JUST ANOTHER BIT OF BLOODSHED ON OUR JOURNEY...

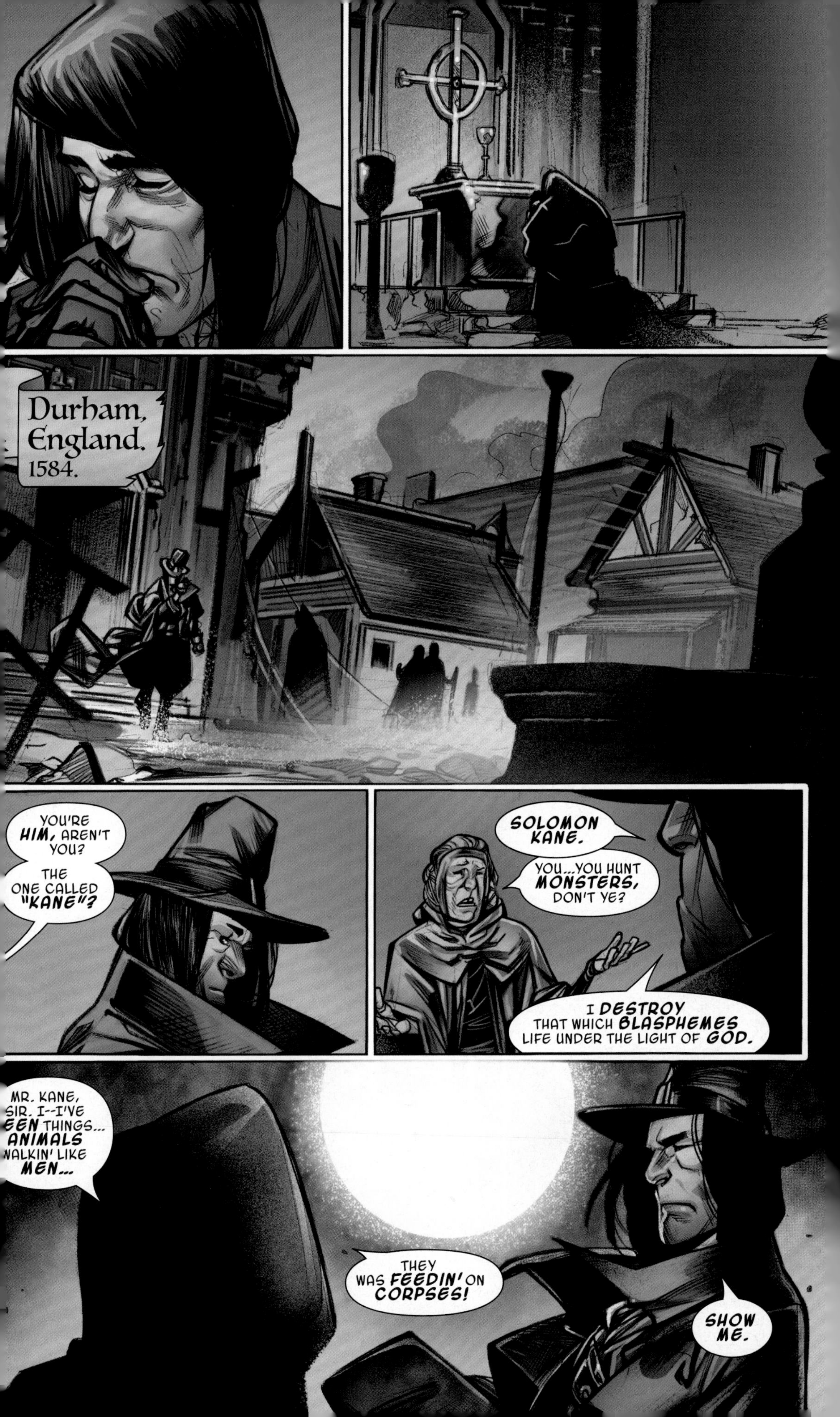
Durham, England. 1584.
YOU'RE HIM, AREN'T YOU?
THE ONE CALLED "KANE"?
SOLOMON KANE.
YOU...YOU HUNT MONSTERS, DON'T YE?
I DESTROY THAT WHICH BLASPHEMES LIFE UNDER THE LIGHT OF GOD.
MR. KANE, SIR. I--I'VE EEN THINGS... ANIMALS WALKIN' LIKE MEN...
THEY WAS FEEDIN' ON CORPSES!
SHOW ME.

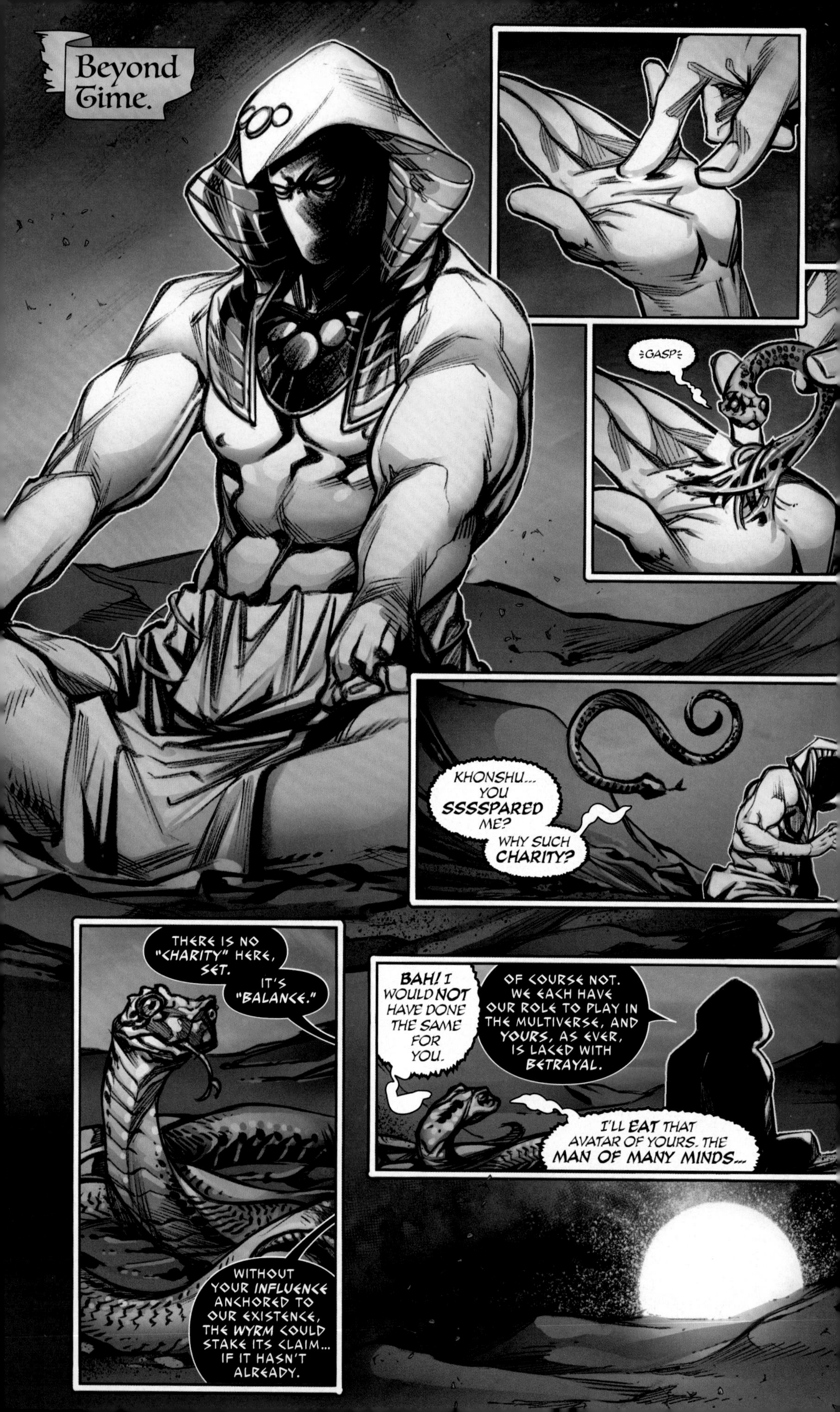
Beyond Time.
GASP
KHONSHU... YOU SSSSPARED ME? WHY SUCH CHARITY?
THERE IS NO "CHARITY" HERE, SET.
IT'S "BALANCE."
BAH! I WOULD NOT HAVE DONE THE SAME FOR YOU.
OF COURSE NOT. WE EACH HAVE OUR ROLE TO PLAY IN THE MULTIVERSE, AND YOURS, AS EVER, IS LACED WITH BETRAYAL.
I'LL EAT THAT AVATAR OF YOURS. THE MAN OF MANY MINDS...
WITHOUT YOUR INFLUENCE ANCHORED TO OUR EXISTENCE, THE WYRM COULD STAKE ITS CLAIM... IF IT HASN'T ALREADY.

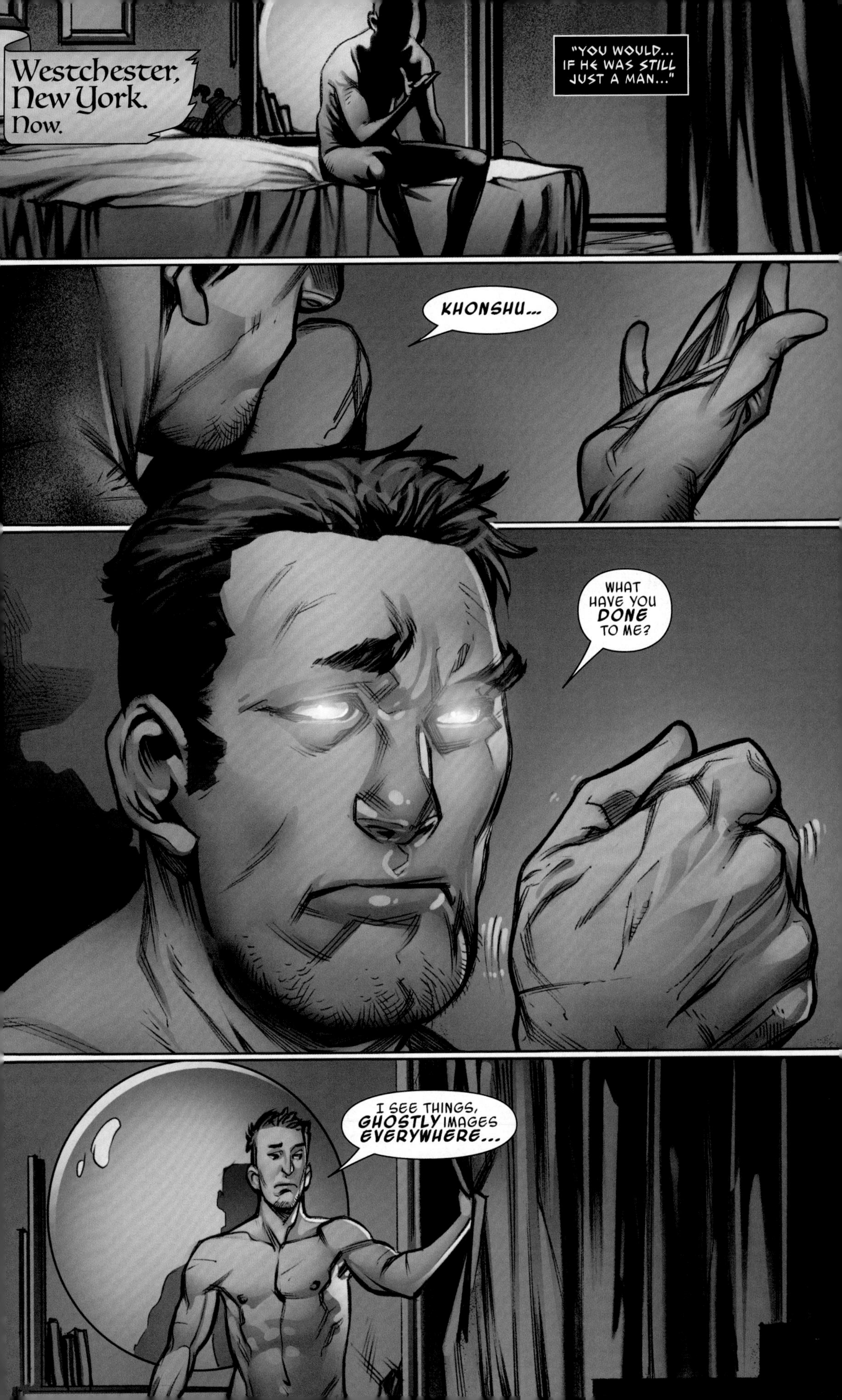
Westchester, New York. Now.
"YOU WOULD... IF HE WAS STILL JUST A MAN..."
KHONSHU...
WHAT HAVE YOU DONE TO ME?
I SEE THINGS, GHOSTLY IMAGES EVERYWHERE...

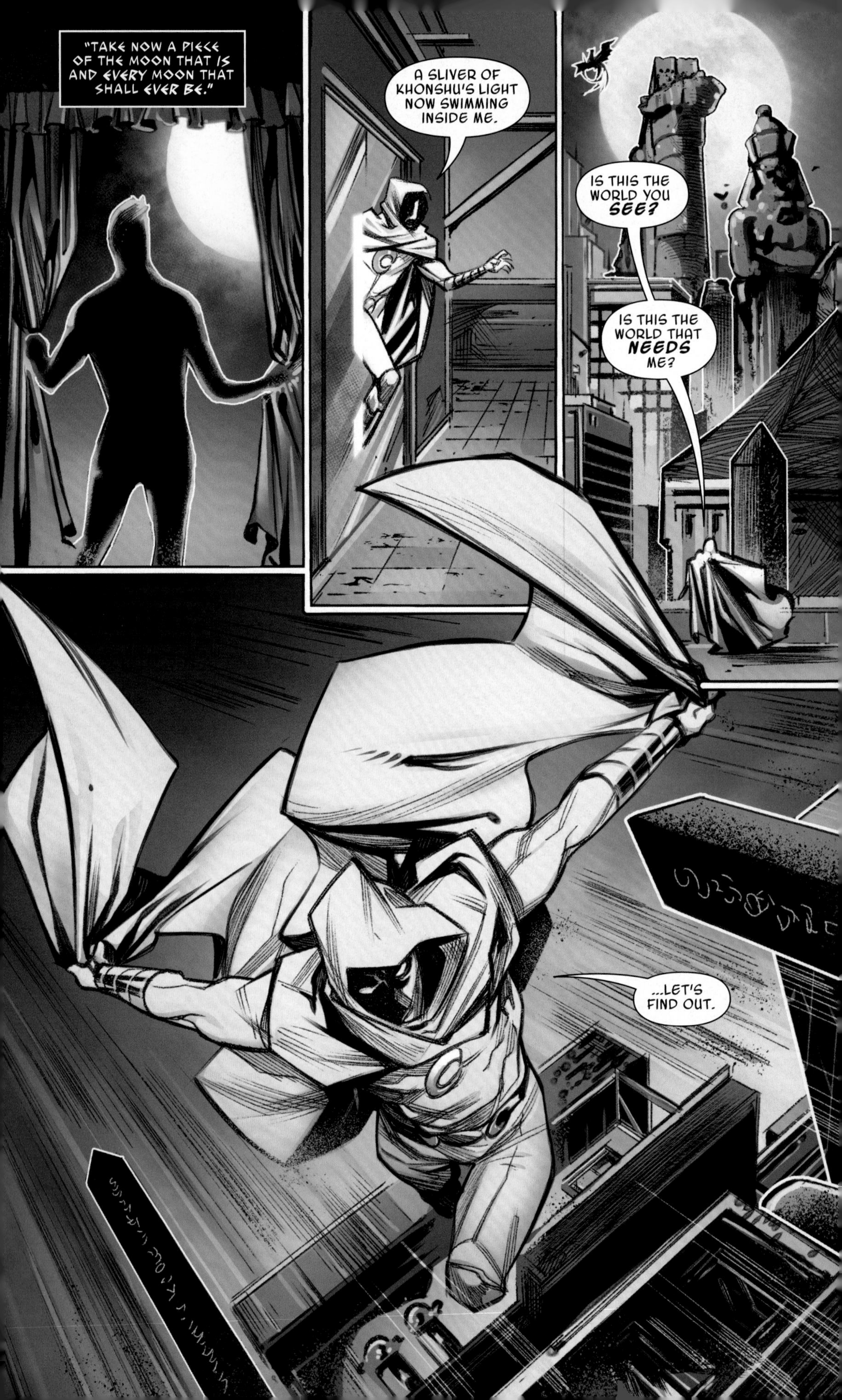
"TAKE NOW A PIECE OF THE MOON THAT IS AND EVERY MOON THAT SHALL EVER BE."
A SLIVER OF KHONSHU'S LIGHT NOW SWIMMING INSIDE ME.
IS THIS THE WORLD YOU SEE?
IS THIS THE WORLD THAT NEEDS ME?
...LET'S FIND OUT.

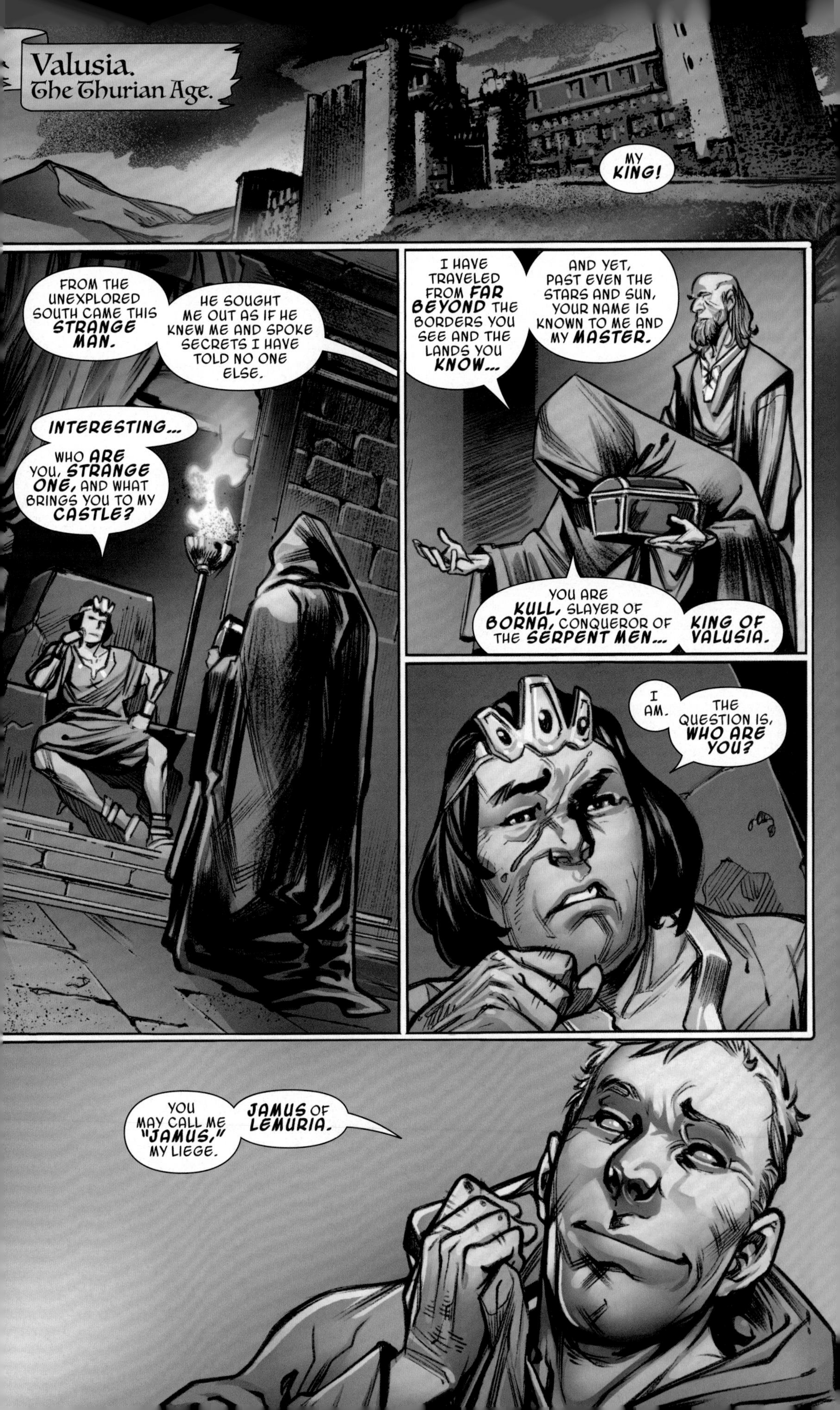
Valusia. The Thurian Age.
MY KING!
FROM THE UNEXPLORED SOUTH CAME THIS STRANGE MAN.
HE SOUGHT ME OUT AS IF HE KNEW ME AND SPOKE SECRETS I HAVE TOLD NO ONE ELSE.
INTERESTING...
WHO ARE YOU, STRANGE ONE, AND WHAT BRINGS YOU TO MY CASTLE?
I HAVE TRAVELED FROM FAR BEYOND THE BORDERS YOU SEE AND THE LANDS YOU KNOW...
AND YET, PAST EVEN THE STARS AND SUN, YOUR NAME IS KNOWN TO ME AND MY MASTER.
YOU ARE KULL, SLAYER OF BORNA, CONQUEROR OF THE SERPENT MEN...
KING OF VALUSIA.
I AM.
THE QUESTION IS, WHO ARE YOU?
YOU MAY CALL ME "JAMUS," MY LIEGE.
JAMUS OF LEMURIA.

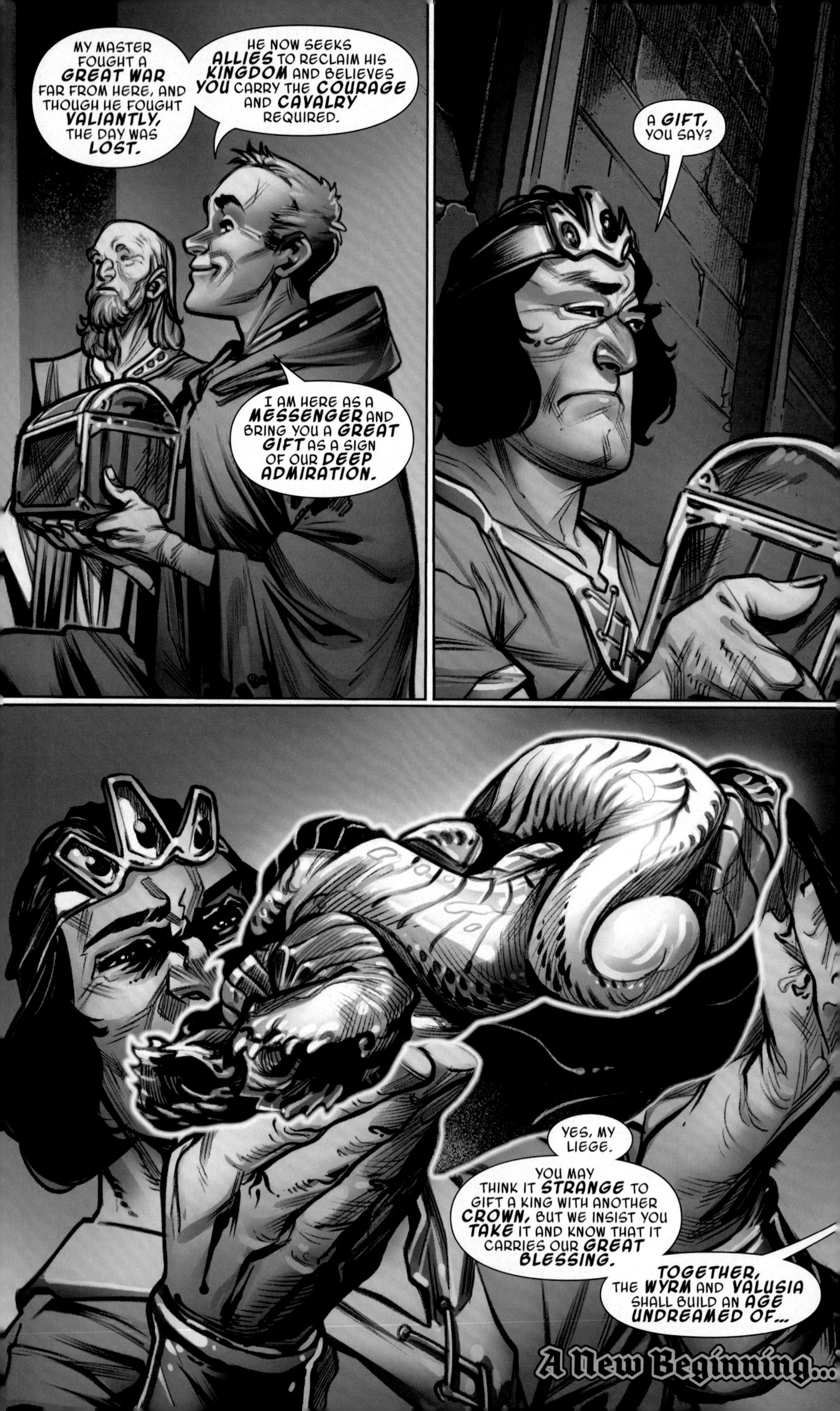
MY MASTER FOUGHT A GREAT WAR FAR FROM HERE, AND THOUGH HE FOUGHT VALIANTLY, THE DAY WAS LOST.
HE NOW SEEKS ALLIES TO RECLAIM HIS KINGDOM AND BELIEVES YOU CARRY THE COURAGE AND CAVALRY REQUIRED.
I AM HERE AS A MESSENGER AND BRING YOU A GREAT GIFT AS A SIGN OF OUR DEEP ADMIRATION.
A GIFT, YOU SAY?
YES, MY LIEGE.
YOU MAY THINK IT STRANGE TO GIFT A KING WITH ANOTHER CROWN, BUT WE INSIST YOU TAKE IT AND KNOW THAT IT CARRIES OUR GREAT BLESSING.
TOGETHER, THE WYRM AND VALUSIA SHALL BUILD AN AGE UNDREAMED OF...
A New Beginning...

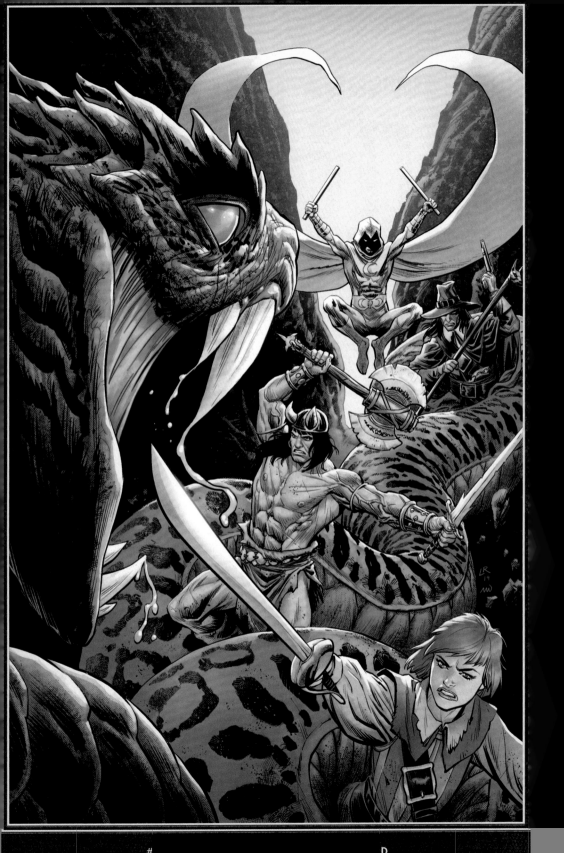

SUPERNATURAL THRILLERS

MARVEL COMICS GROUP ™

APPROVED BY THE COMICS CODE AUTHORITY

20¢ 3 APR 02164

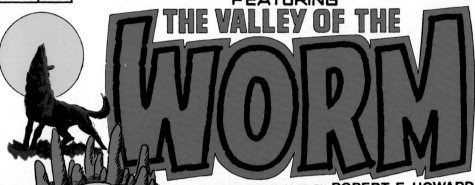

SUPERNATURAL THRILLERS
FEATURING
THE VALLEY OF THE
WORM

ADAPTED FROM THE CHILLER BY ROBERT E. HOWARD

ONE OF THE GREATEST **MONSTER EPICS** OF ALL TIME!!

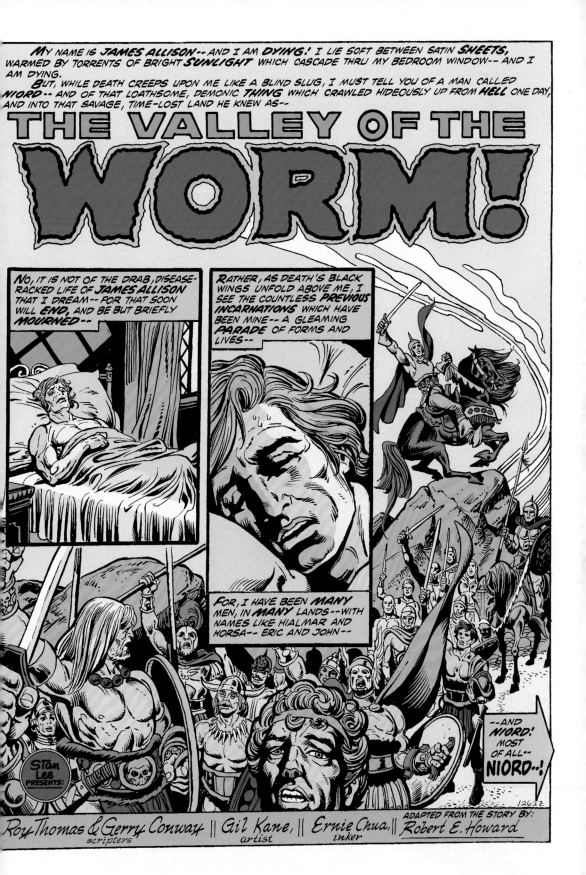

MY NAME IS *JAMES ALLISON*-- AND I AM *DYING!* I LIE SOFT BETWEEN SATIN *SHEETS,* WARMED BY TORRENTS OF BRIGHT *SUNLIGHT* WHICH CASCADE THRU MY BEDROOM WINDOW-- AND I AM DYING.

BUT, WHILE DEATH CREEPS UPON ME LIKE A BLIND SLUG, I MUST TELL YOU OF A MAN CALLED *NIORD*-- AND OF THAT LOATHSOME, DEMONIC *THING* WHICH CRAWLED HIDEOUSLY UP FROM *HELL* ONE DAY, AND INTO THAT SAVAGE, TIME-LOST LAND HE KNEW AS--

THE VALLEY OF THE WORM!

NO, IT IS NOT OF THE DRAB, DISEASE-RACKED LIFE OF *JAMES ALLISON* THAT I DREAM-- FOR THAT SOON WILL *END,* AND BE BUT BRIEFLY *MOURNED*--

RATHER, AS DEATH'S BLACK WINGS UNFOLD ABOVE ME, I SEE THE COUNTLESS *PREVIOUS INCARNATIONS* WHICH HAVE BEEN MINE -- A GLEAMING *PARADE* OF FORMS AND LIVES--

FOR, I HAVE BEEN *MANY* MEN, IN *MANY* LANDS-- WITH NAMES LIKE HIALMAR AND HORSA-- ERIC AND JOHN--

--AND *NIORD!* MOST OF ALL-- NIORD--!

Stan Lee PRESENTS:

Roy Thomas & Gerry Conway scripters || *Gil Kane,* artist || *Ernie Chua,* inker || ADAPTED FROM THE STORY BY: *Robert E. Howard*

12622

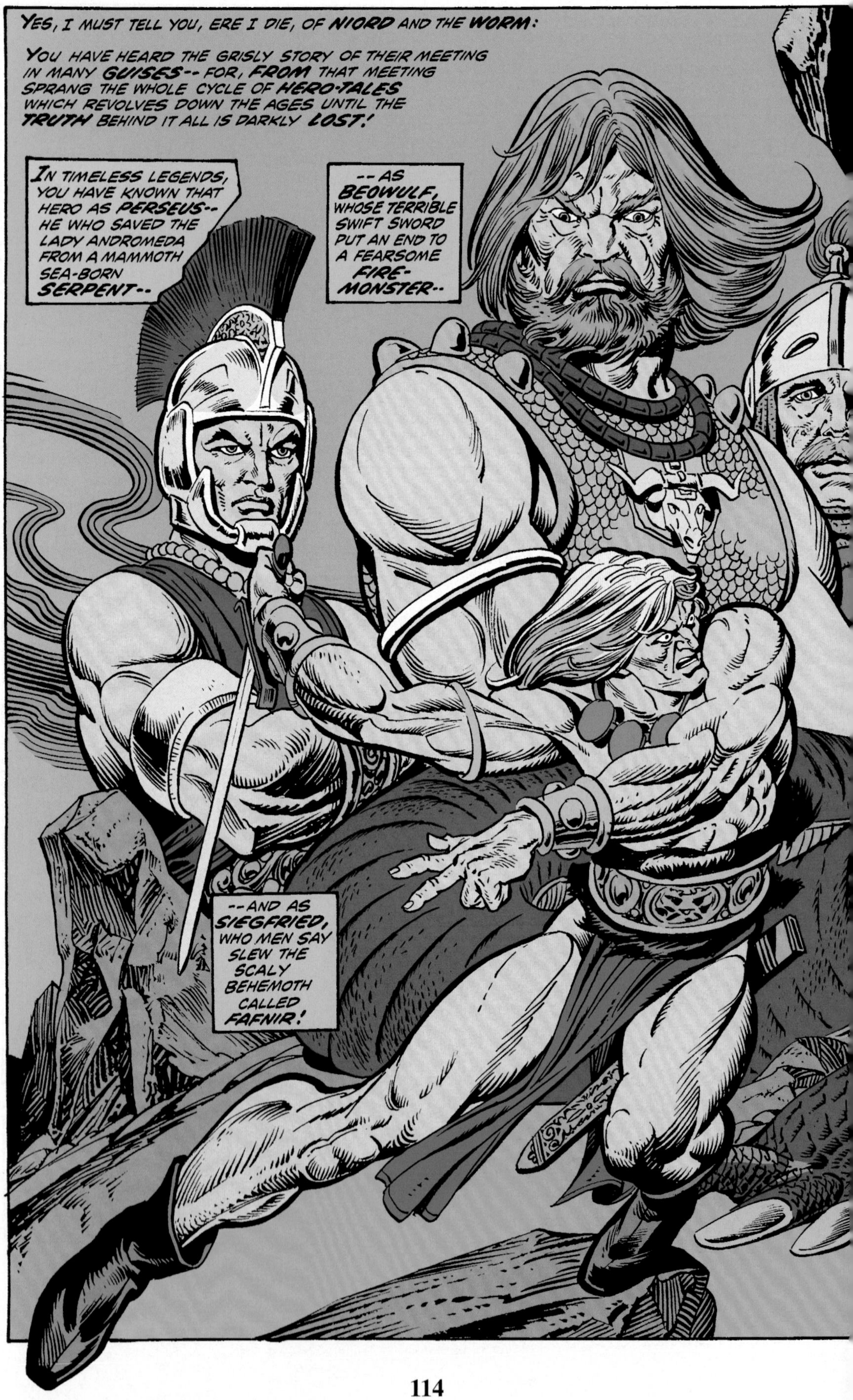
YES, I MUST TELL YOU, ERE I DIE, OF NIORD AND THE WORM:
YOU HAVE HEARD THE GRISLY STORY OF THEIR MEETING IN MANY GUISES-- FOR, FROM THAT MEETING SPRANG THE WHOLE CYCLE OF HERO-TALES WHICH REVOLVES DOWN THE AGES UNTIL THE TRUTH BEHIND IT ALL IS DARKLY LOST!
IN TIMELESS LEGENDS, YOU HAVE KNOWN THAT HERO AS PERSEUS-- HE WHO SAVED THE LADY ANDROMEDA FROM A MAMMOTH SEA-BORN SERPENT--
--AS BEOWULF, WHOSE TERRIBLE SWIFT SWORD PUT AN END TO A FEARSOME FIRE-MONSTER--
--AND AS SIEGFRIED, WHO MEN SAY SLEW THE SCALY BEHEMOTH CALLED FAFNIR!

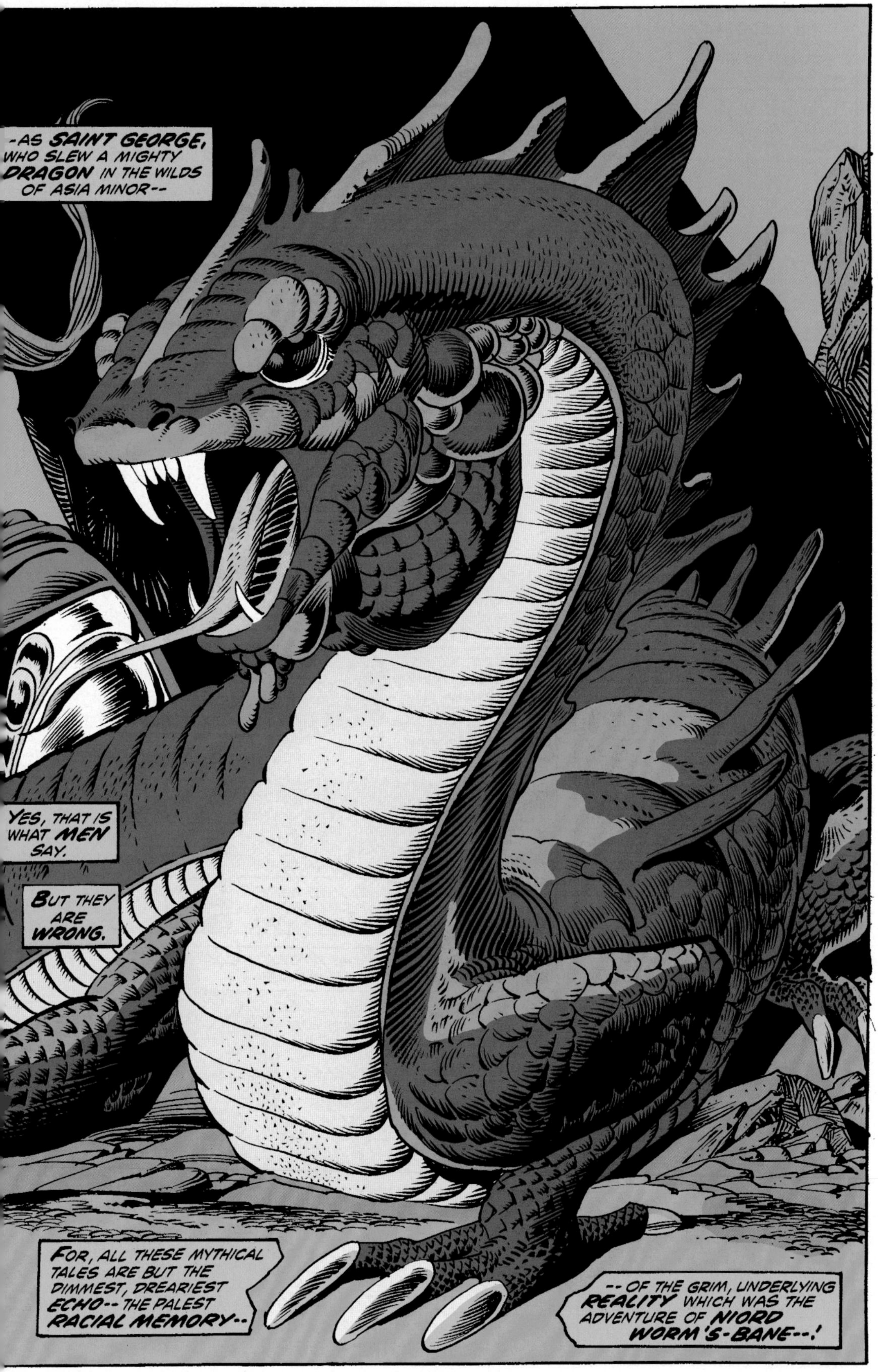
-AS SAINT GEORGE, WHO SLEW A MIGHTY DRAGON IN THE WILDS OF ASIA MINOR--
YES, THAT IS WHAT MEN SAY.
BUT THEY ARE WRONG.
FOR, ALL THESE MYTHICAL TALES ARE BUT THE DIMMEST, DREARIEST ECHO-- THE PALEST RACIAL MEMORY--
-- OF THE GRIM, UNDERLYING REALITY WHICH WAS THE ADVENTURE OF NIORD WORM'S-BANE--!

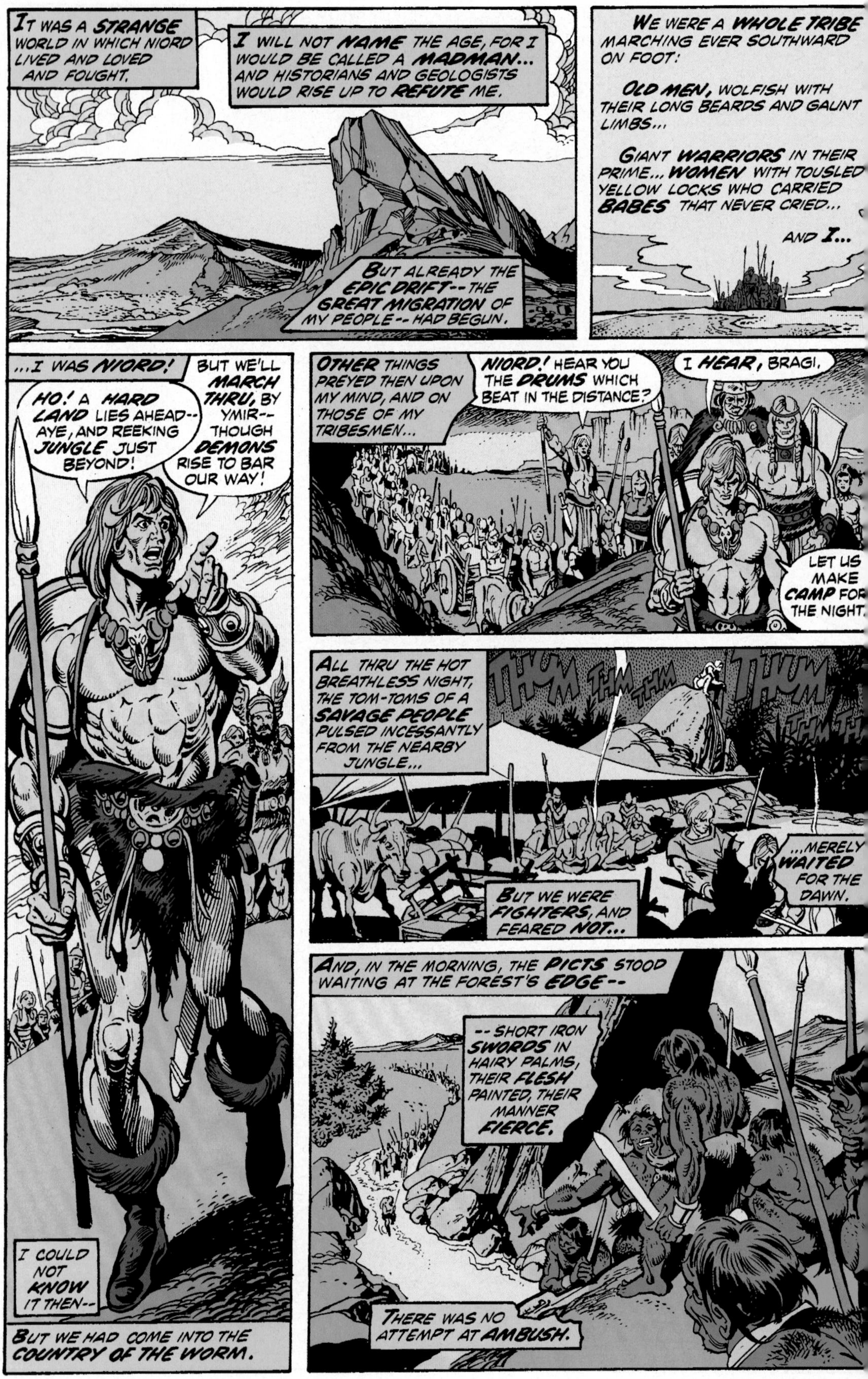
IT WAS A STRANGE WORLD IN WHICH NIORD LIVED AND LOVED AND FOUGHT.
I WILL NOT NAME THE AGE, FOR I WOULD BE CALLED A MADMAN... AND HISTORIANS AND GEOLOGISTS WOULD RISE UP TO REFUTE ME.
BUT ALREADY THE EPIC DRIFT--THE GREAT MIGRATION OF MY PEOPLE--HAD BEGUN.
WE WERE A WHOLE TRIBE MARCHING EVER SOUTHWARD ON FOOT:
OLD MEN, WOLFISH WITH THEIR LONG BEARDS AND GAUNT LIMBS...
GIANT WARRIORS IN THEIR PRIME... WOMEN WITH TOUSLED YELLOW LOCKS WHO CARRIED BABES THAT NEVER CRIED...
AND I...
...I WAS NIORD!
HO! A HARD LAND LIES AHEAD--AYE, AND REEKING JUNGLE JUST BEYOND!
BUT WE'LL MARCH THRU, BY YMIR--THOUGH DEMONS RISE TO BAR OUR WAY!
I COULD NOT KNOW IT THEN--
BUT WE HAD COME INTO THE COUNTRY OF THE WORM.
OTHER THINGS PREYED THEN UPON MY MIND, AND ON THOSE OF MY TRIBESMEN...
NIORD! HEAR YOU THE DRUMS WHICH BEAT IN THE DISTANCE?
I HEAR, BRAGI.
LET US MAKE CAMP FOR THE NIGHT.
ALL THRU THE HOT BREATHLESS NIGHT, THE TOM-TOMS OF A SAVAGE PEOPLE PULSED INCESSANTLY FROM THE NEARBY JUNGLE...
THUM THM THM THUM THM TH
BUT WE WERE FIGHTERS, AND FEARED NOT...
...MERELY WAITED FOR THE DAWN.
AND, IN THE MORNING, THE PICTS STOOD WAITING AT THE FOREST'S EDGE--
--SHORT IRON SWORDS IN HAIRY PALMS, THEIR FLESH PAINTED, THEIR MANNER FIERCE.
THERE WAS NO ATTEMPT AT AMBUSH.

THEY SANG *THEIR* WAR-SONGS... AND WE SANG *OURS*.

THEY SENT THEIR DEATH-TIPPED *ARROWS* AMONG US...

AND *WE*, MAD WITH THE JOY OF BATTLE, *DROPPED* OUR OWN BOWS...

...AND RAN TO *MEET* THEM!

I CANNOT PAINT WITH *WORDS* THE SLAUGHTER, THE FURY, ABOVE ALL THE MERCILESS *SAVAGERY* OF IT ALL -- OR ELSE YOU WOULD RECOIL IN HORROR --

BUT EVEN I, *JAMES ALLISON*, STAND AGHAST AS I REVIEW THE BUTCHERY IN WHICH I, *NIORD*, TOOK PART!

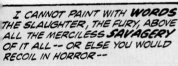

AT LAST, WE *PREVAILED* --

BUT IT WAS A VICTORY *HARD-WON!*

AND AS THE PICTS FLED, OUR *WOMEN* CAME FORWARD TO BRAIN THE WOUNDED ENEMIES WITH STONES... OR CUT THEIR THROATS WITH COPPER KNIVES.

WE DID NOT *TORTURE.*

WE MERELY *SLEW* THOSE WHO WOULD HAVE SLAIN *US.*

I, NIORD, WAS OCCUPIED WITH AN ESPECIALLY *VALIANT* FOE.

LIKE *ALL* HIS RACE, HE CAME SCARCELY TO MY *CHIN* -- YET HE WAS A SOLID KNOT OF *STEEL-SPRING MUSCLES*...

NOW *THERE* WAS A FIGHT TO GLUT EVEN *MY* BATTLE-LUSTING SOUL!

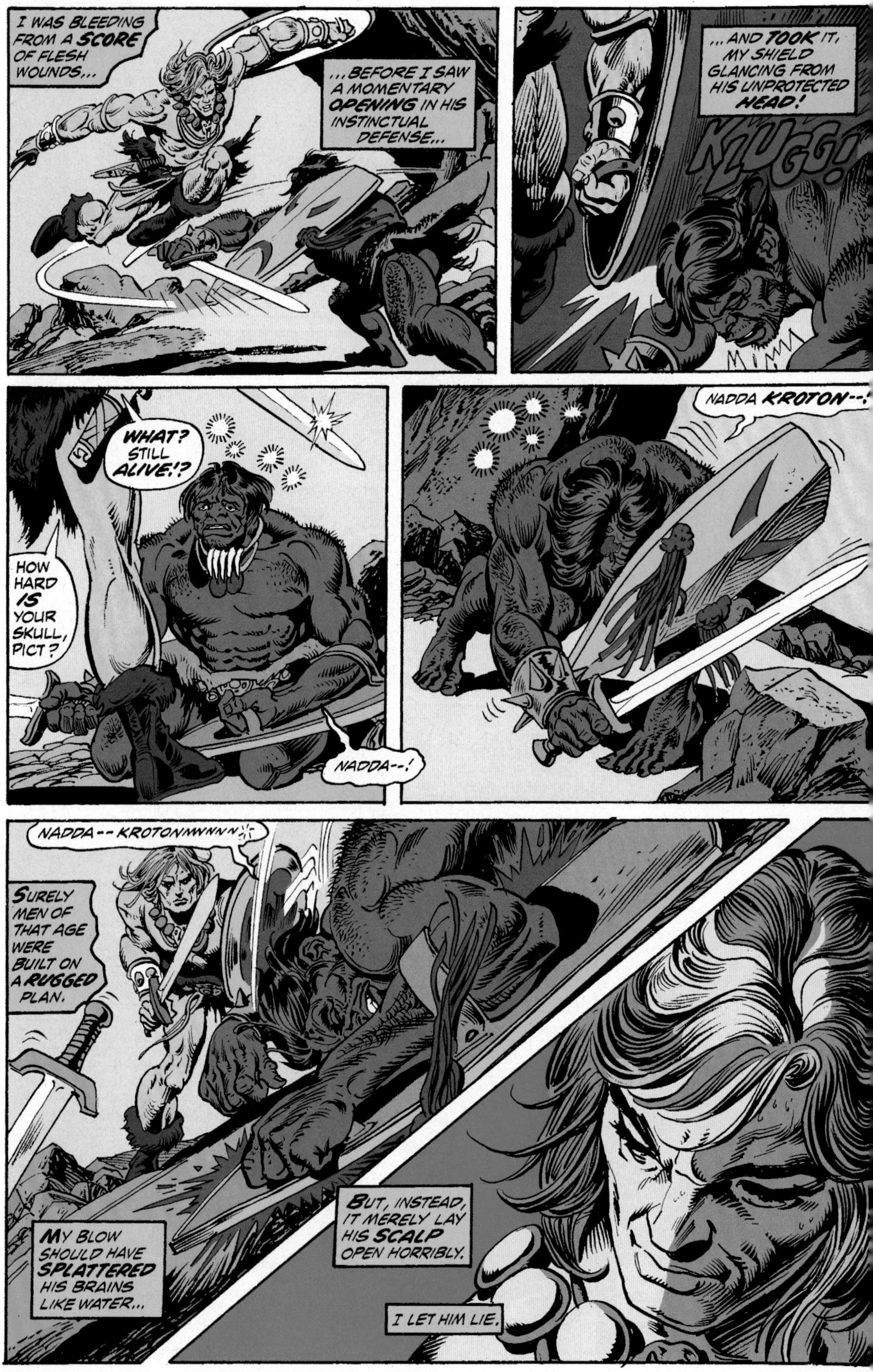
I WAS BLEEDING FROM A SCORE OF FLESH WOUNDS...
...BEFORE I SAW A MOMENTARY OPENING IN HIS INSTINCTUAL DEFENSE...
...AND TOOK IT, MY SHIELD GLANCING FROM HIS UNPROTECTED HEAD!
KLUGG!
WHAT? STILL ALIVE!?
HOW HARD IS YOUR SKULL, PICT?
NADDA--!
NADDA KROTON--!
NADDA--KROTONMNNNN!
SURELY MEN OF THAT AGE WERE BUILT ON A RUGGED PLAN.
MY BLOW SHOULD HAVE SPLATTERED HIS BRAINS LIKE WATER...
BUT, INSTEAD, IT MERELY LAY HIS SCALP OPEN HORRIBLY.
I LET HIM LIE.

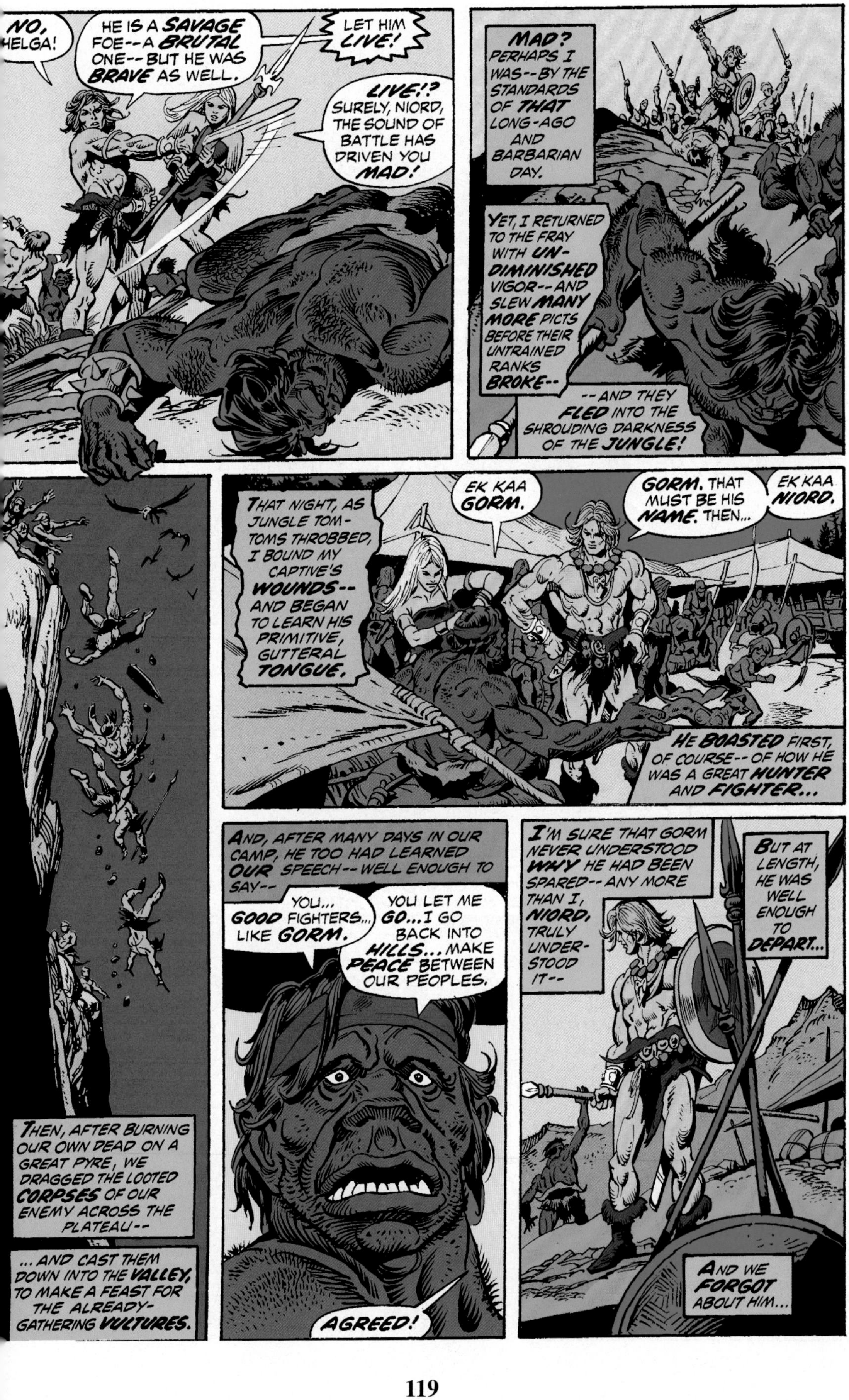
NO, HELGA!
HE IS A SAVAGE FOE--A BRUTAL ONE--BUT HE WAS BRAVE AS WELL.
LET HIM LIVE!
LIVE!? SURELY, NIORD, THE SOUND OF BATTLE HAS DRIVEN YOU MAD!
MAD? PERHAPS I WAS--BY THE STANDARDS OF THAT LONG-AGO AND BARBARIAN DAY.
YET, I RETURNED TO THE FRAY WITH UN-DIMINISHED VIGOR--AND SLEW MANY MORE PICTS BEFORE THEIR UNTRAINED RANKS BROKE--
--AND THEY FLED INTO THE SHROUDING DARKNESS OF THE JUNGLE!
THEN, AFTER BURNING OUR OWN DEAD ON A GREAT PYRE, WE DRAGGED THE LOOTED CORPSES OF OUR ENEMY ACROSS THE PLATEAU--
... AND CAST THEM DOWN INTO THE VALLEY, TO MAKE A FEAST FOR THE ALREADY-GATHERING VULTURES.
THAT NIGHT, AS JUNGLE TOM-TOMS THROBBED, I BOUND MY CAPTIVE'S WOUNDS--AND BEGAN TO LEARN HIS PRIMITIVE, GUTTERAL TONGUE.
EK KAA GORM.
GORM. THAT MUST BE HIS NAME, THEN...
EK KAA NIORD.
HE BOASTED FIRST, OF COURSE--OF HOW HE WAS A GREAT HUNTER AND FIGHTER...
AND, AFTER MANY DAYS IN OUR CAMP, HE TOO HAD LEARNED OUR SPEECH--WELL ENOUGH TO SAY--
YOU... GOOD FIGHTERS... LIKE GORM.
YOU LET ME GO...I GO BACK INTO HILLS...MAKE PEACE BETWEEN OUR PEOPLES.
AGREED!
I'M SURE THAT GORM NEVER UNDERSTOOD WHY HE HAD BEEN SPARED--ANY MORE THAN I, NIORD, TRULY UNDER-STOOD IT--
BUT AT LENGTH, HE WAS WELL ENOUGH TO DEPART...
AND WE FORGOT ABOUT HIM...

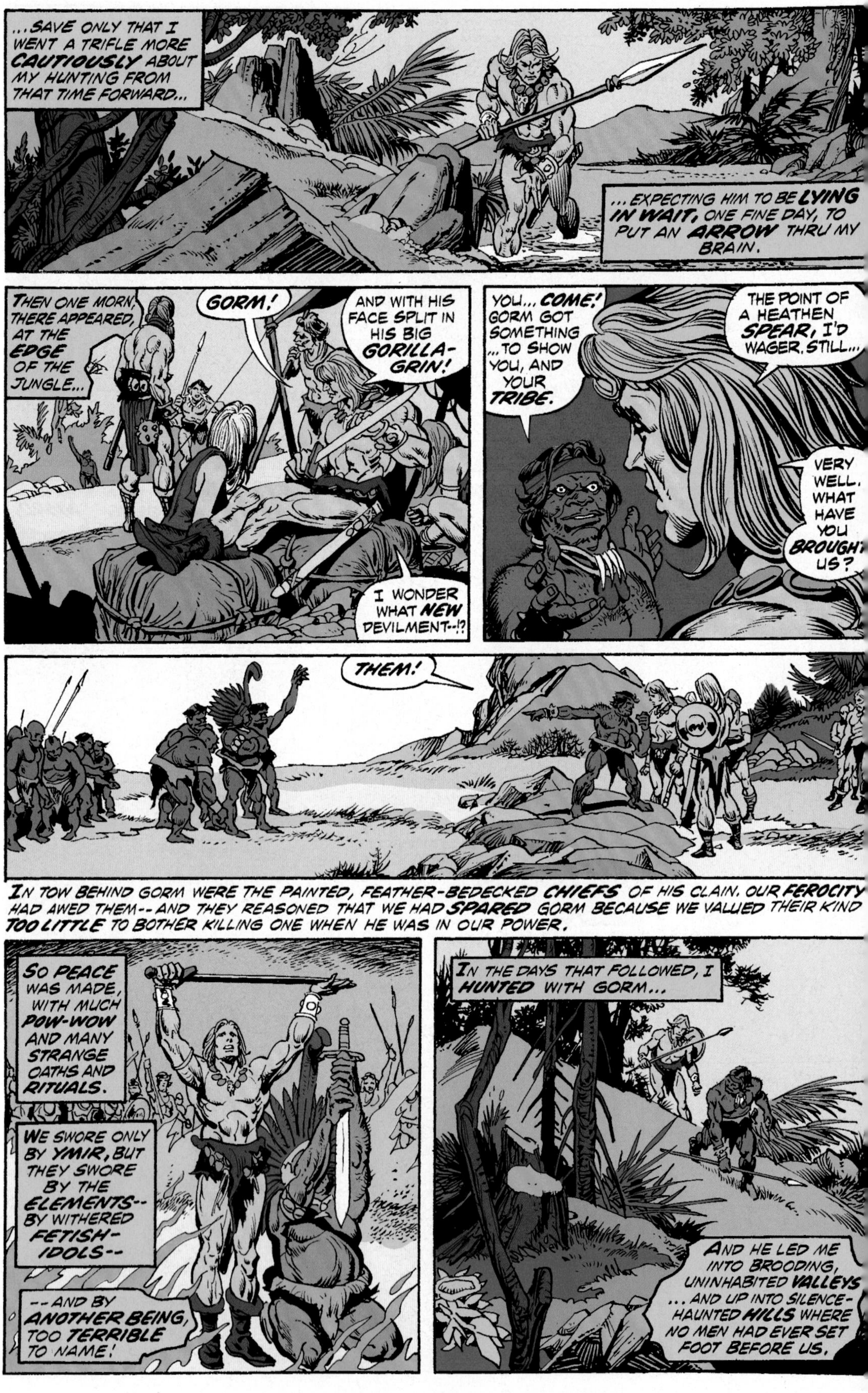

...SAVE ONLY THAT I WENT A TRIFLE MORE CAUTIOUSLY ABOUT MY HUNTING FROM THAT TIME FORWARD...
...EXPECTING HIM TO BE LYING IN WAIT, ONE FINE DAY, TO PUT AN ARROW THRU MY BRAIN.
THEN ONE MORN, THERE APPEARED, AT THE EDGE OF THE JUNGLE...
GORM!
AND WITH HIS FACE SPLIT IN HIS BIG GORILLA-GRIN!
I WONDER WHAT NEW DEVILMENT--!?
YOU... COME! GORM GOT SOMETHING ...TO SHOW YOU, AND YOUR TRIBE.
THE POINT OF A HEATHEN SPEAR, I'D WAGER. STILL...
VERY WELL. WHAT HAVE YOU BROUGHT US?
THEM!
IN TOW BEHIND GORM WERE THE PAINTED, FEATHER-BEDECKED CHIEFS OF HIS CLAN. OUR FEROCITY HAD AWED THEM-- AND THEY REASONED THAT WE HAD SPARED GORM BECAUSE WE VALUED THEIR KIND TOO LITTLE TO BOTHER KILLING ONE WHEN HE WAS IN OUR POWER.
SO PEACE WAS MADE, WITH MUCH POW-WOW AND MANY STRANGE OATHS AND RITUALS.
WE SWORE ONLY BY YMIR, BUT THEY SWORE BY THE ELEMENTS-- BY WITHERED FETISH-IDOLS--
--AND BY ANOTHER BEING, TOO TERRIBLE TO NAME!
IN THE DAYS THAT FOLLOWED, I HUNTED WITH GORM...
AND HE LED ME INTO BROODING, UNINHABITED VALLEYS ...AND UP INTO SILENCE-HAUNTED HILLS WHERE NO MEN HAD EVER SET FOOT BEFORE US.

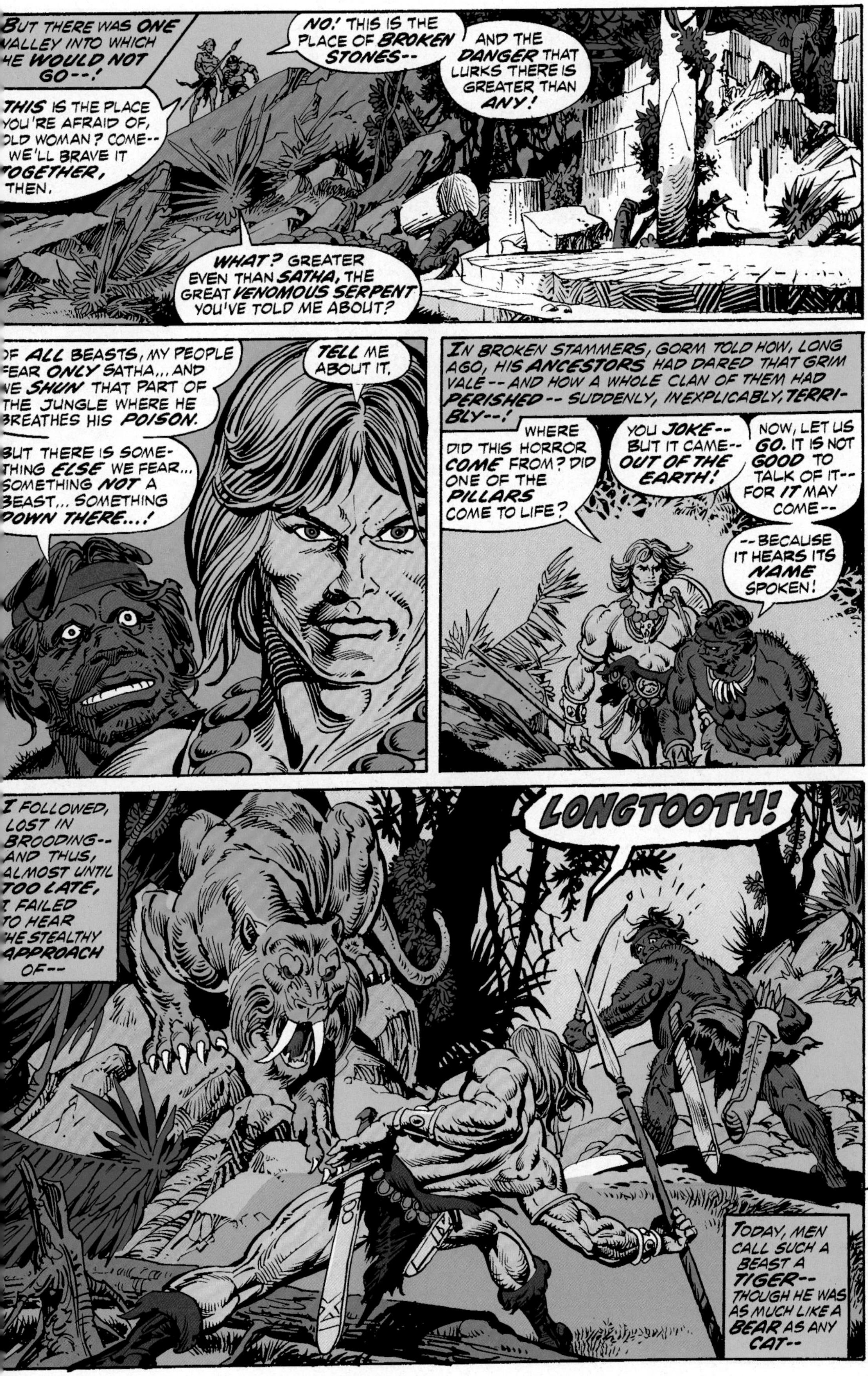

BUT THERE WAS ONE VALLEY INTO WHICH HE WOULD NOT GO--!
NO! THIS IS THE PLACE OF BROKEN STONES--
AND THE DANGER THAT LURKS THERE IS GREATER THAN ANY!
THIS IS THE PLACE YOU'RE AFRAID OF, OLD WOMAN? COME-- WE'LL BRAVE IT TOGETHER, THEN.
WHAT? GREATER EVEN THAN SATHA, THE GREAT VENOMOUS SERPENT YOU'VE TOLD ME ABOUT?
OF ALL BEASTS, MY PEOPLE FEAR ONLY SATHA... AND WE SHUN THAT PART OF THE JUNGLE WHERE HE BREATHES HIS POISON.
BUT THERE IS SOMETHING ELSE WE FEAR... SOMETHING NOT A BEAST... SOMETHING DOWN THERE...!
TELL ME ABOUT IT.
IN BROKEN STAMMERS, GORM TOLD HOW, LONG AGO, HIS ANCESTORS HAD DARED THAT GRIM VALE -- AND HOW A WHOLE CLAN OF THEM HAD PERISHED -- SUDDENLY, INEXPLICABLY, TERRIBLY--!
WHERE DID THIS HORROR COME FROM? DID ONE OF THE PILLARS COME TO LIFE?
YOU JOKE-- BUT IT CAME-- OUT OF THE EARTH!
NOW, LET US GO. IT IS NOT GOOD TO TALK OF IT-- FOR IT MAY COME--
--BECAUSE IT HEARS ITS NAME SPOKEN!
I FOLLOWED, LOST IN BROODING-- AND THUS, ALMOST UNTIL TOO LATE, I FAILED TO HEAR THE STEALTHY APPROACH OF--
LONGTOOTH!
TODAY, MEN CALL SUCH A BEAST A TIGER-- THOUGH HE WAS AS MUCH LIKE A BEAR AS ANY CAT--

LONGTOOTH: MASSIVE-LIMBED, WITH LOW-SLUNG HEAVY *BODY*...

ORGANIC DEVELOPMENT GONE *MAD*--

-- AND RUN TO *FANGS* AND *TALONS*

--TO *SLAUGHTER* AND *DESTRUCTION*--!

AND YET, I *KILLED* LONGTOOTH, IN A BATTLE THAT WOULD MAKE A SAGA IN ITSELF-- AND WOULD HAVE *DIED* THAT DAY, HAD NOT *GORM* BEEN THERE TO CARRY ME BACK TO OUR *CAMP*.

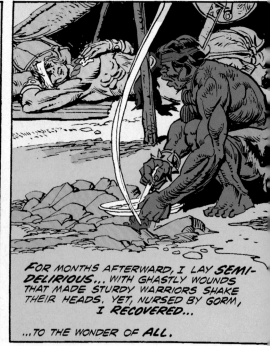

FOR MONTHS AFTERWARD, I LAY *SEMI-DELIRIOUS*... WITH GHASTLY WOUNDS THAT MADE STURDY WARRIORS SHAKE THEIR HEADS. YET, NURSED BY GORM, I *RECOVERED*...

...TO THE WONDER OF *ALL*.

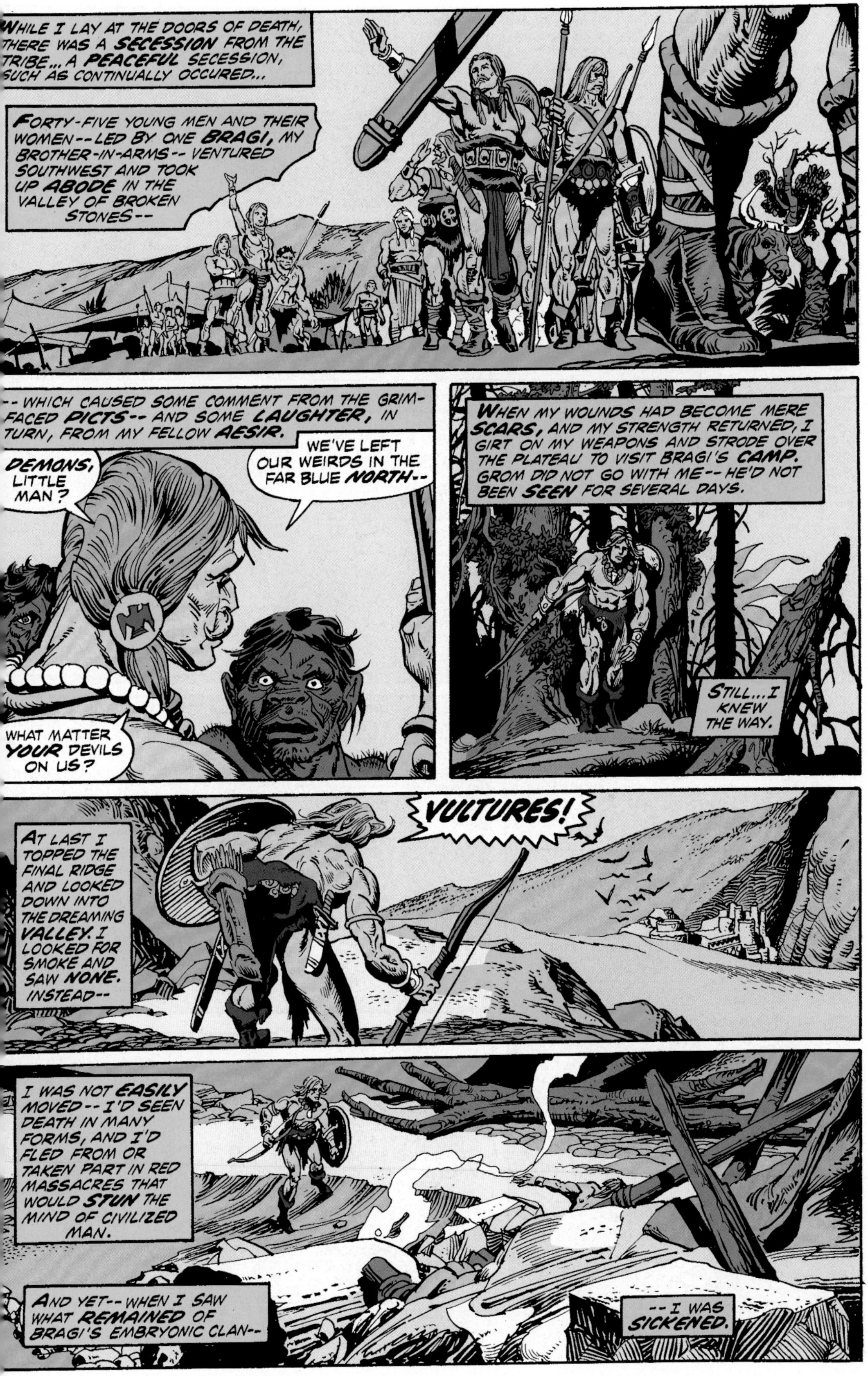
WHILE I LAY AT THE DOORS OF DEATH, THERE WAS A SECESSION FROM THE TRIBE... A PEACEFUL SECESSION, SUCH AS CONTINUALLY OCCURED...
FORTY-FIVE YOUNG MEN AND THEIR WOMEN--LED BY ONE BRAGI, MY BROTHER-IN-ARMS--VENTURED SOUTHWEST AND TOOK UP ABODE IN THE VALLEY OF BROKEN STONES--
--WHICH CAUSED SOME COMMENT FROM THE GRIM-FACED PICTS--AND SOME LAUGHTER, IN TURN, FROM MY FELLOW AESIR.
DEMONS, LITTLE MAN?
WE'VE LEFT OUR WEIRDS IN THE FAR BLUE NORTH--
WHAT MATTER YOUR DEVILS ON US?
WHEN MY WOUNDS HAD BECOME MERE SCARS, AND MY STRENGTH RETURNED, I GIRT ON MY WEAPONS AND STRODE OVER THE PLATEAU TO VISIT BRAGI'S CAMP. GROM DID NOT GO WITH ME--HE'D NOT BEEN SEEN FOR SEVERAL DAYS.
STILL...I KNEW THE WAY.
AT LAST I TOPPED THE FINAL RIDGE AND LOOKED DOWN INTO THE DREAMING VALLEY. I LOOKED FOR SMOKE AND SAW NONE. INSTEAD--
VULTURES!
I WAS NOT EASILY MOVED--I'D SEEN DEATH IN MANY FORMS, AND I'D FLED FROM OR TAKEN PART IN RED MASSACRES THAT WOULD STUN THE MIND OF CIVILIZED MAN.
AND YET--WHEN I SAW WHAT REMAINED OF BRAGI'S EMBRYONIC CLAN--
--I WAS SICKENED.

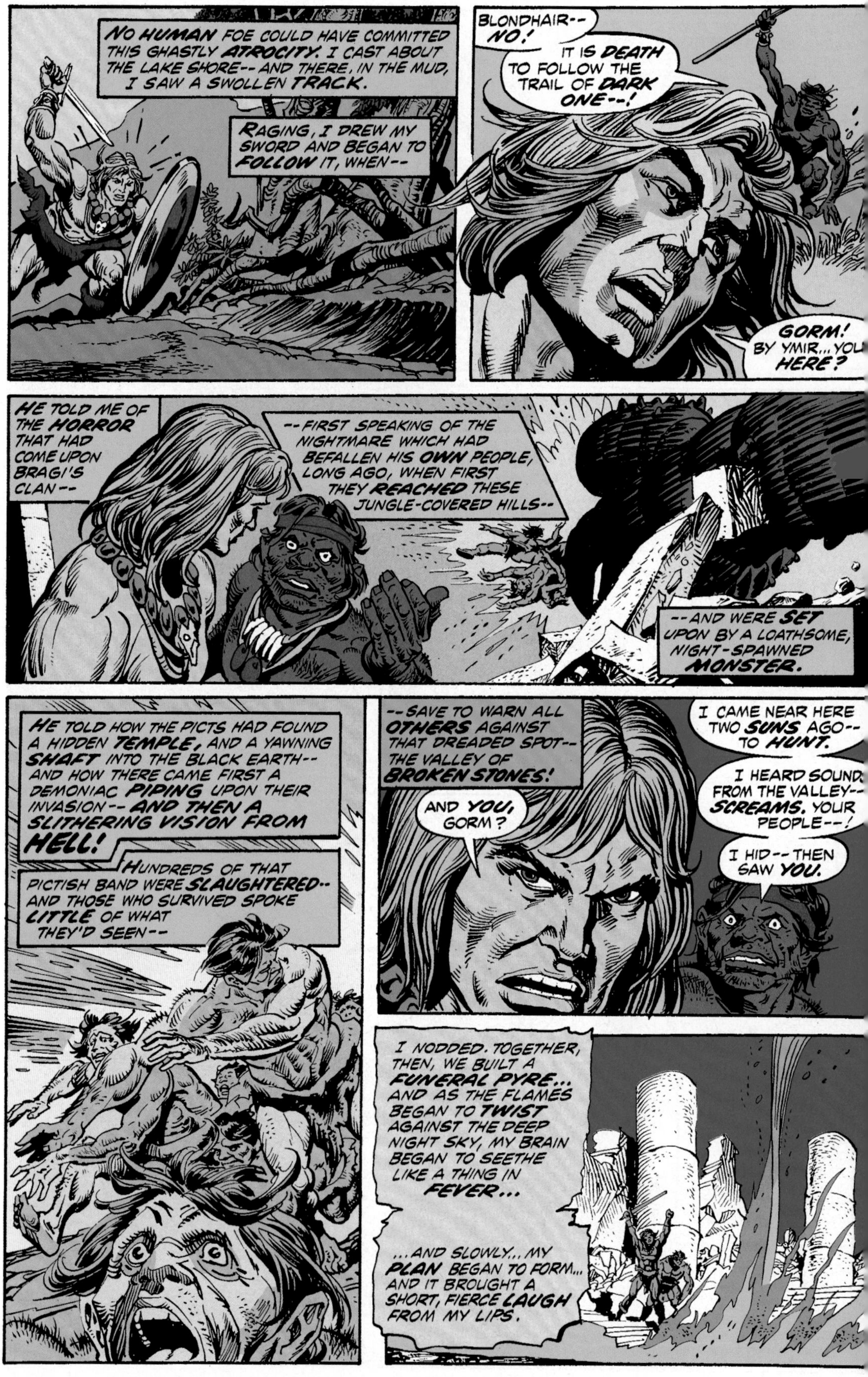
NO HUMAN FOE COULD HAVE COMMITTED THIS GHASTLY ATROCITY. I CAST ABOUT THE LAKE SHORE-- AND THERE, IN THE MUD, I SAW A SWOLLEN TRACK.
RAGING, I DREW MY SWORD AND BEGAN TO FOLLOW IT, WHEN--
BLONDHAIR-- NO!
IT IS DEATH TO FOLLOW THE TRAIL OF DARK ONE--!
GORM! BY YMIR... YOU HERE?
HE TOLD ME OF THE HORROR THAT HAD COME UPON BRAGI'S CLAN--
--FIRST SPEAKING OF THE NIGHTMARE WHICH HAD BEFALLEN HIS OWN PEOPLE, LONG AGO, WHEN FIRST THEY REACHED THESE JUNGLE-COVERED HILLS--
--AND WERE SET UPON BY A LOATHSOME, NIGHT-SPAWNED MONSTER.
HE TOLD HOW THE PICTS HAD FOUND A HIDDEN TEMPLE, AND A YAWNING SHAFT INTO THE BLACK EARTH-- AND HOW THERE CAME FIRST A DEMONIAC PIPING UPON THEIR INVASION-- AND THEN A SLITHERING VISION FROM HELL!
HUNDREDS OF THAT PICTISH BAND WERE SLAUGHTERED-- AND THOSE WHO SURVIVED SPOKE LITTLE OF WHAT THEY'D SEEN--
--SAVE TO WARN ALL OTHERS AGAINST THAT DREADED SPOT-- THE VALLEY OF BROKEN STONES!
AND YOU, GORM?
I CAME NEAR HERE TWO SUNS AGO-- TO HUNT.
I HEARD SOUND FROM THE VALLEY-- SCREAMS. YOUR PEOPLE--!
I HID-- THEN SAW YOU.
I NODDED. TOGETHER, THEN, WE BUILT A FUNERAL PYRE... AND AS THE FLAMES BEGAN TO TWIST AGAINST THE DEEP NIGHT SKY, MY BRAIN BEGAN TO SEETHE LIKE A THING IN FEVER...
...AND SLOWLY... MY PLAN BEGAN TO FORM... AND IT BROUGHT A SHORT, FIERCE LAUGH FROM MY LIPS.

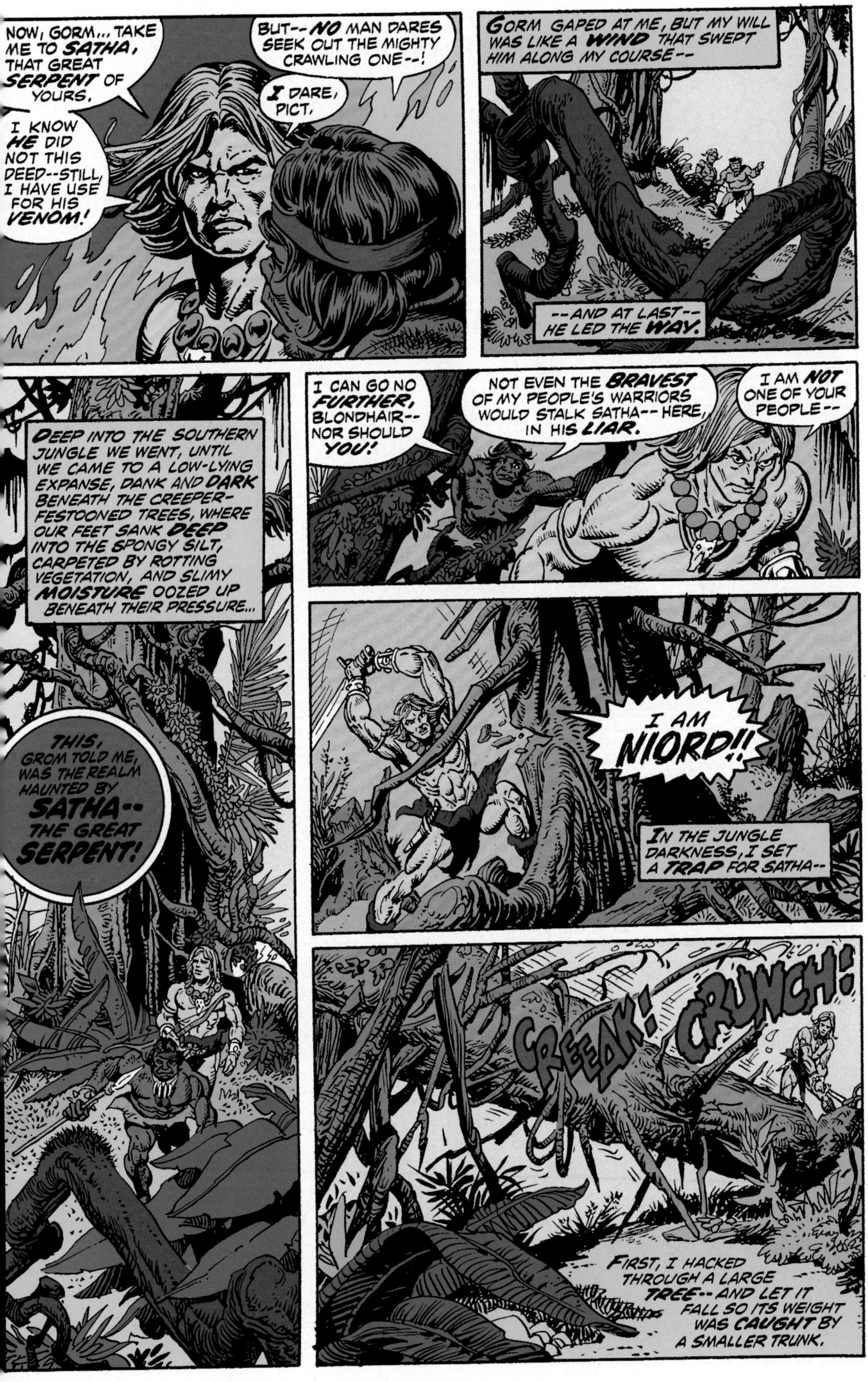

NOW, GORM... TAKE ME TO SATHA, THAT GREAT SERPENT OF YOURS.
BUT-- NO MAN DARES SEEK OUT THE MIGHTY CRAWLING ONE--!
I DARE, PICT.
I KNOW HE DID NOT THIS DEED--STILL, I HAVE USE FOR HIS VENOM!
GORM GAPED AT ME, BUT MY WILL WAS LIKE A WIND THAT SWEPT HIM ALONG MY COURSE--
--AND AT LAST-- HE LED THE WAY.
DEEP INTO THE SOUTHERN JUNGLE WE WENT, UNTIL WE CAME TO A LOW-LYING EXPANSE, DANK AND DARK BENEATH THE CREEPER-FESTOONED TREES, WHERE OUR FEET SANK DEEP INTO THE SPONGY SILT, CARPETED BY ROTTING VEGETATION, AND SLIMY MOISTURE OOZED UP BENEATH THEIR PRESSURE...
THIS, GROM TOLD ME, WAS THE REALM HAUNTED BY SATHA-- THE GREAT SERPENT!
I CAN GO NO FURTHER, BLONDHAIR-- NOR SHOULD YOU!
NOT EVEN THE BRAVEST OF MY PEOPLE'S WARRIORS WOULD STALK SATHA-- HERE, IN HIS LIAR.
I AM NOT ONE OF YOUR PEOPLE--
I AM NIORD!!
IN THE JUNGLE DARKNESS, I SET A TRAP FOR SATHA--
CREEAK! CRUNCH!
FIRST, I HACKED THROUGH A LARGE TREE-- AND LET IT FALL SO ITS WEIGHT WAS CAUGHT BY A SMALLER TRUNK.

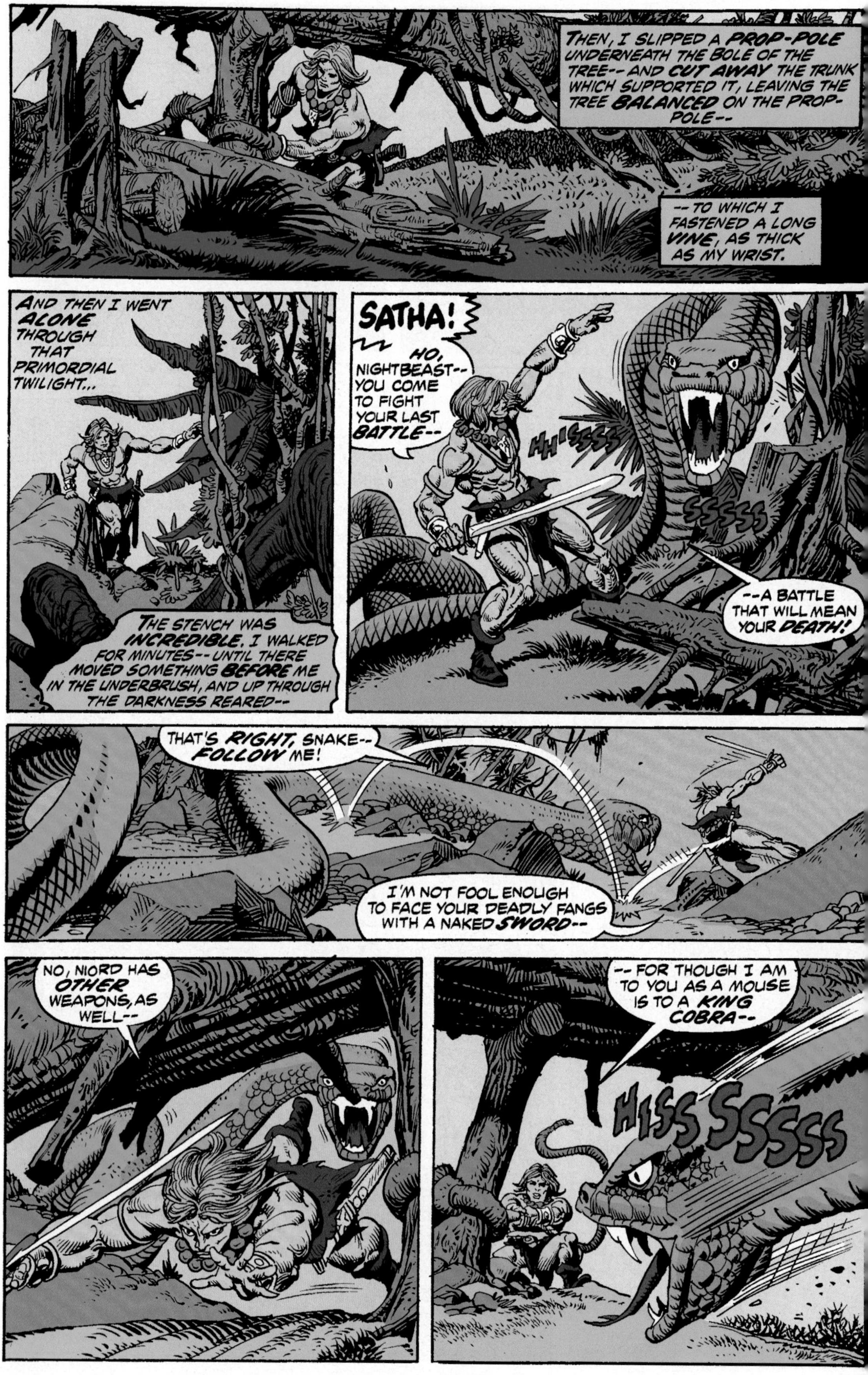
THEN, I SLIPPED A PROP-POLE UNDERNEATH THE BOLE OF THE TREE-- AND CUT AWAY THE TRUNK WHICH SUPPORTED IT, LEAVING THE TREE BALANCED ON THE PROP-POLE--
--TO WHICH I FASTENED A LONG VINE, AS THICK AS MY WRIST.
AND THEN I WENT ALONE THROUGH THAT PRIMORDIAL TWILIGHT...
THE STENCH WAS INCREDIBLE. I WALKED FOR MINUTES-- UNTIL THERE MOVED SOMETHING BEFORE ME IN THE UNDERBRUSH, AND UP THROUGH THE DARKNESS REARED--
SATHA!
NO, NIGHTBEAST-- YOU COME TO FIGHT YOUR LAST BATTLE--
HHISSSS
SSSSSS
--A BATTLE THAT WILL MEAN YOUR DEATH!
THAT'S RIGHT, SNAKE-- FOLLOW ME!
I'M NOT FOOL ENOUGH TO FACE YOUR DEADLY FANGS WITH A NAKED SWORD--
NO, NIORD HAS OTHER WEAPONS, AS WELL--
-- FOR THOUGH I AM TO YOU AS A MOUSE IS TO A KING COBRA--
HISS SSSSSS

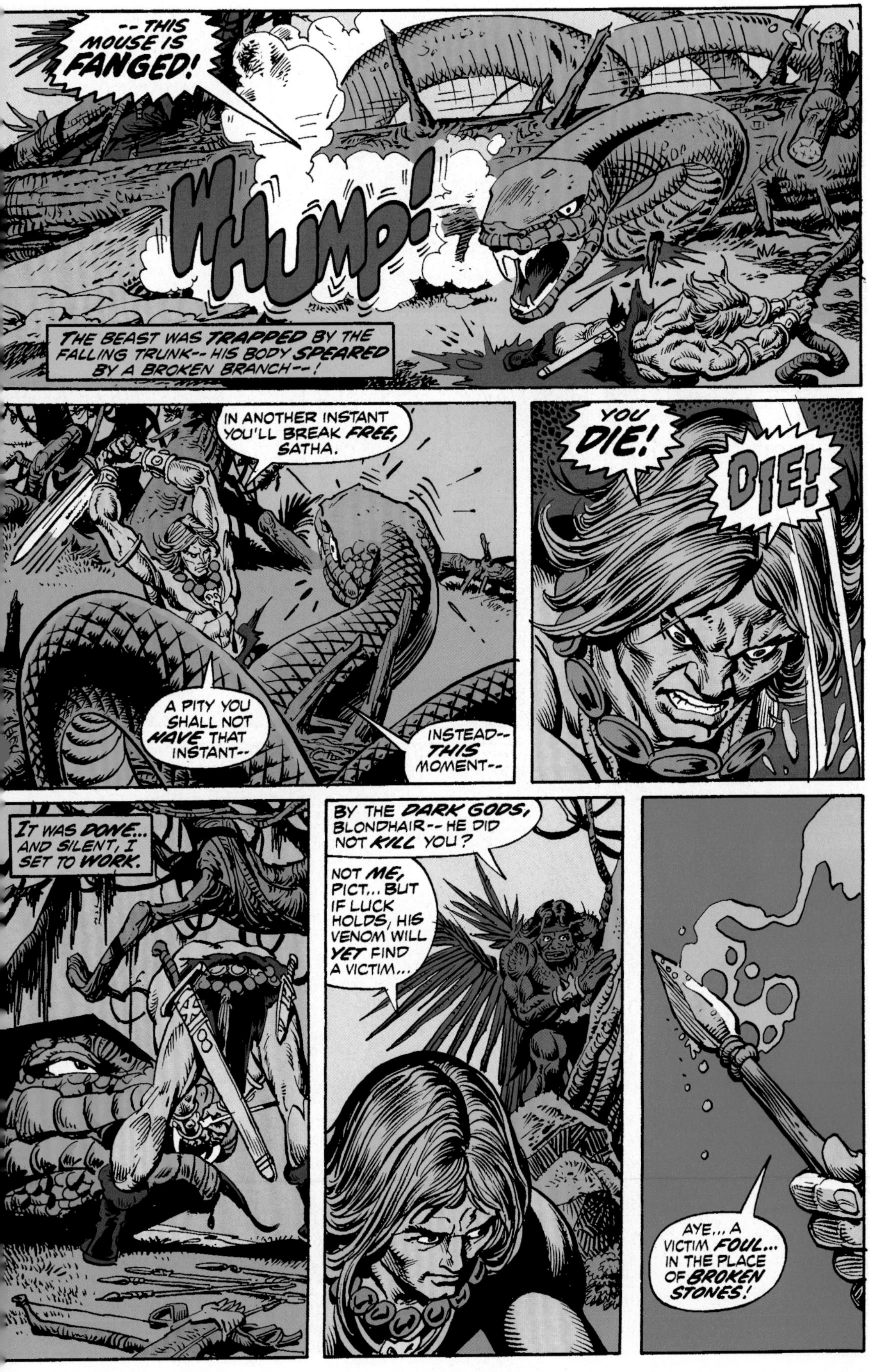
-- THIS MOUSE IS FANGED!
WHUMP!
THE BEAST WAS TRAPPED BY THE FALLING TRUNK-- HIS BODY SPEARED BY A BROKEN BRANCH--!
IN ANOTHER INSTANT YOU'LL BREAK FREE, SATHA.
A PITY YOU SHALL NOT HAVE THAT INSTANT--
INSTEAD-- THIS MOMENT--
YOU DIE!
DIE!
IT WAS DONE... AND SILENT, I SET TO WORK.
BY THE DARK GODS, BLONDHAIR-- HE DID NOT KILL YOU?
NOT ME, PICT... BUT IF LUCK HOLDS, HIS VENOM WILL YET FIND A VICTIM...
AYE... A VICTIM FOUL... IN THE PLACE OF BROKEN STONES!

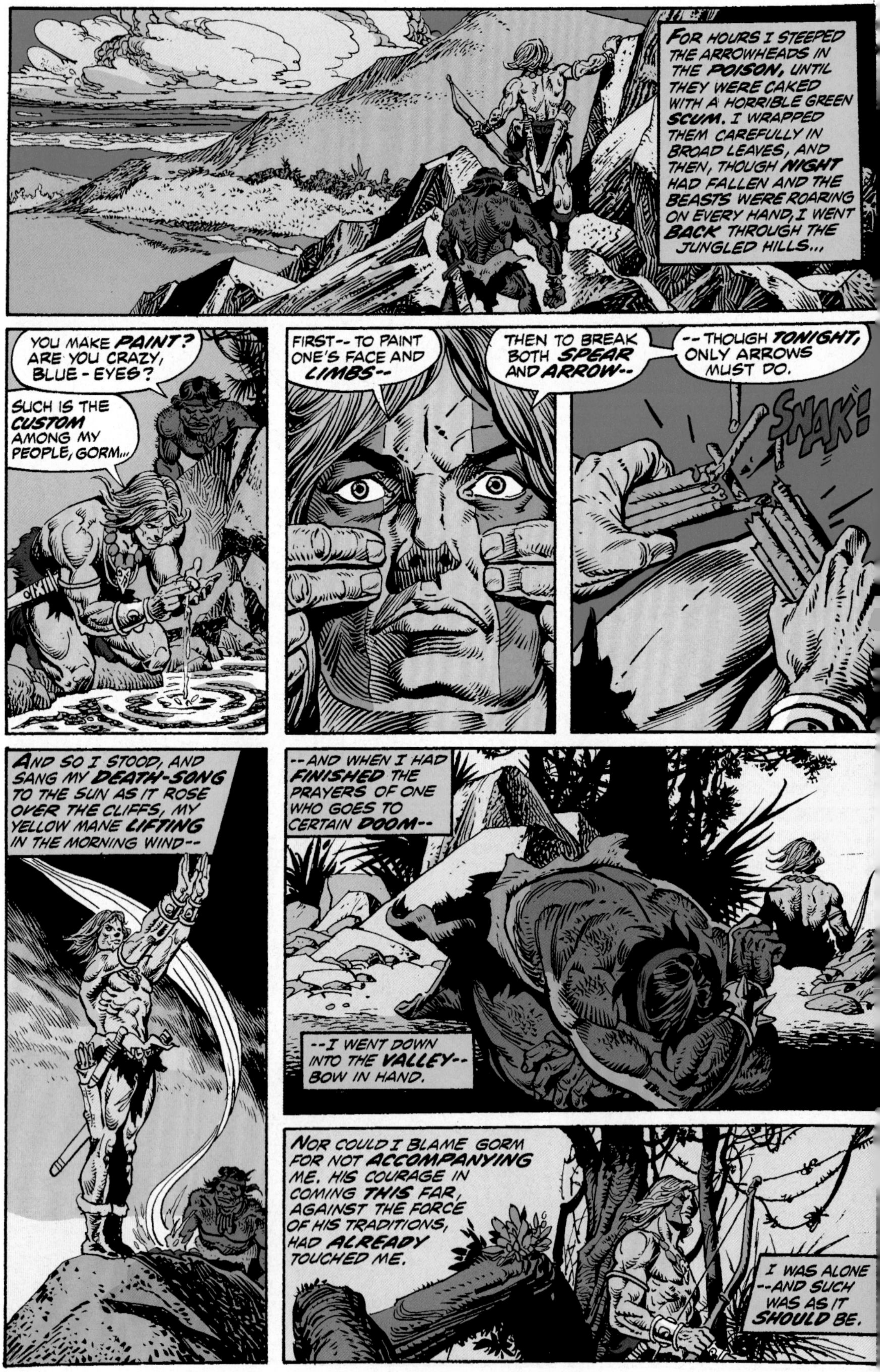
FOR HOURS I STEEPED THE ARROWHEADS IN THE POISON, UNTIL THEY WERE CAKED WITH A HORRIBLE GREEN SCUM. I WRAPPED THEM CAREFULLY IN BROAD LEAVES, AND THEN, THOUGH NIGHT HAD FALLEN AND THE BEASTS WERE ROARING ON EVERY HAND, I WENT BACK THROUGH THE JUNGLED HILLS...
YOU MAKE PAINT? ARE YOU CRAZY, BLUE-EYES?
SUCH IS THE CUSTOM AMONG MY PEOPLE, GORM...
FIRST-- TO PAINT ONE'S FACE AND LIMBS--
THEN TO BREAK BOTH SPEAR AND ARROW--
-- THOUGH TONIGHT, ONLY ARROWS MUST DO.
SNAK!
AND SO I STOOD, AND SANG MY DEATH-SONG TO THE SUN AS IT ROSE OVER THE CLIFFS, MY YELLOW MANE LIFTING IN THE MORNING WIND--
--AND WHEN I HAD FINISHED THE PRAYERS OF ONE WHO GOES TO CERTAIN DOOM--
--I WENT DOWN INTO THE VALLEY-- BOW IN HAND.
NOR COULD I BLAME GORM FOR NOT ACCOMPANYING ME. HIS COURAGE IN COMING THIS FAR, AGAINST THE FORCE OF HIS TRADITIONS, HAD ALREADY TOUCHED ME.
I WAS ALONE --AND SUCH WAS AS IT SHOULD BE.

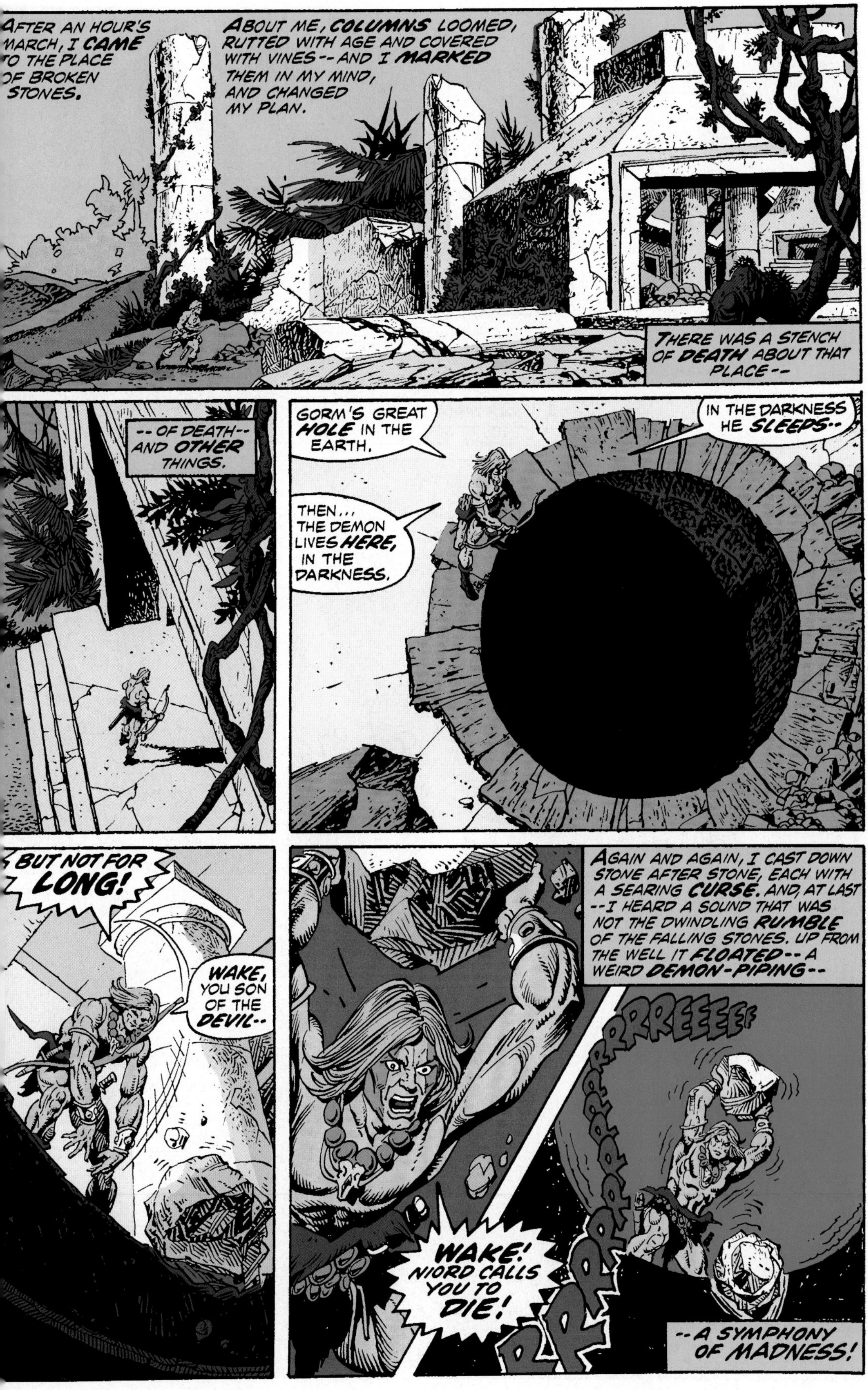
AFTER AN HOUR'S MARCH, I CAME TO THE PLACE OF BROKEN STONES.
ABOUT ME, COLUMNS LOOMED, RUTTED WITH AGE AND COVERED WITH VINES -- AND I MARKED THEM IN MY MIND, AND CHANGED MY PLAN.
THERE WAS A STENCH OF DEATH ABOUT THAT PLACE --
-- OF DEATH -- AND OTHER THINGS.
GORM'S GREAT HOLE IN THE EARTH.
THEN... THE DEMON LIVES HERE, IN THE DARKNESS.
IN THE DARKNESS HE SLEEPS..
BUT NOT FOR LONG!
WAKE, YOU SON OF THE DEVIL..
AGAIN AND AGAIN, I CAST DOWN STONE AFTER STONE, EACH WITH A SEARING CURSE. AND, AT LAST -- I HEARD A SOUND THAT WAS NOT THE DWINDLING RUMBLE OF THE FALLING STONES. UP FROM THE WELL IT FLOATED -- A WEIRD DEMON-PIPING --
WAKE! NIORD CALLS YOU TO DIE!
PRRRRRRRRRRRREEEEEE
-- A SYMPHONY OF MADNESS!

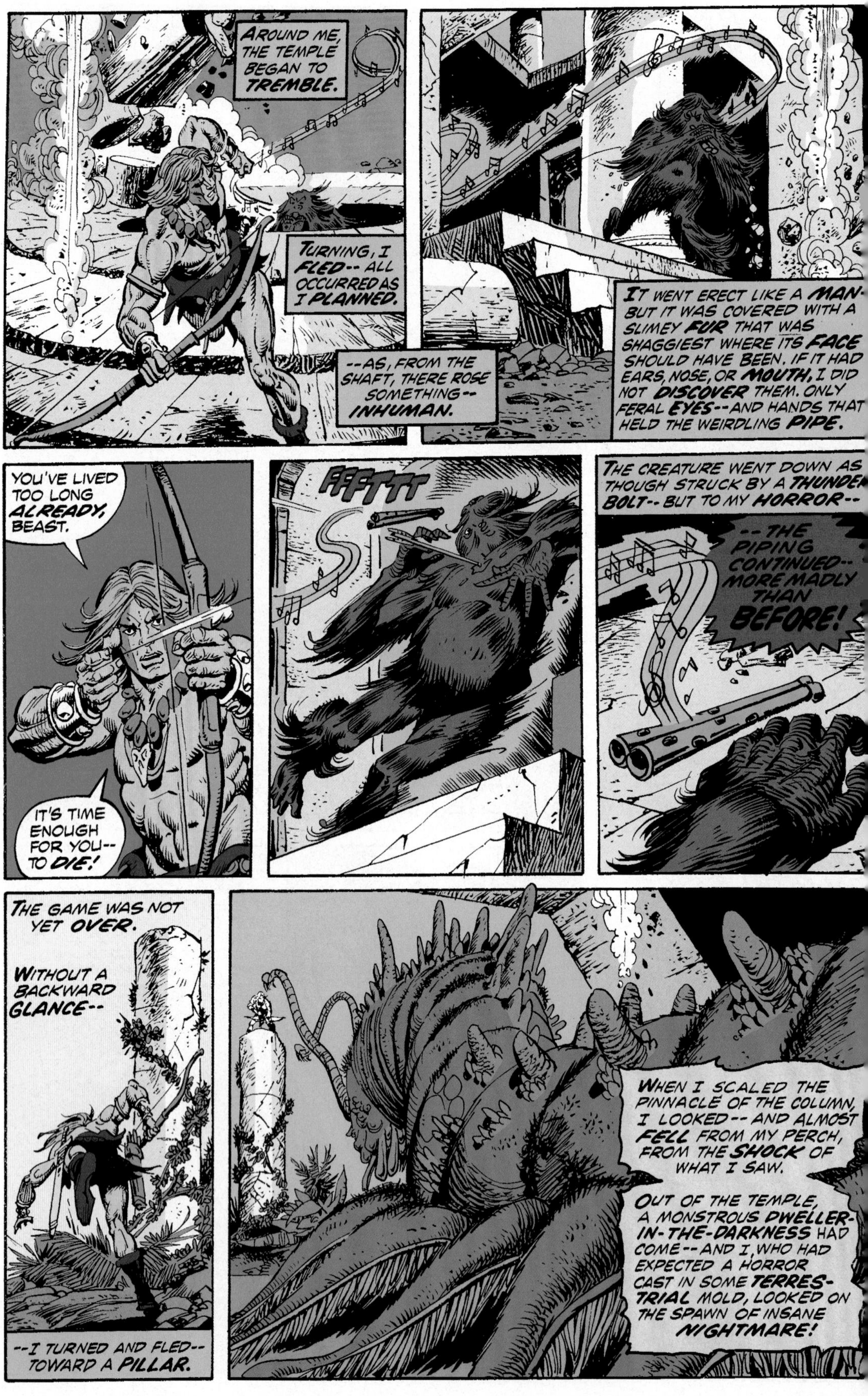
AROUND ME, THE TEMPLE BEGAN TO TREMBLE.
TURNING, I FLED-- ALL OCCURRED AS I PLANNED.
--AS, FROM THE SHAFT, THERE ROSE SOMETHING-- INHUMAN.
IT WENT ERECT LIKE A MAN-- BUT IT WAS COVERED WITH A SLIMEY FUR THAT WAS SHAGGIEST WHERE ITS FACE SHOULD HAVE BEEN. IF IT HAD EARS, NOSE, OR MOUTH, I DID NOT DISCOVER THEM. ONLY FERAL EYES--AND HANDS THAT HELD THE WEIRDLING PIPE.
YOU'VE LIVED TOO LONG ALREADY, BEAST.
IT'S TIME ENOUGH FOR YOU-- TO DIE!
FFFTTTT
THE CREATURE WENT DOWN AS THOUGH STRUCK BY A THUNDER-BOLT-- BUT TO MY HORROR--
--THE PIPING CONTINUED-- MORE MADLY THAN BEFORE!
THE GAME WAS NOT YET OVER.
WITHOUT A BACKWARD GLANCE--
--I TURNED AND FLED-- TOWARD A PILLAR.
WHEN I SCALED THE PINNACLE OF THE COLUMN, I LOOKED-- AND ALMOST FELL FROM MY PERCH, FROM THE SHOCK OF WHAT I SAW.
OUT OF THE TEMPLE, A MONSTROUS DWELLER-IN-THE-DARKNESS HAD COME-- AND I, WHO HAD EXPECTED A HORROR CAST IN SOME TERRESTRIAL MOLD, LOOKED ON THE SPAWN OF INSANE NIGHTMARE!

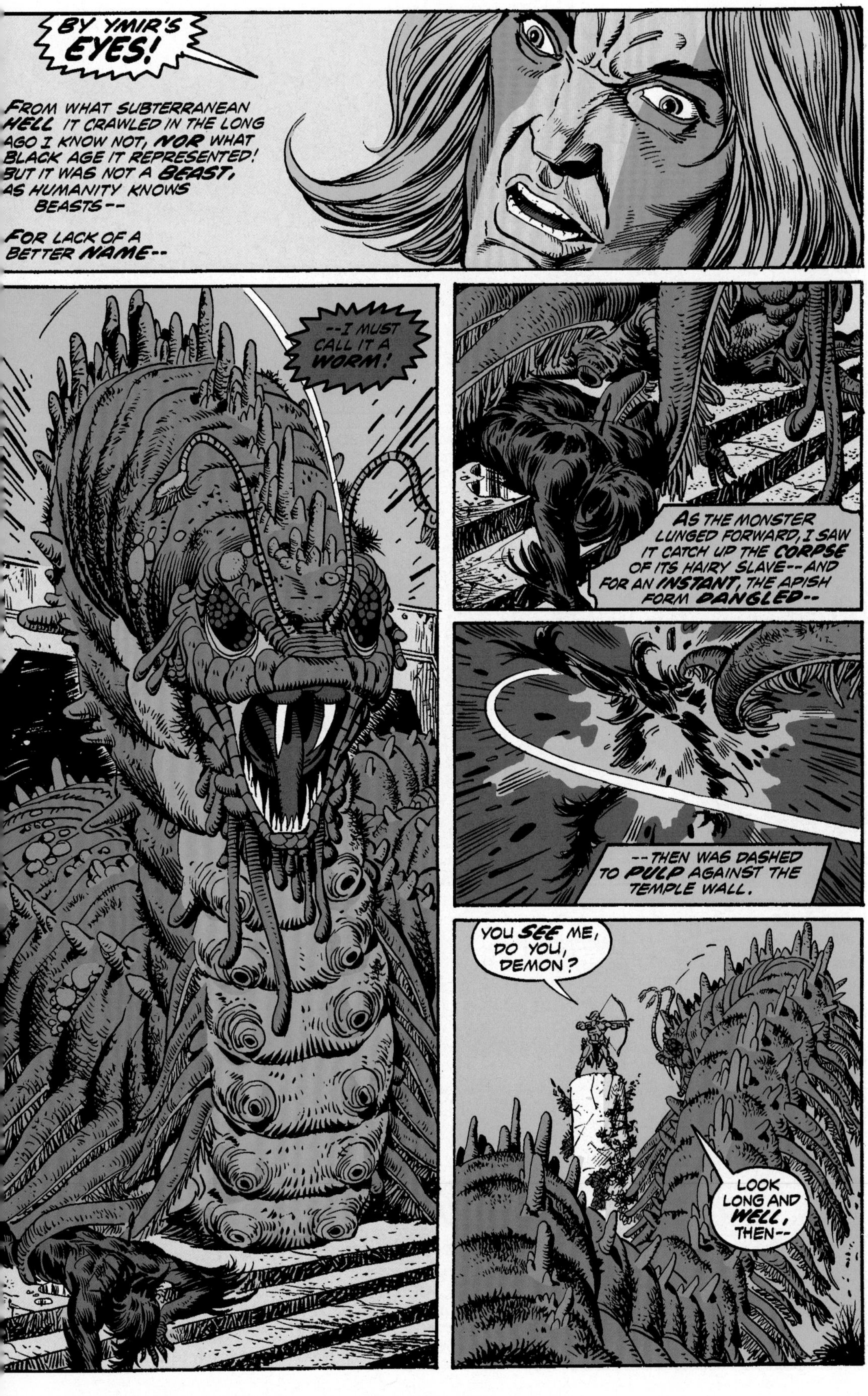
BY YMIR'S EYES!
FROM WHAT SUBTERRANEAN HELL IT CRAWLED IN THE LONG AGO I KNOW NOT, NOR WHAT BLACK AGE IT REPRESENTED! BUT IT WAS NOT A BEAST, AS HUMANITY KNOWS BEASTS--
FOR LACK OF A BETTER NAME--
--I MUST CALL IT A WORM!
AS THE MONSTER LUNGED FORWARD, I SAW IT CATCH UP THE CORPSE OF ITS HAIRY SLAVE--AND FOR AN INSTANT, THE APISH FORM DANGLED--
--THEN WAS DASHED TO PULP AGAINST THE TEMPLE WALL.
YOU SEE ME, DO YOU, DEMON?
LOOK LONG AND WELL, THEN--

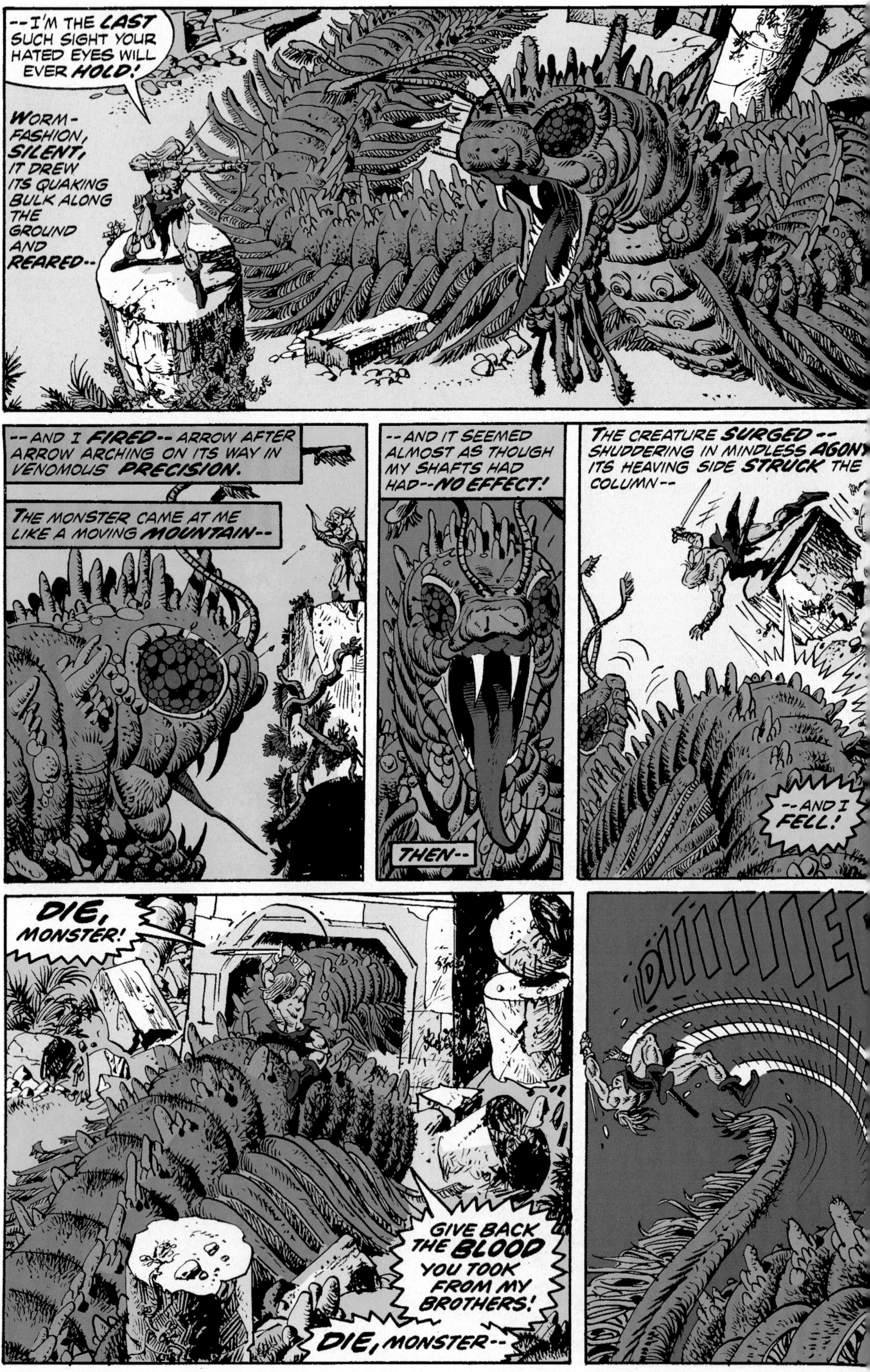
--I'M THE LAST SUCH SIGHT YOUR HATED EYES WILL EVER HOLD!
WORM-FASHION, SILENT, IT DREW ITS QUAKING BULK ALONG THE GROUND AND REARED--
--AND I FIRED-- ARROW AFTER ARROW ARCHING ON ITS WAY IN VENOMOUS PRECISION.
THE MONSTER CAME AT ME LIKE A MOVING MOUNTAIN--
--AND IT SEEMED ALMOST AS THOUGH MY SHAFTS HAD HAD--NO EFFECT!
THEN--
THE CREATURE SURGED--SHUDDERING IN MINDLESS AGONY ITS HEAVING SIDE STRUCK THE COLUMN--
--AND I FELL!
DIE, MONSTER!
GIVE BACK THE BLOOD YOU TOOK FROM MY BROTHERS!
DIE, MONSTER--

THE IMPACT MUST HAVE *SPLINTERED* HALF THE BONES IN MY FRAME-- YET EVEN SO, THROUGH THE RED BLAZE OF INCREDIBLE *PAIN,* I COULD HEAR THE BEGINNINGS OF A DISTANT *RUMBLE--*

--AND THOUGH I COULD NOT *SIT UP,* STILL I COULD *SEE--!*

I *WATCHED* AS THE CREATURE SLID HOME--

-- AND AS THE MONSTER VANISHED INTO THE TEMPLE WELL, WITH A RENDING, GRINDING *GROAN* THE RUINED WALLS CRUMPLED--TOTTERED--AND *COLLAPSED* IN A CLOUD OF RISING *DUST.*

BLOND-HAIR-- DO YOU *LIVE?*

I SAW THE FIGHT-- I *CAME--*

MY *SWORD,* GORM,....! GIVE ME... MY SWORD...

YOUR WOUNDS ARE *GREAT,* BLONDHAIR.

GORM WILL TAKE YOU *HOME.*

TOO LATE...

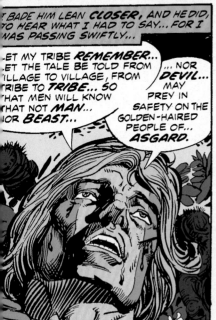

I BADE HIM LEAN *CLOSER,* AND HE DID, TO HEAR WHAT I HAD TO SAY... FOR I WAS PASSING SWIFTLY...

ET MY TRIBE *REMEMBER...* ET THE TALE BE TOLD FROM ILLAGE TO VILLAGE, FROM RIBE TO *TRIBE...* SO THAT MEN WILL KNOW HAT NOT *MAN...* OR *BEAST...*

... NOR *DEVIL...* MAY PREY IN SAFETY ON THE GOLDEN-HAIRED PEOPLE OF... *ASGARD.*

THERE WAS *MORE* THAT I SAID-- BUT ALREADY IT *FADED,* AS THE LIFE FLOWED FROM ME. I *FINISHED* MY FEW WORDS--

--AND THEN, WHILE GORM HOWLED AND BEAT HIS HAIRY BREAST...

DEATH CAME TO ME...

...IN THE VALLEY OF THE WORM...!

FINI

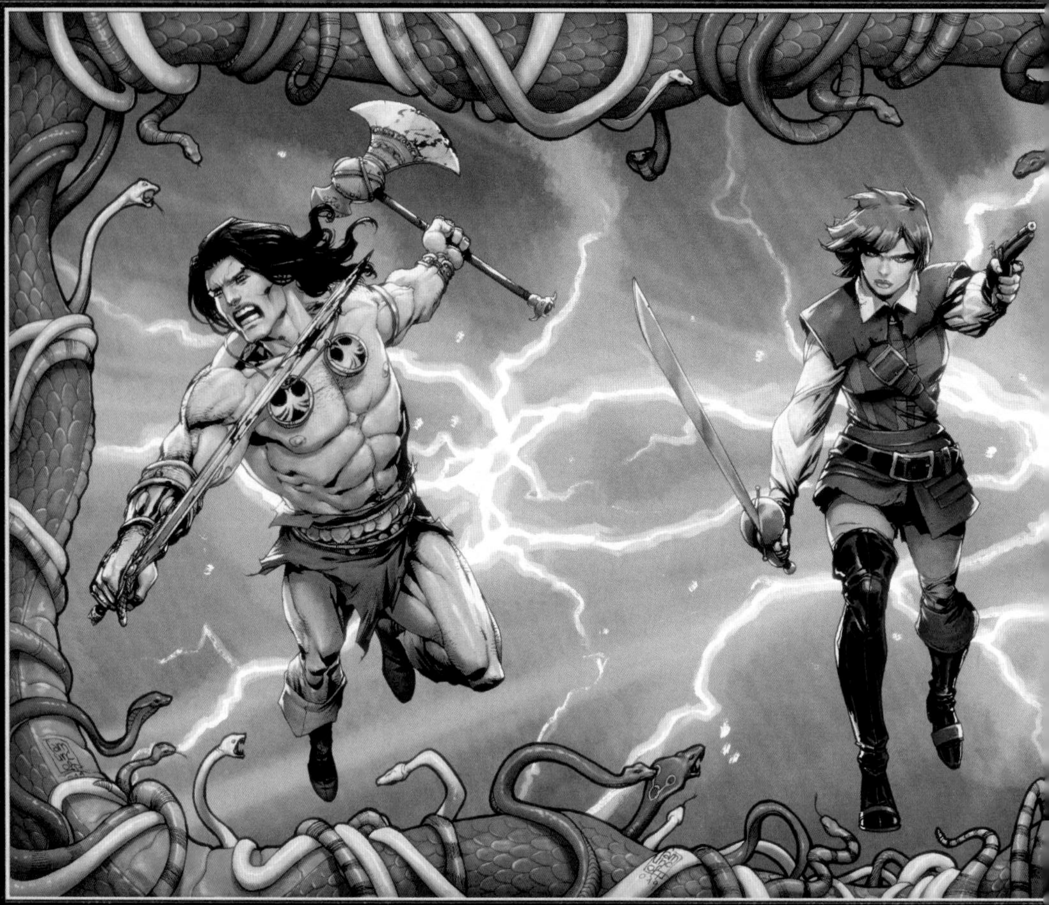

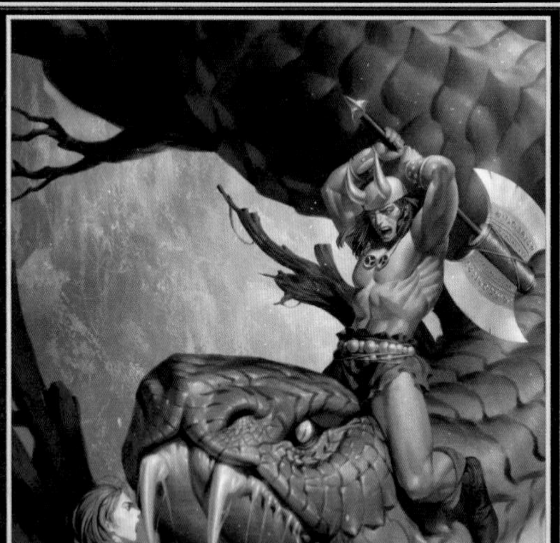

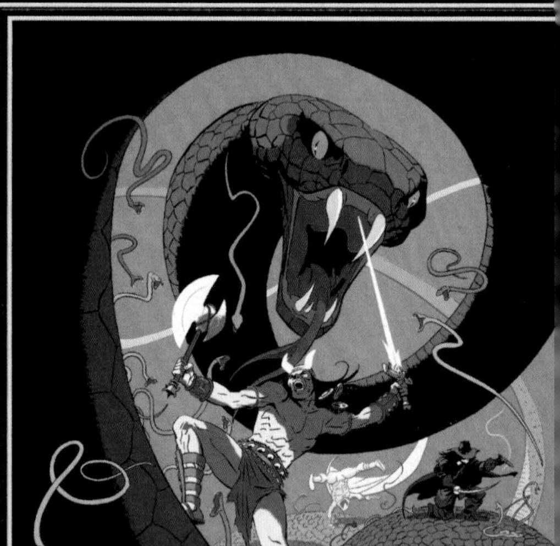

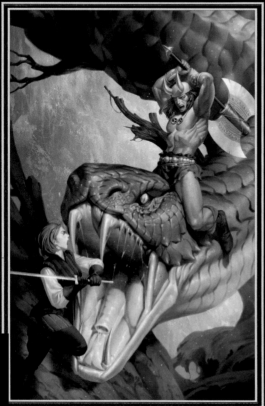

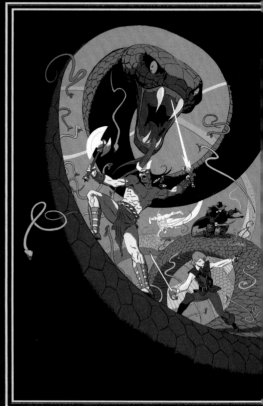

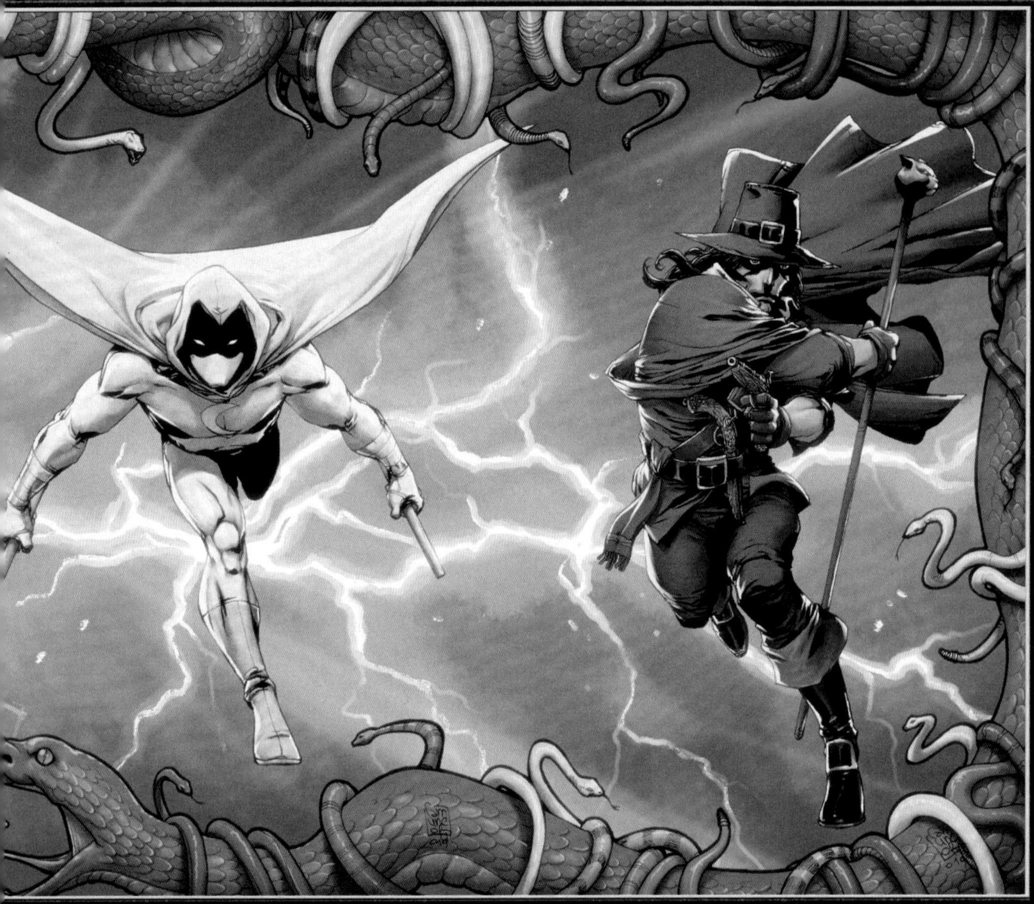

#1-4 CONNECTING VARIANTS BY GIUSEPPE CAMUNCOLI & JEAN-FRANÇOIS BEAULIEU

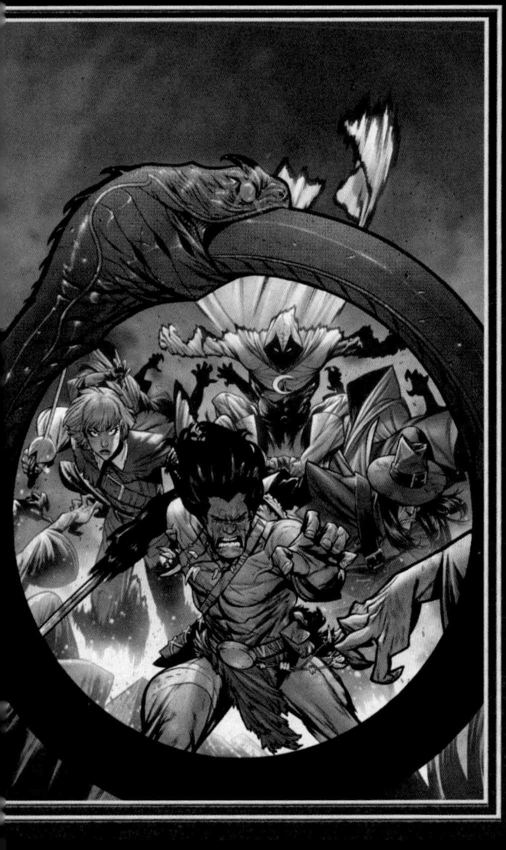

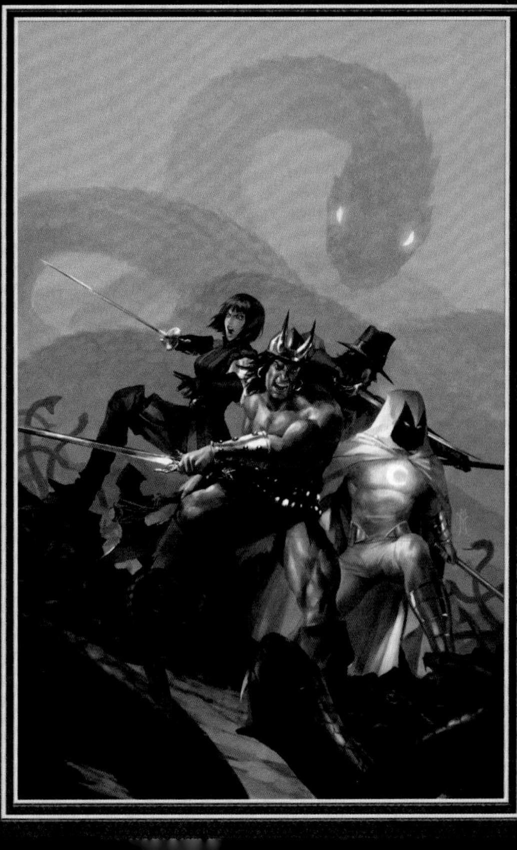

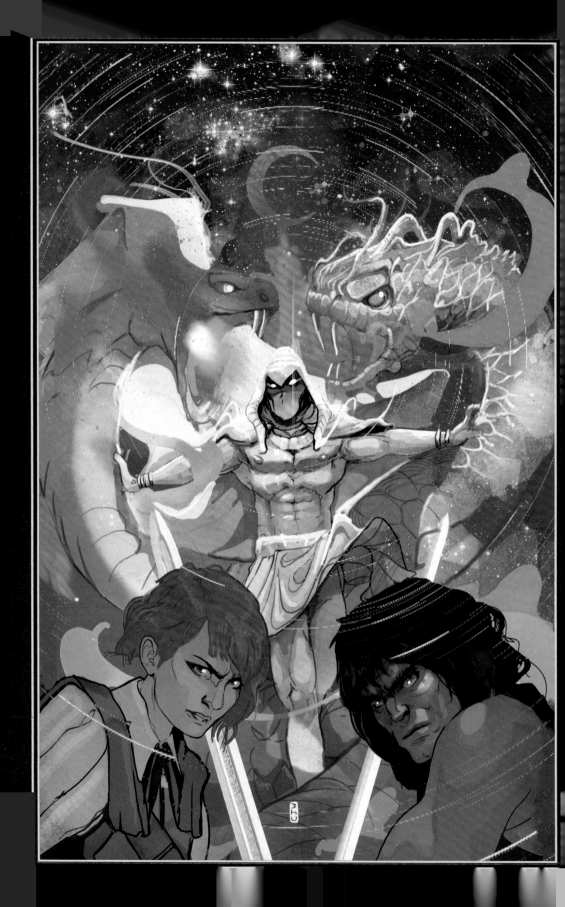